SOCIALIST ALTERNATIVE

This book is meant to be read as part of the introductory discussion groups run regularly by Socialist Alternative, Australia's biggest revolutionary socialist organisation.

We have branches in most major cities and student clubs on university campuses across the country.

Sign up to discuss the book with us and get involved – a member of SA from your area will get in touch. Just scan the QR code below or go to **redflag.org.au/getinvolved**

INTRODUCING MARXISM

a theory of revolutionary change

Tom Bramble

R RED FLAG
BOOKS

Tom Bramble has been a socialist activist since the 1970s in Britain and Australia. He is a founding member of Socialist Alternative and a member of its National Executive. He writes regularly for *Red Flag* and *Marxist Left Review*. His most recent book is *The Fight for Workers' Power: Revolution and Counter-Revolution in the 20th Century* (with Mick Armstrong).

Introducing Marxism: A theory of revolutionary change by Tom Bramble

ISBN 978-1-922927-13-2

First published in 2015

This second edition published by Red Flag Books
Melbourne, January 2024

Red Flag Books is an imprint of Socialist Alternative
redflag.org.au // sa.org.au
books@redflag.org.au

Cover
Oscar Sterner

Subediting and proofing
Tess Lee Ack

Layout and production by Oscar Sterner
Printed by IngramSpark

Contents

Introduction 1

1. What's wrong with capitalism? 5

2. The capitalist state 29

3. Workers' struggle and revolution 51

4. Socialism 83

5. Trade unions 101

6. Imperialism 121

7. Class and racial oppression 147

8. Women's and LGBTI oppression 179

9. The Russian Revolution 207

10. The defeat of the Russian Revolution 245

11. The revolutionary party and our project today 263

Socialist Alternative's Statement of Principles 283

Further reading 287

Acknowledgments for the first edition

Every book builds on the achievements of others, and this is even more the case with this book than for most. I must first acknowledge the direct contribution made by several authors, in particular Paul D'Amato, Sandra Bloodworth, Rick Kuhn, Louise O'Shea and Mick Armstrong, whose work appears here in several chapters in condensed form with their permission. I have acknowledged others whose work I have incorporated at the beginning of the relevant chapter. The book's structure was developed in consultation with Vashti Kenway, Liz Walsh and Corey Oakley, who, together with Louise O'Shea, provided valuable feedback on draft chapters. Diane Fieldes edited the final draft of the book. Tess Lee Ack did proofreading and layout.

Acknowledgements for the second edition

This edition fully updates and adds new material to account for questions that have come to the fore since the book was first published in 2015. I would like to thank Socialist Alternative comrades who have suggested changes to the text based on their experience running Marxism discussion groups, in particular Jasmine Duff, Luca Tavan and Liam Parry who made further suggestions on the draft in progress. I also acknowledge those comrades whose work I have incorporated for permission to do so. I hope that the new edition continues to challenge, educate and inspire readers to take up the fight for socialism.

Introduction

The Communists disdain to conceal their views and aims. They openly declare that their ends can be attained only by the forcible overthrow of all existing social conditions. Let the ruling classes tremble at a Communistic revolution. The proletarians have nothing to lose but their chains.

They have a world to win.

—Karl Marx and Friedrich Engels,
The Communist Manifesto

MARXISM IS THE THEORY of international working-class revolution. This simple statement forms the basis of this book, which aims to introduce some of the key ideas of Marxism today.

This book is an unabashedly partisan volume that aims to educate people not for mere intellectual satisfaction, although I hope it achieves that, but also to convince you, the reader, to commit to the project expounded by the founders of Marxism, Karl Marx and Friedrich Engels, nearly two centuries ago: that of workers' revolution. In Australia today, that means throwing your lot in with Socialist Alternative.

When we look at the world today, who but those who grow fat off the misery of the many could doubt that we need a total transformation? We see food being destroyed while people die of starvation for lack of the money to buy it. We see people living on the streets or in miserable shacks while millions of homes lie empty because property developers and landlords cannot sell or rent them out at a profit. We see money handed out to fossil fuel companies while the earth is heading towards climate catastrophe. We see Indigenous people killed by police who get off scot-free. We see trillions of dollars spent on wars and occupations, yet money is ripped out of public funding of hospitals. We see billionaires pay themselves another bonus while driving down the wages and conditions of low-paid workers. We see governments elected by the people but serving only the wealthy and powerful. We see the mainstream media that trumpets its commitment to press freedom but uses its privileged position to lie and slander the country's most oppressed people – Indigenous people, refugees, Muslims, and low-paid workers – to keep us divided and fearful.

Every one of these crimes should rouse us to action. To cry out against injustice. The point of this book is to explain how all these things are part of the same cruel system that puts profits for the few ahead of the needs of the many. It is also, however, to show that, brutal though the system may be, it is not impregnable. The capitalist system, with all its fortifications – its legions of police, generals and spies, newspaper editors, public service bosses and university vice-chancellors – is subject to one fatal weakness: it depends for its immense wealth on those it exploits. The working class which it brings into existence, not just in one country, not just in one continent but now on a truly global basis, is its gravedigger because the working class has both the interest in and the capacity to overthrow the capitalists and take power.

There has never been a shortage of popular revolts by the exploited masses throughout recorded history – from the revolt of the slaves in Rome led by the gladiator Spartacus to the risings in the Global South and Black Lives Matter in more recent times. The modern working class is unique in that it can take power into its own hands and prepare the way for a transition to a classless society. Such a society will know no disparities between rich and poor. It will treat with contempt the ills of our society, which we are expected to regard as natural or unavoidable, even admirable.

For the working class to rise and overthrow the capitalist class, it has to be armed with a theory that stands in complete contradiction to every accepted norm of the capitalist status quo. That theory is Marxism, developed over nearly two centuries by the working class's revolutionary struggle for liberation and by intellectuals committed to the workers' revolution who have distilled the lessons of this struggle based on their own connections to it.

The working class needs more than just to be armed with revolutionary theory. This has to take a concrete form, and that is the revolutionary party. Such a party must bring together the most politically conscious members of the working class to convince their sisters and brothers of the need for a revolutionary challenge to capitalism, not one that stops halfway or tries to compromise with it. The party must, further, organise to take the practical steps to bring a revolutionary struggle to a successful conclusion. There will be plenty of other forces active in the working class trying to confuse it and divert it from the measures needed to smash the capitalist state. Only the intervention and involvement of a revolutionary party based solidly in the working class can defeat these attempts to shunt the struggle into a cul-de-sac.

Nowhere in the world does a party of this nature currently exist, standing hundreds of thousands of strong. Socialist Alternative does not pretend to be such a party. But we are taking the steps today to contribute to building such a party here in Australia. To do that more successfully, however, we need to grow so that we can count in our ranks not the hundreds but the thousands. If you agree with what you read in this book, not necessarily every word, but the bulk of it, then don't simply put it aside, but commit yourself to our common struggle and join Socialist Alternative. In small numbers, or as individuals, we are ineffectual; only together can we have an effect. We cannot guarantee that the struggle ahead will be easy, but nothing less than the future of humanity is at stake.

Tom Bramble
January 2024

Chapter one

What's wrong with capitalism?

Society as a whole is more and more splitting up into two great hostile camps, into two great classes directly facing each other – Bourgeoisie and Proletariat.

—Marx and Engels, *The Communist Manifesto*

TODAY, CAPITALISM SPANS THE GLOBE. It wreaks havoc everywhere, enabling the exploitation of the vast majority of people by a small ruling class. Capitalism is not, like democracy or dictatorship, a system of government that varies from nation to nation. Capitalism is the worldwide economic system that dominates every country. It is a class-divided system in which the capitalist class, who own and control the enormous resources of our planet, oppress and exploit the rest of us. Capitalism is fundamentally undemocratic. Even in countries with a parliamentary system, ordinary people do not have any power over those who own the mines, the farms or any of the other resources and productive equipment that are necessary to make our world run. And the key economic decisions in our world are based upon profit-making rather than human need.

Everywhere you look, the world is divided into haves and have-nots. This is not an accident but is knitted into the very fabric of the system. The richest 1 percent of the world's population, owns nearly one-half of all global wealth. The CEOs of America's top 350 firms "earned" on average $28 million in 2021, 399 times more than the average worker. For much of the world's population, though, poverty is their lot. Over 800 million people experience hunger, and nearly one-quarter of the world's children are stunted for lack of food. War and pandemics are increasing the number of hungry people and are directly responsible for millions of deaths every year.[1]

The priorities of the system stink. Providing universal access to safe drinking water and sanitation in 140 low- and middle-income countries would cost US$114 billion per year. That may sound a lot, but it's equivalent to only three weeks of global military spending. COVID vaccines have saved many millions of lives in the pandemic, but money determines whose lives are saved: access to such vaccines is low or non-existent in many poorer countries, resulting in double the death rate compared to wealthier nations.

Poverty is not just the preserve of the Global South. In the United States, one in nine households, 37 million people, live below the poverty line. For Hispanic Americans, the poverty rate is one in six and for Black Americans, one in five. Millions depend on food stamps. Homelessness is at crisis levels as rents are soaring. In England, underinvestment in the National Health Service, leading to years-long waits for hospital treatment, is costing the lives of more than 100,000 people every year.[2]

For many decades, capitalism promised rising living standards. But many young people in the world's wealthiest countries now face worse prospects than their parents and grandparents, as exorbitant student debt, stagnant wages and soaring rents and house prices cruel their futures.

Australia is no exception to this picture of polarisation of wealth and class. In 2019, the top 20 percent of households held 63 percent of the national wealth, which was 90 times greater than that of the bottom 20 percent. Even this, however, understates the inequality that matters, the disparity of ownership and control over the assets that, when set into motion by workers, generate or distribute more wealth – the factories, offices, mines, banks, media and communications, farms, shopping malls, warehouses, trucks, railways, aeroplanes and ports. Here, the people that matter are only a fraction of the top 1 percent, at the top of which stand the nation's billionaires. In 2023, the combined wealth of the country's 50 richest stood at $213 billion, a hefty 70 percent jump from 2019.[3]

The Australian government does its best to ensure that those with money keep it, with tax breaks and subsidies galore doled out to big business and the wealthy. But when it comes time to give back to the Treasury, the corporations are missing. One-third of the country's biggest 2,700 companies paid no income tax in 2022.[4]

Just as governments coddle the rich, they penalise the poor. The welfare state in Australia is threadbare compared to other wealthy nations, with one-half or more of those in households reliant on welfare remaining in poverty. For a brief period during the first year of the COVID-19 pandemic, governments doubled social security payments, slashing poverty, but these were quickly withdrawn, forcing welfare claimants back into hardship. Getting a job is not enough to escape poverty – nearly 3 million people struggle to survive on the minimum wage.[5]

Hundreds of thousands of households in Australia suffer food insecurity, where family members, usually mothers, are sometimes forced to starve themselves for days because budgets don't stretch far enough to feed everyone. Food bank queues are getting longer, and cases of scurvy are now being reported in our big cities – scurvy in one of the world's richest countries! But there's no lack of food. There's a lack of money in the hands of the working class because the capitalists are pushing up prices and rents to fill their pockets.[6]

Wage theft is rampant everywhere, from farms to universities. Hundreds of thousands of workers, most non-citizens on a range of work and study visas, are not even paid the minimum wage. Even workers on union agreements have seen their wages fall in recent years after the rising cost of food, rents, insurance and utility prices is taken into account.

Home ownership has become an impossible dream for many workers. Those without wealthy parents and stuck on low wages are now forced to compete with other desperate people for the privilege of securing a rental property where they will pay a third of their incomes to a grasping landlord. Decades of under-investment in public housing by state governments has seen the stock of public housing collapse. Those households on average incomes who do get on the first rung of the home-ownership ladder are paying 30 percent of their incomes on mortgage repayments. The banks, however, continue to rake it in, with the big four racking up billions of dollars in profit every year.

These enormous divisions between the rich and the poor are not just unfortunate facts of life. They reflect the division of society into classes: the capitalists and their hangers-on, who live off the proceeds of the working class's labour, and the workers who work all their lives to earn enough to live and sometimes barely even that.

Our class position affects us even before we see the light of day. Wealthier women have access to higher quality and more specialised care and have, on average, healthier babies. Poor diet damages the health of children born to poor and working-class families. From being underweight as babies, children in poor families are more likely to be overweight. Children born to wealthy parents also share a range of other benefits. They are much more likely to inherit money and will live, on average, six years longer than those born to poor families.[7]

Schooling further entrenches this divide. Working-class and poor children are concentrated in under-resourced schools, while wealthy children enjoy abundant educational opportunities. The result is that children who attend schools in low socioeconomic status areas lag, on average, three years behind their counterparts in wealthier neighbourhoods.

Government funding to private and Catholic schools is racing ahead of that going to state schools. The funding disparity communicates who matters in our society. This shapes the self-image, expectations and aspirations of young people in myriad ways and helps prepare them for life either of privilege and control or submission and oppression. The situation is no better in higher education. Students from private schools are more likely to enrol in tertiary education compared to those from government schools, which sets them up for lucrative careers. Even once enrolled, students from poorer backgrounds find things tough, with most worrying about their financial situation.

The class divide in the education system prepares people for working life. The children of the rich enter adulthood having gained a sense of superiority, an expectation of control and access to resources, a competitive nature, extensive social networks among the privileged and the ability to give orders, all of which the private school system, elite colleges and wealthy social cliques function to equip them with. Children of the working class, by the time they embark on working life, are much more likely to have become accustomed to taking orders, deferring to the more privileged and living with a sense of alienation from the powerful institutions that dominate social and working life. This lack of control and an acceptance of that reality, to a greater or lesser degree, is a central aspect of working-class oppression under capitalism.

Once employed, the stress of not being able to provide for children, working long hours, and fear of unemployment is a persistent feature of working-class life. It has not and never will be for those at the top. This has serious health consequences for workers. Insecure or unfavourable working conditions and low self-esteem, depression and physical and mental health problems disproportionately affect workers and those with less power in society. In addition, the workplace itself is unsafe for many workers: four out of every 100 workers will experience a work-related injury or illness in any year. Around 170 workers are killed each year in Australia, with manual workers facing the highest risk of death at work.[8] Many more die due to long-term work-related health conditions such as silicosis.

If work is bad, unemployment is worse. Woeful social security damages the self-esteem of recipients, and the government's punitive approach means that the unemployed are forced to accept degrading treatment at the hands of parasitic "mutual obligation" agencies, forcing many to stop looking for work altogether. The situation is even worse for Aboriginal people, nearly half of whom are unemployed or not in the labour force.

Once workers are old or their bodies are wrecked, they no longer have any value in capitalist terms. The capitalist class resents supporting those who make no contribution to profits and who are not independently wealthy. Winding back age pension entitlements, raising the pension age and the "marketisation" of aged care have thus been long-term aims of governments and corporations worldwide.

Class matters

Class matters at every stage of our lives and in every sphere. But what is it exactly? A Marxist approach identifies class, grounded in social relationships in production, as the basis of power in our society. Who makes critical decisions, the nature of those decisions and who benefits or suffers from them are shaped by class. Marxism also provides a framework for understanding the treatment of oppressed groups and social conflict as symptoms of a class-divided society.

The contradictory nature of their relationship defines the fundamental classes in societies. The capitalist class (or bourgeoisie) comprises those who own or control significant productive resources and compete for profit. Key figures in the Australian capitalist class include those with huge personal fortunes, such as Gina Rinehart, Andrew "Twiggy" Forrest, Harry Triguboff and Frank Lowy. Much is made in the Forbes Rich List of the alleged entrepreneurial talents of the wealthy in Australia. The stories of migrants arriving with a suitcase and building fortunes are not untrue. Such cases occur. Then there are others who start up a technology company and make hundreds of millions of dollars, sometimes billions, in a few years. And it's also true that some capitalists lose their money in ill-advised business ventures or stock market crashes and are forced into wage labour. The capitalist class is not a rigid social caste system impervious to change. As we shall see, capitalism is a dynamic system in which fortunes can be made or destroyed. But it is not a system of meritocracy where hard work can simply make your fortune. Out of the ten richest Australians named in the 2023 Forbes Rich List, five individuals either inherited their wealth or came from families that had already started significant businesses, which they subsequently expanded.

On top of those who own large businesses, we may add to the capitalist class the executives in charge of the big banks, supermarkets and industrial companies, the telecommunications, media, gambling and entertainment companies and the logistics, transport and warehousing companies. Occasional conflicts notwithstanding, these managers have the same goals as big business owners: maximising profit and expanding the business. That many top managers themselves own shares in the companies they oversee reinforces their identification with capitalist priorities.

The senior functionaries of the state apparatus carefully guard the interests of the capitalists. Some, like members of the federal and state cabinets, the heads of the public service departments and government business enterprises, the armed forces chiefs of staff, the police commissioners and the vice-chancellors of the universities are, with their control over immense financial and human resources, little different from the chief executives of any private sector business, even if some of them do not trade on the market. Others, like High Court judges or Opposition shadow ministers, are ideologically embedded in the same state machine and are rewarded for their loyalty to it. That they often hail from the same schools, socialise in the same circles and marry into each other's families contributes further to their loyalty to the big capitalists. If not narrowly capitalists, these state functionaries are still members of the ruling class. The capitalist class and those directly serving it comprise 1 percent of the population.

Standing in polar opposition to the capitalist class are the working class, those whose only means of making a living is to sell their ability to work to an employer. The working class includes retail workers, nurses, construction workers, fruit pickers, schoolteachers, flight attendants and process workers in a factory, along with a host of other occupations. Their class position is defined by their relationship to their employer and the productive resources they require to work, not how much they earn. Some mineworkers, for example, may own motorboats or a holiday home, but they do not own the machinery with which they work or the ore they dig out of the ground, and nor do they vote for their supervisors – they are bossed about, not the boss. Some workers think they are middle-class and vote Liberal – but this does not prevent them from being exploited by the bosses daily. The working class includes spouses and children dependent on a wage. Unemployed people, who are unable to labour or cannot get a job and therefore have to survive on meagre social security payments, are also part of the working class, as are old-age pensioners and retired workers. The working class accounts for about two-thirds of the population.

Then there are middle layers, which share some characteristics with capitalists and others with wage earners. The traditional middle class (or petty bourgeoisie) own small amounts of productive resources like a truck, a shop, the tools of their trade or other kinds of equipment for which they often incur enormous debts. Unlike capitalists, members of the petty bourgeoisie primarily depend on their own labour, perhaps aided by family or a few employees. Some professionals, such as independent solicitors, accountants and doctors, are also part of the middle class.

Another element of the middle class is the array of senior supervisors, professionals and middle managers working in big private and public sector bureaucracies. Specialised professionals, engineers, lawyers or accountants in such bureaucracies may have considerable autonomy in their work. Supervisors have power over subordinates. But they do not take part in major decisions about employment levels, large-scale investments or the business their organisation is in. Then there are those who play an important ideological role for capitalism and have a substantial amount of control over their own labour: university professors and senior journalists, people running NGOs, and so on. Their social role is to provide the ruling class with ideological cover. The middle classes, taken together, account for about one-quarter of the population.

Exploitation

Exploitation conjures up images of sweatshop factories in the developing world or dodgy contractors paying migrant workers cash-in-hand for farm work. But for Marxists, exploitation is not simply a disparaging term for a few wicked bosses. Nor is it the result of the system being abused. It is the typical, everyday functioning of capitalist production.

All class societies throughout history rest on exploitation: a tiny minority live off the labour of the vast majority. How this exploitation is organised and how the exploiting class distribute among themselves the wealth they expropriate from the labour of others defines the mode of production – slave society, feudalism, capitalism and so on.

In slave societies, the labourers are themselves property, bought and sold, receiving only enough to keep them alive and able to work. Under feudalism, peasants worked for a certain number of days on their own land, producing what their families needed, and for the rest of the working week, they worked for their lord. Or they had to hand over a certain amount of their produce to the lord for the right to farm on his estate. The exploitation was obvious. The lords were supported by the powerful ideology of the church that God ordained everyone's place in the world. If that failed and any peasants thought this was an unjust situation, the lords had their armed retainers to back up their social privilege and authority with brutal force.

Under capitalism, the situation is different. Unlike the peasants, workers have no control over any means of production – machinery, tools, technology – except for the most basic tools a tradesperson may have. They work not to produce their necessities but for a wage with which they can buy those necessities.

It seems as if workers are paid a fair day's pay for a fair day's work. But when we look more closely, we have to ask: if the capitalists paid their workers the whole value they created in that day, where would their profits come from? There would be none. Here we come to the rub. No capitalist would want to employ any workers because their whole reason for investing is to make profits and to accumulate more capital from the process.

Capitalists can only make profits by paying their workers less than the value they create each day.[9] Workers employed by Australian business take, on average, the first four hours of an eight-hour working day to produce the value of goods and services required to pay the wages that will allow them to sustain themselves and be fit to work the following day.[10] The remaining value – the additional four hours of goods and services workers produce – goes to their employer. This is what Marx called surplus value. The relationship is exploitative, as it was under feudalism, but the exploitation is now hidden behind the apparent equality of boss and worker who confront each other as buyer and seller of labour power on the job market. Whether you're the average worker in Australia on an hourly rate of $48 or a textile worker in Bangladesh being paid 70 cents an hour, you are being paid far less than the value of the wealth you create.

Ruling class ideologists try to convince us that the rich make their wealth from hard work and talent and that, inequitable as the system may be, such rewards are essential to drive society forward. Even leaving aside those bosses whose only hard work was ensuring that they were born into the right families, those at the top contribute nothing to society. If Gina Rinehart lay in bed for a month, iron ore would still be dug out and shipped to China. But if those who dig the ore down tools and go on strike, supplies would dry up in days, and no profits would be made. The capitalists grow rich not because they contribute to wealth creation or the day-to-day running of society but because of a process of legalised theft.

Competition and waste

Capitalism never stands still. As Marx and Engels wrote in the *Communist Manifesto* in 1848:

> The bourgeoisie cannot exist without constantly revolutionising the instruments of production, and thereby the relations of production, and with them the whole relations of society... Constant revolutionising of production, uninterrupted disturbances of all social conditions, everlasting uncertainty and agitation distinguish the bourgeois epoch from all earlier ones... all new-formed [relations] become antiquated before they can ossify. All that is solid melts into air.

To confirm that this remains the case, we only need to reflect on the astonishing growth of the Chinese urban working class since the 1980s, drawn out of their villages in their hundreds of millions. The qualitative leaps in computer power, alongside the closure of automotive production in Australia and the shuttering of Detroit, are also testimony to capitalist dynamism, which has lifted the productive capacity of humanity. We can produce more with less labour. Between 1995 and 2023, the output of the average Australian worker rose by two-thirds.[11]

So, with all this wealth and ability to provide for people, why do we still see starvation, poverty, misery and injustice? The simple answer is that no exploiting class organises production for the good of the exploited. They are intent on staying in power, filling their own pockets and surrounding themselves with the trappings that emphasise their power over society. But to answer the question in more depth, we need to look at the competition that drives the capitalist system and how the market works.

Capitalism is driven by competition between capitalists. They are constantly finding new ways to produce things more cheaply by introducing new technology and machinery or developing new products to substitute for existing ones to out-sell their rivals. The capitalists do not just use the surplus value they rip off from their workers to buy luxuries for themselves (although they do). To stay in business and remain competitive, they must reinvest most of their surplus value in "revolutionising the means of production".[12] Marx described this capital accumulation as the "self-expansion of value". Any capitalist who gives up on this drive to accumulate ever more capital in order to make more profits to invest falls by the wayside. You cannot be a capitalist if you stagnate. Competitors will drive your business to the wall and possibly buy you up on the cheap, leaving you with debts.

The capitalists argue that the dynamism of the system produces wealth for all. "A rising tide lifts all boats," they say. From this perspective, it is justifiable for workers whose roles are made redundant by technological advances to be thrown on the scrap heap for the "greater good".

But the reality is quite different. More often than not, productivity gains result in more profits for the bosses, with no commensurate improvement in pay and conditions for workers. But we should also consider the what, where, when and how of production. Capitalism produces a multitude of outright harmful or useless things. The global arms industry is worth an estimated $1.5 trillion annually and is devoted to producing goods and services whose primary purpose is destruction. Hundreds of billions are spent globally on advertising, and the media empires churn out what have aptly been described as "weapons of mass distraction". Vast amounts of labour and resources are spent on constructing luxury playthings for the rich – the super-yachts, mansions, sports cars and so on whose main purpose is the ostentatious display of wealth. Even when products are useful, they are made to be obsolete in a relatively short time. Cars, computers, home appliances, shoes and clothing could easily be produced to last. But, for the sake of constantly selling them, they will probably require replacement in a few short years or less.

The "free market" which supposedly drives the system is a myth. Three or four companies dominate almost every sector of consumer and industrial goods and services in Australia. In the United States, supposedly the heartland of the free market, three investment companies, BlackRock, Vanguard and State Street, are, combined, the largest shareholders in almost 90 percent of Wall Street's top 500 companies, owning on average 20 percent of their stock. A similar story can be told in Europe and Japan. Such holdings of wealth give these companies enormous influence over the economy. Fewer than 750 interlocking corporations control 80 percent of the planet's entire business wealth between them.[13]

And far from shunning state protection – something they advocate all the time for the poor – big business sucks up public funds. Just look at the tens of trillions of dollars handed to big business during the 2008–09 global financial crisis or in the first year of the COVID-19 pandemic. Consider the hundreds of millions of dollars doled out to private transport operators, fossil fuel corporations, infrastructure companies and business consultancies by state and federal governments in Australia.[14] Handing over public services to the big corporations does not mean "small government"; it means the closer integration of state and business interests.

Crisis

Economic crises regularly wrack the capitalist system and waste resources on a stupendous scale. Capitalists invest where they think they will make money, not based on human need. But they can't be certain they will make a profit because the very competition that drives the system causes dislocation and crisis. Under capitalism, only when the products of people's labour are compared and exchanged on a market after the production process is complete does it become clear whether the products can be sold and where labour has been unnecessarily expended. So, the capitalists invest in raw materials, machinery, tools and buildings, and they hire workers. The workers are put to work using all these means of production to produce surplus value. Then the commodities produced have to be transported, possibly to the other side of the globe, and they have to be displayed and marketed. By then, other capitalists may have been producing the same kind of commodity. Unaware of each other's plans, the capitalists have now produced more commodities than can be sold – either because not enough people want them or they can't afford them; it makes no difference. Lack of buyers amounts to over-production, whether or not people need the things. That's why there can be what seems to be over-production of food while people starve, or why houses can lie empty while the homeless sleep in parks. The capitalists cannot guarantee that they will realise the profits they hope for because they can't know exactly what their competitors, suppliers and customers will do.

More importantly, there is no correlation between people's needs and what is produced. That's why money can keep pouring into the production of polluting cars instead of public transport, even though humanity urgently needs something done about global warming. Under capitalism, investment can't be democratically organised, with surplus value employed rationally. Instead, it is invested with the sole purpose of making a profit.

The orthodox economists' dream that the market is the most rational or natural way for humans to organise production is laughable when you look at how capitalist markets work. Capitalism has always followed a pattern of frenetic economic activity followed by a more or less severe economic slump. Even mainstream economists acknowledge this boom-slump cycle. It is not a matter of government policy or something the capitalists can avoid. It is built into the way the system operates. This is how Marx and Engels summarised the situation:

> Modern bourgeois society, with its relations of production, of exchange and of property, a society that has conjured up such gigantic means of production and of exchange, is like the sorcerer who is no longer able to control the powers of the nether world whom he has called up by his spells.[15]

When markets are on the up, capitalists pour money into the economy. Investment increases, and jobs become more plentiful. Sales rise. But then shortages develop, pushing up the price of raw materials. Factory and office rents climb. Wages are pushed up. At some point, some capitalists start to think that the rising price of everything is squeezing their profits. So they hesitate. Do they really want to risk losing their money? Perhaps they'll bank it, gamble on the stock market or spend it on luxuries. They begin to sack workers as they cut back, and then the entire cycle goes into reverse. Unemployment climbs, and wages fall. As investment stalls, demand across the entire economy falls back. Unsold items accumulate in warehouses. Profits shrivel. As companies go bust, others swallow them up, further concentrating industry into fewer hands.

These recessions devastate millions of lives, throwing people into unemployment, while there is terrible waste as factories lie idle and products rot, not for want of potential consumers, but for lack of consumers who can buy them. During the 2008–09 global financial crisis, world industrial output fell 13 percent, international trade dropped by 20 percent and unemployment rose by two-thirds. And in every slump, governments and business tell us there isn't enough to go around and that we need to pull in our belts and sacrifice for the common good.

We are taught to think that there is nothing we can do about any of this – the laws governing the way we produce the things we need to survive are supposedly outside of human control. This makes no sense. The capacity for collective, planned production is one of the key things that define humanity as a species. Imagining the changes we want to make to the world before engaging in the activity needed to achieve it is what separates complex human society from that of the bees making their hives. The problem under capitalism is that our ability to work out how to meet our collective needs has been taken from us and replaced by "market forces" that absolve the rich of moral responsibility for their actions. But they *are* responsible, no matter what they say. That's why if we want a different world, we need to take them on.

If economic competition produces booms and busts that ruin people's lives, even worse are the effects of the military competition that is an outgrowth. There has not been a day without war in the last 100 years. Historian Eric Hobsbawm calculated that 187 million people died from wars in the twentieth century, equivalent to 10 percent of the entire world population in 1913.[16] The twenty-first century is no different as the competition for domination by the world's major powers gathers pace. Russia's invasion of Ukraine in 2022 has seen a major land war in Europe for the first time since 1945, with hundreds of thousands of casualties. Growing tensions in the Asia-Pacific are creating many flashpoints, with the potential for a regional war, potentially even a third world war. Governments around the world are ratcheting up military spending. The Australian government is no exception. Spending this money on housing the homeless or lifting living conditions for Aboriginal people in remote communities would support lives rather than destroy them. But the ruling class sees no benefit for themselves in doing these things, so they are not done: guns must come before butter. In chapter six we return to the topic of war and imperialism and how they are embedded in capitalism.

Moreover, the anarchic capitalist system has a profound impact on the natural environment. The success of global capitalism relies on the relentless destruction of our planet. Giant fossil fuel corporations are plundering resources that, when burned, are propelling us toward a catastrophic future. Global heating is spiralling out of control, breaking temperature records and causing more frequent droughts. The rising sea levels pose a direct threat to low-lying areas and Pacific islands, putting their very existence at risk. Climate change and habitat devastation are wiping out species at an alarming rate. Formerly temperate regions are succumbing to desertification, leading to the destruction of entire communities and a decline in local food production. The decline in insect populations, likely linked to the widespread use of pesticides and chemicals, jeopardises global food supplies by threatening pollination. Microplastics have proliferated exponentially in the past 15 years, infiltrating every corner of our planet, from the ocean floor to the highest mountains, and even reaching unborn babies. This destruction of ecosystems will force millions of people to seek refuge in other countries where they face racist immigration authorities who will try to repel them, driving them back to sea or confining them in cages or barges.

The fossil fuel and chemical CEOs do not care about these disasters. After all, they lead incredibly profitable businesses, and the largest banks in the world are heavily invested in them. If there were a sudden shift to publicly owned renewable energy sources, it would severely impact their immense wealth and negatively affect thousands of the world's richest individuals. Naturally, they will not allow that to happen. Furthermore, the wealthy elite might be able to adapt to a future characterised by catastrophic global warming and environmental collapse. If the situation becomes unsustainable, they can simply retreat to heavily guarded enclaves and pay desperate individuals to maintain their accustomed living conditions. This is precisely why, despite repeated warnings from the UN Intergovernmental Panel on Climate Change about the impending climate disaster, nothing substantial is being done. Governments have become entangled with industries that wreak havoc on the environment. In Australia, the Albanese government, which took office amid widespread hopes it would reject the environmental vandalism of its conservative predecessor, is following much the same path, modestly increasing the targeted reduction in carbon emissions while green-lighting dozens of new coal, gas and oil projects that will contribute to the global crisis.

Australian governments promote the interests of the fossil fuel industry for the same reasons they support corporate tax cuts. But imperialist ambitions are also to blame. The war machine of every country depends on burning fossil fuels, which is why even the inadequate carbon emission targets now in place exclude emissions from the military. War itself, most obviously nuclear war, would accelerate the climate catastrophe that has already been set in train. Governments can introduce this or that reform, but the entire system has to go if the planet is to be saved.

The multiplying crises in the capitalist system are having a political effect. The neoliberal agenda pursued by the mainstream Western capitalist parties since the 1980s has eroded their electoral support, sometimes wiping them off the electoral map. As the centre parties weaken, polarisation to left and right has emerged.

On the European left, we have seen various new parties or developments inside existing parties emerge, giving hope to the left and working class after years of betrayal by the centrist mainstream. These have included Podemos in Spain, Communist Refoundation in Italy and SYRIZA in Greece, but there have been many others. In the United States, Bernie Sanders drew crowds of tens of thousands of Democrat supporters looking for a left alternative to Wall Street's favourite candidate, Hillary Clinton, in the presidential primaries for the 2016 election. In every case, however, these parties and leaders have been drawn into governing on behalf of the capitalist class and become defenders of the system. They have backed imperialist wars and supported right-wing economic policies.

The failure of the left to provide an alternative to the neoliberal centre has opened the space for the hard right-leaders such as India's Narendra Modi, the US's Donald Trump and Argentina's Javier Milei, along with others who have done little to disguise their fascist roots. Promising the rebirth of national pride, authoritarian leadership, cuts to taxes on business and the rich, an offensive against "woke elites", a crackdown on immigration, rejection of climate science and assertion of "traditional values" (sexism, homophobia), the hard right has gone from the fringes to the centre of politics in many countries, making what were once extreme right-wing policies part of the mainstream. Centre-right parties have, in turn, shifted to the right to stem the leaching of their vote and have formed coalitions with parties they once rejected.

The 2024 presidential elections will tell if Trump can take the White House again, but even if he fails, Trump and his like leave a legacy of a strengthened far-right current in US politics. By mainstreaming the most extreme irrationalism and conspiratorial ideas, socially reactionary politics and a pro-business agenda, Trump has brought together many of the ingredients needed for a mass far-right movement to grow and that will continue to shape US politics for years to come.

The far right in Australia has not yet made the same inroads. However, the Liberal Party has been veering to the right in recent years and is channelling and cohering the reactionary rage of its right-wing supporter base, most recently in the 2023 referendum on the Indigenous Voice to Parliament. Given that the Liberal Party is, for the foreseeable future, the only alternative government to the ALP, its right-wing trajectory heralds a dangerous trend for Australian society in coming years, especially as Labor also pursues a right-wing agenda delivering nothing for its supporters.

Liberal commentators are now worried that the world system is in danger. In 2022, *Financial Times* journalist Martin Wolf explained to his readers:

> We are now moving into a new era of world disorder, marked by domestic mistakes and global friction… This new epoch of the world is creating huge challenges. It is possible – perhaps even probable – that the world system will shatter.[17]

But there is nothing worth saving about "the world system". It has never worked in the interests of most of the world's people. Socialists would welcome its shattering. Capitalism is an inherently exploitative and profit-driven system, it is irreformable. It needs to be ripped out root and branch. Any political project that seeks to run capitalism in a nicer way will end up defending and apologising for the system – that's what the experience of Labor, and all the reformist and centre-left forces across the world show. Our goal is to get rid of capitalism. The working class is the force that can do this.

Capitalism's gravedigger: the working class

The working class are not only victims but hold enormous power in their hands if they choose to use it. Workers have played a role in many of the revolts and upheavals of the past thirty years by flooding the streets and squares of Europe, Latin America, the Middle East and Africa. The working class has power in numbers, but they also have something even more powerful: the ability to shut down capitalist industry. In 2011, mass strikes in factories and ports helped bring down dictatorial regimes in Egypt and Tunisia. In 2019, when the masses of Sudan stood up against their dictator, strikes by workers shut down the nation's infrastructure and threatened the country's economy. Workers' power rests on the fact that because their labour is the source of all new value and the capitalists contribute nothing, capitalists depend upon workers.

From a small portion of the world's population when Marx and Engels wrote the *Communist Manifesto* in 1848, restricted to pockets of Europe, North America and small enclaves in Asia, the working class now straddles the globe and outnumbers the formerly dominant peasants. In medieval times, most peasants lived in villages and had little knowledge of the world beyond village boundaries. Capitalist development, however, has brought workers together in enormous numbers in big cities. In 1800, only 3 percent of the global population was urban. Today, more than one-half of the world's population lives in cities, a figure the UN slates to rise to two-thirds by 2050. In 1900, only 16 cities in the world, in nine countries, had more than one million inhabitants; today, there are 519 such cities in 125 countries.[18]

As capitalism concentrates workers in large numbers, it creates new battalions for the class struggle. The Foxconn campus in Shenzhen in southern China, a city that has grown from just a few hundred thousand in 1980 to 18 million today, makes Apple products. Foxconn employs 300,000 workers in 15 factories across an area of three square kilometres, complete with dormitories, a fire station, a TV network and a bank. Another 200,000

Foxconn workers are employed in Zhengzhou, the capital of central Henan province with a population of 13 million, where they assemble iPhones. Such workers have enormous collective leverage if they use it. As the popular union song "Solidarity Forever" has it: "Without our brain and muscle, not a single wheel would turn". When labour organises and refuses to work, the wheels of industry cease to turn, and the bosses' source of profits dries up. Strikes spark fear in capitalists because they are a reminder, to quote Russian revolutionary Vladimir Lenin, that "it is the workers and not they who are the real masters".[19] A strike of thousands of workers in a factory that produces some essential part can shut down an entire industry. A transport workers' strike can shut down an entire city, even an entire country. It is this power that explains why industrial workers have been at the centre of most of the successful struggles for democracy over the past century.[20] As Marx and Engels wrote in the *Communist Manifesto*: "What the bourgeoisie therefore produces, above all, are its own gravediggers".

Workers are also a cooperative class. Peasants toiled on the land, separated from each other. Their fondest wish was to own their own plot of land from which they might sell their own produce in competition with others. The capitalist mode of production, on the other hand, is cooperative. Not in the sense that the bosses cooperate with the workers – they do their best to screw them – but in the sense that the labour process brings together workers in a cooperative chain: the car worker making engine blocks works with other workers making tyres, gearboxes, ignition systems, windscreens and so on. The nurse caring for patients works with radiographers, ward staff, cleaners and lab technicians. Everyone is connected in the capitalist division of labour. The large workplaces – the factories, assembly lines, hospitals, warehouses, airports, shopping malls, universities and offices – teach workers collective discipline. They learn how to organise production cooperatively. It is not the chief executives who know best how to run things in any big workplace – many of them would not have the first clue – but the workers themselves. This cooperation is now a global phenomenon: computer chips and other components produced in Taiwan are assembled into tablets in China, using Chinese-made steel produced from Australian coal and iron ore and Silicon Valley know-how to sell on German markets. Every link in the chain brings workers from one country into connection with the others, even if they never meet.

The capitalist division of labour compels workers to work together if they are to win their battles against the bosses. A strike is a collective act: it has to bring everyone out together if it is to be successful. The same applies to the broader struggle for power. Peasants in medieval times could revolt, but they could never come together to take power from the landlords. They could burn down the lords' manor houses, but they could never impose themselves as a new ruling class because they were divided among themselves. Once peasant parties came onto the scene, they were led not by peasants themselves but by urban middle-class figures; the peasants could not represent themselves but had to be represented by others.

The working class are different. A car worker making engines cannot take their equipment home and make cars on their own, nor can a nurse take home a piece of the hospital. If workers want to take over the means of production – to operate the whole car factory or hospital – they have to do so collectively through a committee formed by workers and accountable to the workers. If they want to link up their workplaces to coordinate their efforts and then to link up one city to another, this also has to be done the same way through city-wide councils, or as they were called in Russia in 1917, soviets. The working class has no other way to exercise its power; you cannot just elect an MP to abolish the profit-driven capitalist system.

One more thing that distinguishes the working class is that they are what Marx called "a universal class", "a class which is the dissolution of all classes", since they have no interest in exploiting or oppressing any other group. Bourgeois revolutions, like the 1789 French Revolution, which saw the rising bourgeoisie dismantle the old feudal aristocracy, were carried out in the name of equality for all before the law. However, because the new bourgeois rulers depended on exploiting the emerging working class, the new rights they offered for the great mass of people, even at their most radical, were limited.

The working class are the labouring majority; they have no class to exploit when they control society. For the working class, political freedom without social and economic liberation counts for little. Real liberation for workers can only come by dismantling the entire edifice of society, and that means challenging every form of injustice that the system generates. As Marx and Engels wrote in the *Communist Manifesto*:

> All previous historical movements were movements of minorities, or in the interest of minorities. The proletarian movement is the self-conscious, independent movement of the immense majority, in the interest of the immense majority. The proletariat, the lowest stratum of our present society, cannot stir, cannot raise itself up, without the whole superincumbent strata of official society being sprung into the air.

The sheer comprehensiveness of its exploitation and oppression make the working class a subversive force – a class in short, "with radical chains".[21]

But we are running ahead of our story here, and we will return to the working class in chapter four when we look at how socialism might work.

To summarise. Capitalism itself makes the case for its overthrow. It produces poverty for the many on the one hand and luxury for the few on the other, with the gap between rich and poor getting bigger year after year. The system is wasteful, its chase for profits creating starvation alongside piles of unsold food and homelessness alongside empty apartments. The profits come not from the capitalists' ingenuity or hard work but from the sweat of the working class. And far from using some of the surplus produced by workers to provide better healthcare, education and pensions, the capitalists and governments around the world are stripping back social provisions, causing poverty and anxiety in tens of millions of households and increasing the risks of more deadly pandemics. Even when the system appears to be running smoothly, it diverts trillions of dollars into military spending, and we are now faced with the prospect of a third world war with devastating consequences. The prioritisation of profits before all else also threatens the very habitat we depend upon to live, as climate change endangers the planet's future.

If capitalism threatens our world, it is imperative that we get rid of it before it destroys us all. The working class are the social force that can do this because they have an interest in doing so and the power to do it. But the working class cannot do this if the reformist parties continue to dominate. We need political organisations that reject any collaboration with capitalism and organise the working class everywhere across the world to overthrow it. There is nothing more urgent today than building revolutionary organisation that can lead the working class in its historic task of smashing this rotten system. This is Socialist Alternative's project today.

Notes

1. *Forbes*, "The 2023 List: Facts and Figures", https://www.forbes.com/billionaires/; UBS, *Global Wealth Report 2023*, 2023, p.22; Josh Bivens and Jori Kandra, "CEO pay has skyrocketed 1,460% since 1978", Economic Policy Institute, 4 October 2022; FAO, IFAD, UNICEF, WFP and WHO, The State of Food Security and Nutrition in the World 2023, Rome, 2023.

2. Emily A. Shrider, Melissa Kollar, Frances Chen and Jessica Semega, *Income and Poverty in the United States: 2020*, US Census Bureau, 14 September 2021; Denis Campbell, "'National tragedy': figures show large rise in people dying while on NHS waiting list", *The Guardian*, 31 August 2023.

3. P. Davidson, B. Bradbury, B. Wong and T. Hill, *Inequality in Australia 2023: Overview*, Australian Council of Social Services and UNSW Sydney, 2023; Naazneen Karmali and Nicole Lindsay, "Australia's Richest 2023", *Forbes*, 15 February 2023.

4. Australian Taxation Office, "2021–22 Report of Entity Tax Information", 9 November 2023.

5. P. Davidson, B. Bradbury and M. Wong, Poverty in Australia 2023: Who is affected? Poverty and Inequality Partnership Report no. 20, Australian Council of Social Service and UNSW, 2023.

6. NSW Council of Social Services, *Barely Hanging On: The cost of living crisis in NSW*, NSW Council of Social Services, 2023.

7. Australian Institute of Health and Welfare (AIHW), *Australian Burden of Disease Study: impact and causes of illness and death in Australia 2018*, Australian Burden of Disease Study series no. 23. Cat. no. BOD 29, AIHW, 2021.

8. Safe Work Australia, *Key work health and safety statistics Australia 2022*, 2022.

9. This is true for capitalism as a system. Obviously, individual capitalists can and do make profits by using monopoly power to gouge consumers, by fiddling their taxes or by outright theft, but in the final analysis, these constitute a drain on, rather than an addition to, the total pool of surplus value created by the working class.

10. Calculated using data on industry value added and wages and salaries paid in selected industries, published in Australian Bureau of Statistics, *Australian Industry 2020–21*, ABS 8155.0DO0001_202021.

11. In the market sector. Australian Bureau of Statistics, *Australian System of National Accounts*, Cat. No. 5204.0, Table 13.

12. Between 1995 and 2023, capitalists in Australia doubled their investments in capital relative to money outlaid on employing workers, what economists call the "capital-labour ratio". Australian Bureau of Statistics, *Australian System of National Accounts*, Cat. No. 5204.0, Table 13.

13. Jan Fichtner and Eelke M. Heemskerk, "The New Permanent Universal Owners: Index Funds (Im)patient Capital, and the Claim of Long-termism", 2019, https://papers.ssrn.com/sol3/papers.cfm?abstract_id=3321597; James B. Glattfelder, Stefano Battiston, "The architecture of power: Patterns of disruption and stability in the global ownership network", 2019, https://papers.ssrn.com/sol3/papers.cfm?abstract_id=3314648; Bruce Upbin, "The 147 companies that control everything," *Forbes*, October 22, 2011; Stefania Vitali, James B. Glattfelder, and Stefano Battiston, "The network of global corporate control", paper written for the Federal Institute of Technology, Zurich, Switzerland, September 2011, http://arxiv.org/pdf/1107.5728.pdf.

14.   Australia Institute, *Fossil Fuel Subsidies in Australia 2023*, 2023; Tom Lowrey, "Public service audit reveals \$20.8b spent on external contractors and consultants in 2021–22", ABC News, 6 May 2023.

15.   Karl Marx and Friedrich Engels, *The Communist Manifesto*, 1848.

16.   Eric Hobsbawm, "War and Peace in the 20th Century", *London Review of Books*, Vol. 24, no. 4, 21 February 2002.

17.   Martin Wolf, "In an era of disorder, open trade is at risk", *Financial Times*, 29 June 2022.

18.   Mark Beissinger, *The Revolutionary City: Urbanization and the Global Transformation of Rebellion*, Princeton University Press, 2022, pp.6, 67.

19.   V.I. Lenin, *On Strikes*, 1899.

20.   Sirianne Dahlum, Carl Henrik Knudsen and Tore Wig, "Who revolts? Empirically revisiting the social origins of democracy", *The Journal of Politics*, 81 (4), 2019.

21.   Karl Marx, *A Contribution to the Critique of Hegel's Philosophy of Right*, 1843.

Chapter two

The capitalist state[1]

The executive of the modern state is but a committee for managing the common affairs of the whole bourgeoisie.

—Marx and Engels, *The Communist Manifesto*

T HE CAPITALIST CLASS does not just dominate the factories, warehouses and offices; it dominates the state as well. The state is the coercive institution whose purpose is to enforce the rule of one class over others. It monopolises the means of organised violence in its hands – the police, the army, the courts and the jails – to secure the domination of the ruling class. This differs from what schools, universities and politicians tell us about the state. They tell us it is a neutral institution designed to uphold the law and secure peace in the land. In the absence of a state, they say, society will tear itself apart in "a war of all against all", in the words of seventeenth-century philosopher Thomas Hobbes.[2] But the apparent neutrality of the state is a façade. As Engels put it, the state is, "as a rule, the state of the most powerful, economically dominant class, which, through the medium of the state, becomes also the politically dominant class, and thus acquires new means of keeping down and exploiting the oppressed class".

> Thus, the state of antiquity was above all the state of the slave owners for keeping down the slaves, as the feudal state was the organ of the nobility for keeping down the peasant serfs and villeins, and the modern representative state is an instrument for the exploitation of wage labour by capital.[3]

No class system can survive by naked force alone. By definition, a class society involves the exploitation of the many by the few. What is to stop the many from seizing back the wealth they have produced? Unless there are to be endless rounds of conflict, class rule must rest at least in part on the consent of the exploited. And for that, the ruling class relies on the efforts of ideologists – traditionally priests, but today, the media and the education system – who seek to convince us that the current society, even if flawed, is the best possible. An important part of this legitimation process is parliamentary democracy. But when wealth is dominated by the few, the political equality that we enjoy in Australia today, where the worker's vote is equal to that of Gina Rinehart, is merely a screen disguising the rule of the capitalist class. As Lenin put it:

> Bourgeois democracy, although a great historical advance in comparison with medievalism, always remains, and under capitalism is bound to remain, restricted, truncated, false, hypocritical – a paradise for the rich and a snare and deception for the exploited, for the poor.[4]

Conventionally, states are understood as comprising three arms: the legislative, executive and judicial. The Commonwealth, State and Territory parliaments, along with local councils, form the state's legislative arm. In them, our elected representatives are said to make the most important decisions for our society. These take the form of policies, laws and by-laws. The executive comprises governments, the public service, the police and the armed forces. It includes other institutions set up under particular laws, like the Australian Broadcasting Corporation (ABC), Reserve Bank, Australia Post and public universities. Executive agencies are supposed to carry out the legislative decisions. In practice, most state decisions are formulated if not made by ministers, their advisers and allies – who may or may not hold any public office – and senior public servants. Judges and magistrates are the most important figures in the third arm of the state, the judiciary, which is supposed to act as the neutral adjudicator of disputes about the application of laws.

This "separation of powers" between the three arms of the state, the basis of the Westminster system of government, is said to ensure genuine democracy and the rule of the people through their representatives in parliament. It is, however, a cover for the dictatorship of capital. This may not be immediately obvious. After all, in parliamentary democracy, the politicians, the judges, and the senior public servants are mostly not capitalists – politicians, for example, are disproportionately from legal backgrounds. In our system, those who govern do not own; those who own do not govern. Things worked differently under feudal society, where those who owned property and those in charge of the state were often the same people: any peasant hauled up before the local court would likely find their landlord as the judge. Today, however, in liberal democracies like Australia, the capitalists leave running the state machine to political functionaries and administrators and tend not to concern themselves with every part of its operations.

Why and how does the state, even in a democratic country like Australia, pursue the interests of the capitalist class? One obvious means the capitalist class has at their disposal is lobbying and bribery. Scarcely a day goes by that we don't hear of some company donating to the ALP or Coalition to sway political decisions, and well-paid careers await those politicians who do their bidding. But in the scheme of things, this is unimportant. Even the "cleanest" government under capitalism would still serve the capitalist class. The chief reason that the state serves the capitalists, even in a parliamentary democracy, is because it depends on capital. The decisions made by members of the capitalist class have huge effects on employment, production, investment and exports. These issues dominate the financial pages of the newspapers and preoccupy government leaders and senior bureaucrats. "Business confidence" surveys signal to governments which policies are acceptable, and which are not. And when a government threatens to introduce measures the capitalists don't like, they go on strike – they refuse to invest and withdraw their money, dragging down the economy. With rare exceptions, governments buckle.

Those in charge of the state machine respond to pressure from the capitalists because politicians' electoral prospects and the job security or chances of promotion of senior public servants suffer when growth slows, and unemployment rises. The incomes of all public employees also come, via taxation and state charges, from the part of the economy producing commodities. So politicians and state managers encourage economic growth, which entails trying to boost the profitability of capital in the territory they preside over.

Just as the state depends on capital, capitalists rely on states. The armed forces, far from defending the nation, defend the interests of those with money. The British state used military power to take the land from Indigenous people as a crucial first step in developing Australian capitalism. Thereafter, the armed forces have been used to secure the interests of the Australian ruling class against rival ruling classes with designs on Australia's neighbourhood and its self-declared sphere of influence in the South Pacific. This battle for control has been the basis for several wars and military operations in the past century. Even if Australian military intervention has sometimes been couched in terms of humanitarian interventions, the rationale is always about what is best for the ruling class. The Australian military has not only fought overseas; it has broken strikes by Australian workers. The army also has contingency plans for repressing protests and demonstrations free from parliamentary scrutiny.

The armed forces reproduce all the class distinctions of civil society. At the top are the generals – highly paid and vested with enormous power, including the right to order thousands to their deaths. They are conservative and form part of the ruling class; on retirement from the armed forces, many have become state governors or governors-general. They will not hesitate to take drastic measures to prop up the capitalist social order. The officer corps reflects all the rotten features of the social order it has to defend, as is clear from the repeated sexual abuse and bastardisation in its training institutions. Attempts to clean up such abuses are irrelevant – dehumanisation is inevitable in an institution whose purpose is to oppress the working class. Below the officers and the NCOs are the dogsbodies, the naval ratings and privates, who form the "working class in uniform", bossed around like workers in a factory.

The police and courts are the front lines of capitalist coercion against the working class. We will spend more time on them below, but for the moment, it's important to understand that the basis of the legal system is the protection of property – if you don't believe that, look at any legal textbook! The more property you have, the more you will enjoy the protection of the courts and police. And if you are believed to be a threat to that property, the courts and police will take a great interest in you. That's why strikers, who cut off the flow of profits to the bosses, are harassed by legal injunctions and police bullying, while businesspeople who rip off consumers or workers get off with a slap on the wrist.

The state helps capital in other ways. It establishes and enforces rules of economic behaviour. It promotes growth and international competitiveness. Special departments, bureaus, divisions, branches and sections promote the well-being of entire sectors of the economy, like manufacturing, agriculture, mining, communications, tourism and transport. Other state institutions fund or regulate essential infrastructures that serve private enterprise (water, electricity, gas, ports, railways, roads, airports, broadcast spectrum).

State and federal welfare, immigration, education and health policies ensure that a suitable supply of labour power is available to the capitalist class. Rules that govern pensions, youth allowance, unemployment benefits, income taxation and the rights of spouses, parents and guardians shape the families in which the next generation of workers is raised and socialised. This is not a benevolent but often a punitive process. Welfare bureaucracies, which are meant to look after those in need, as commonly harass those already downtrodden, as the Robodebt scandal revealed. They play an important role in disciplining working-class communities and, with Indigenous families, breaking them up and ensuring ongoing Stolen Generations. Such interventions are driven not only by cost-cutting measures but also by the need to strike fear into the hearts of the working class and to force workers to accept any low-paid job rather than rely on the welfare state.

The education system produces workers with general abilities and specific skills that employers need. More importantly, the education system trains people to follow orders and accept the status quo. The bureaucratic structures of school and work and the undemocratic authority of teachers and bosses have parallels in the health system, with its complicated rules and the elevated status of doctors.

Governments and state and federal industrial relations commissions determine the conditions under which employers buy workers' labour power, including wages, hours of work, superannuation entitlements, public holidays, and health and safety rules. Their decisions are further opportunities to secure business profitability in Australia and the competitiveness of locally based capitals against their rivals in other countries.

To an important degree, institutions of the state are capitalist institutions which function according to the same logic. Like private corporations, states are large enterprises ruled by strict hierarchies. At the bottom are workers, people who do what they are told and control none of the human or financial resources. In Australia, the state and commonwealth governments are the largest employers. Together, they employ over two million people, the vast majority of them workers who simply sell their labour power. At the top of public sector agencies are state managers (whether senior politicians or bureaucrats), who decide how assets and staff are deployed. As we argued in chapter one, these managers, because of their role in the production relations inside the state, are as much members of the capitalist class as the executives at the top of BHP, Wesfarmers or the Commonwealth Bank. They have common interests with the rest of that class in preserving the authority of management and its control over productive resources and are paid accordingly, around ten times average weekly earnings.

Because of the role they play in securing the reproduction of capital, senior state officials come into close contact with other sections of the capitalist class, as discussed in chapter one. There is movement of personnel in both directions between corporations and the state and, commonly, corporate executives are invited to make policy for governments. The Business Council of Australia and the Australian Chamber of Commerce and Industry are frequently consulted about the drafting of government policy. Common interests and personal ties cohere the bosses, public and private, into a capitalist class that shares the same worldview.

When Marx and Engels wrote that "the executive of the modern state is but a committee for managing the common affairs of the whole bourgeoisie",[5] they did not mean that the state is a puppet of the capitalists. It enjoys some autonomy. In important ways, the state balances the interests of competing capitalists against each other, to do what is best for Australian capitalism. Thus, governments may enact legislation that is in the long-term interests of the capitalists, even if it injures some of them in the short term. And if the working class is mobilising in large numbers, the capitalist state can respond favourably to its demands, albeit only to prevent any further escalation. But if the state is not a puppet, it works intimately with and within the capitalist class and in its interests.

Role of the police and courts

It is worth emphasising the coercive nature of the capitalist state since this runs so much against everything that we are taught. The state exists to enforce property rights, as a study of the police in Australia will confirm.

Australian police have their origins in two projects of early colonial settlement. One was to control the convicts and regulate their labour.[6] The first body to carry out policing functions was the dozen-strong night watch appointed in 1788 by Governor Arthur Phillip from the ranks of convicts who gained preferential treatment in return for carrying out the duties. Ben Hillier and Tom O'Lincoln argue:

> [T]he role of this embryonic police force in the very early years was not so much defending great material privilege – there was little material privilege to defend – but protecting property, maintaining order and helping to establish and enforce the hierarchy of authority.

Justice lay in the hands of magistrates who were drawn from the "respectable" elements of the penal settlement, including surgeons, chaplains and officers. These had a direct personal interest in enriching a narrow minority whose wealth came from grabbing land and appointing convicts to work on their properties. Controlling the labour of convicts became their chief concern; drunkenness, absconding from work and idleness were serious offences and punished by lashes and irons. In the late 1790s, Governor Hunter introduced a pass system that strictly regulated the movement of convicts in the colony; it subjected those found without a pass to hard labour or lashes. Such a system required police informants, whose numbers flourished. By 1814, "constable" was the fourth largest occupational category. The first full-time magistrate, who was also police superintendent, was appointed. Each Sydney district obtained a watch house and district constable.

By the 1830s, British demand for wool led to a surge in colonial settlement beyond the Blue Mountains and south to what is now Victoria as the pastoral industry emerged. Capitalist development now overtook the penal logic of the early colony. The second element of colonial settlement kicked in – the dispossession of the Indigenous population, with the police taking a prominent role in crushing resistance and deploying hunting parties to massacre "troublesome Natives". Wholesale massacres ensued, with mounted police detachments attacking Indigenous groups with impunity. The Queensland Native Police Force alone was responsible for an estimated 24,000 "violent Aboriginal deaths" between 1859 and 1897, according to historian Raymond Evans.[7]

If the Indigenous population was subjected to a campaign of near extermination, this did not mean that the police ignored the expanding labouring classes of the colonies. In 1854, police joined almost 300 mounted and foot troopers to attack the Eureka Stockade in Ballarat to crush insurgent gold miners protesting about the imposition of an unfair tax and the refusal of the governor to listen to their demands. At least 22 miners were killed in the attack. In the 1880s and 1890s, the authorities regularly deputised farmers' sons as special constables to attack striking shearers, wharfies and seafarers demanding higher pay and recognition of their unions. Mass arrests, bashings and frame-ups were the order of the day. This pattern continued throughout the twentieth century, with the police being regularly used to break picket lines, harass strikers and otherwise do the bosses' bidding during industrial disputes.

The class bias of the police and justice system is still apparent today. If a crooked boss robs workers of $1,000 in wages, the police will do nothing. In the rare instance where the employer is prosecuted by a body other than the police, at most they will pay a small fine. But when it comes to $1,000 missing from the till at a shop, police will review surveillance footage to identify which employee stole it and then will prosecute them to the full extent of the law. During the cost-of-living crisis, police are targeting shoplifters but do nothing to stop the supermarkets from pushing up prices and racking up $1 billion in annual profits. The state does not care about the petty possessions of individuals. If you have ever had your wallet or computer stolen, you know it little interests the police, and the clear-up rate is low. With most petty property crimes, police are effectively inspectors for insurance companies.

The state is not interested in preventing what is euphemistically called white-collar crime. A few heads may roll after some particularly scandalous piece of corporate crookery, particularly where this crookery has interfered with profit-making by other capitalists, but the agencies tasked with cracking corporate crime – the Australian Federal Police (AFP) and the Australian Securities and Investigation Commission (ASIC) – generally fail to act even when thousands of people's lives have been ruined. The AFP is too busy raiding trade union offices and the homes of whistleblowing journalists in the service of Liberal governments, while ASIC, stuffed full of former bankers, has allowed banks to extract millions of dollars from customers' accounts. The 2017 Royal Commission into the banking industry noted:

> Too often [the banks] have been treated in ways that would allow them to think that they, not ASIC, not the Parliament, not the courts, will decide when and how the law will be obeyed or the consequences of breach remedied.[8]

The media would have us believe that a thin blue line is the only thing standing between society and criminal mayhem. This is far from true. In 2015, New York police pulled back from harassing Black and Latino communities for minor offences as part of a reactionary campaign against the city mayor. This led to no obvious escalation of crime and a great decrease in the level of fear in working-class communities.[9] Community responder programs, in which New York residents rather than police respond to low-level street crime, have seen rates of homicide, shootings and auto theft drop.[10] A systematic review of 62 studies of police force size and crime in the US between 1971 and 2013 concluded that "the overall effect size for police force size on crime is negative, small, and not statistically significant".[11]

Protecting ordinary people from interpersonal violence is not, and has never been, the reason that governments spend so much money on a police force. After all, workplace accidents and illnesses cause many times more deaths than interpersonal violence. Yet government health and safety agencies do not have anywhere near the independence, powers or funding of the police force.

The police are not about protecting us but crushing us if we ever threaten the capitalist class and their social order. The largest mobilisations of police since the end of World War II have all been to suppress protests. More than 4,000 were mobilised to protect US President George W. Bush and other world leaders at the 2007 APEC forum in Sydney. Five thousand were marshalled from all across Australia and New Zealand to protect the G20 summit in Brisbane in 2014. In 2020, NSW police used COVID-19 pandemic restrictions on public gatherings to suppress Black Lives Matter protests in Sydney, and it was only after 30,000 people had already taken to the streets in defiance of police threats that the court backed down. At the following week's protest, the police mobilised huge numbers to take over the entire CBD and successfully prevented the rally from assembling properly. In "declared zones", police have the legal right to randomly search protesters, seize their possessions, ban items of dress and order demonstrators to leave the area. Climate protesters engaged in direct action risk jail terms under laws designed to protect fossil fuel companies, and even organisers of small demonstrations have been arrested in their homes and detained late at night.

Intimidating displays of weapons are now par for the course at left-wing demonstrations in Sydney and Melbourne, and riot police now have access to high-tech weaponry, including semi-automatic rifles, flash and noise devices and capsicum gas canister bombs.

British socialist Audrey Farrell compared three sets of statistics – crime statistics, police numbers and the level of protests. Her findings were stark: while there is a strong correlation between police numbers and protests, there was no correlation at all between crime rates and police numbers.[12] There is no reason to expect that Australian research findings would differ.

Police officers spend most of their time enforcing property laws that keep the poor poor – prosecuting people for shoplifting or public transport fare evasion, or even harassing homeless people for sleeping in the street. This builds a distrust of and contempt for ordinary people, which makes police more reliable at policing protests. At bottom, police forces are reliable servants of the capitalist order. Many recruits come from working-class backgrounds, but training, tight organisation and the promotion of loyalty to the force suppress feelings of solidarity with other workers. Police are taught how to bully people and ensure that their instructions are obeyed. An effective police force is disciplined, has a strong corporate identity and is separate from ordinary people. An inevitable by-product of giving the police the power and discretion they need, if they are to be a reliable means of enforcing class rule, is endemic corruption. But this is a small price to pay for an institution that is available to smash picket lines, break up demonstrations, intimidate individuals, reinforce racism and foster panics about "law and order".

It is this training and outlook that distinguishes the police from the army. The political loyalty of the armed forces is a vital question for revolutionaries because unless the armed forces split, no revolution will succeed – our side will never have the weapons or training to overcome an army that stands firm to support the status quo. In most times, when the armed forces are called upon, they do the government's bidding. In the 1949 coal strike, the Chifley government sent soldiers to the mines to dig coal. In 1989, the Hawke government used the RAAF to break an airline pilots' strike. Legislation is in place to permit the military to take over civilian government in cases of "disorder".

Breaking strikes and smashing workers' heads, however, is not the reason most soldiers and sailors join the armed forces – they do so because they think they might learn a trade, travel overseas or defend their country from invasion. Nor is harassing workers and the poor part of their daily experience. Soldiers and sailors are not, therefore, immersed in a culture where hating large parts of the civilian population is par for the course, as the police are. And hatred for the officer corps is common. This is why, at times of political crises, if those in the streets or on picket lines appeal to soldiers on the basis of class solidarity – "Don't shoot on your brothers and sisters!" – the armed forces can split. This has been the historical record at many key moments, with soldiers and sailors refusing to follow orders to fire on crowds and, sometimes, handing over their weapons to the masses or joining their ranks. When the armed forces switch sides, that spells the death knell for any regime. Frontline police, however, never mutiny in this way and if they object to orders from their superiors it is usually because they regard the higher-ups as being too "soft" on those they police.

"Law enforcement" overwhelmingly oppresses and punishes the working class, Indigenous people, LGBTI people and ethnic minorities. Rates of arrest for oppressed groups, including workers, are far higher than for the middle and capitalist classes. Indigenous people drinking in the streets are hauled off to court and fined. Business people hiring a marquee in a city square and getting obnoxiously drunk are safe from prosecution. Young workers and Arab or African migrants driving "flash" cars are routinely pulled over and quizzed, while drivers of the same cars in well-off suburbs are never touched. LGBTI people are still bashed by police when they think there are no cameras around. Young Muslim men meeting in groups in Melbourne's Thomastown or Sydney's Lakemba regularly face police harassment, while college boys at Ormond or St John's at Melbourne or Sydney universities are treated with kid gloves as the future leaders that most are.

The prison population reflects these oppressive policing practices. While the rich walk free, those with few resources often face prison when pulled before courts. Those incarcerated are much more likely to have received little formal education, to be unemployed, homeless, addicted to drugs and suffering intellectual disabilities. In particular, they tend to be Aboriginal: Indigenous people are imprisoned at 16 times the rate of non-Indigenous. Overcrowding and the brutality of the prison system further accentuate the disadvantage experienced by prisoners even before they are locked up, making prisoners more likely to self-harm or commit suicide. Nearly 40 percent of those in prison have not been convicted of anything but are on remand, awaiting a court hearing.[13]

Periodic "law and order" campaigns further criminalise those who are the main victims of penny-pinching government policies – the unemployed, youth, those marginalised and discriminated against, as well as individuals and groups most dependent on the social services decimated by cuts and privatisation. Where the state should provide education, healthcare and economic support to workers and the poor, it instead criminalises and incarcerates them. The suburbs most associated in the mass media with crime and delinquent youth, such as Bankstown in western Sydney, also have a youth unemployment rate well above the national average.

The law-and-order agenda also provides a convenient scapegoat for governments looking to blame others for the social decay they are responsible for. Crime and criminal elements are frequently presented as the cause of social breakdown and used as a focus for mass anger and insecurity, rather than the government policies that contribute to unemployment, poverty, drug use and violence. Racist hostility to particular ethnic groups almost always accompanies such scapegoating, with the focus today on Lebanese, Muslim and African youth. Campaigns against "ethnic gangs" are only one part of the law-and-order offensive. Other elements include crackdowns on bikies and anti-terrorism laws. All are used to boost spending on police and prisons while spending on health and education is cut.

On top of the routine policing which targets the working class and political opposition, the state also runs extensive covert operations against the population. Various arms of the state and federal police have compiled voluminous records on what they deem to be subversives and subversive organisations for many decades. Communists, actual or otherwise, were a major target for surveillance and infiltration for half a century. In more recent times, environmental activists have borne much of the brunt. In 2022, NSW police in plain clothes and unmarked cars spied on an encampment of climate activists at a private property north of Sydney. Under the cover of anti-terrorism legislation, snooping on private citizens is being escalated, involving the collection and storage of internet and phone metadata without restriction or court authorisation. Government funding for ASIO more than quadrupled in real terms in the two decades after the 9/11 bombing of the World Trade Center.

Can the state be reformed?

The state is a repressive instrument that operates in the interests of and often as part of the capitalist class. Many of the most important agencies of the state are unelected and, therefore, subject to no direct popular accountability. These include the judges, the public service bureaucrats, the army generals and the police commissioners. But what of the government of the day? It is elected and can fire insubordinate state functionaries trying to frustrate the people's will.

That government can wield the instruments of the state to serve the needs of the working class might seem appealing at first sight and has inspired generations of socialists. This has historically involved workers looking to the ALP as the means to improve their lot. Labor politicians tell us we only need to vote for them to usher in reforms or abolish reactionary laws. In times past, some of them even argued that parliament could introduce socialism in Australia.

Attempting to create socialism through parliamentary reform is doomed to failure. Every attempt at it has been disastrous, and the strength of the capitalist class over the state makes it impossible today. The first set of problems concerns the ability of the working class to get its voice heard and acted upon within the institutions of the capitalist state. Any elected government operates at the mercy of the High Court in relation to its interpretation of the law and the constitution. Judges are conservative, not just because they mostly come from upper-crust social circles and are paid handsome salaries and allowances, but because their job is to defend the constitution, which is the constitution of property owners. As Labor governments have found out in the past, the High Court will strike down any attempt to nationalise the banks on constitutional grounds. By the same token, courts will overrule any attempt by Labor governments to tamper with the sacred rights of bosses to run their workplaces as they see fit, providing they meet basic safety standards and pay workers their correct wages and conditions (although in practice, many fail to do so). The courts will never allow governments to enact legislation requiring bosses to give workers and unions the right to appoint supervisors or managers or to decide whether their workplace should close or stay open.

Even if a reforming government overcomes any legal challenge in the courts, other elements of the state will block it. These include reactionary bureaucrats, army generals and police chiefs. Sometimes, Labor governments may make one or two changes to the ranks of the senior public service personnel, but the new appointees are rarely any more sympathetic to serious reform. Police commanders and military heads of staff are even less vulnerable in their positions – any move to purge police commanders or military heads of staff would lead to deep opposition in the ranks of these institutions. The outcome is that any reforming government invariably finds not only the judges but senior public service bureaucrats and police and army commanders arrayed against it.

Parliamentary elections themselves are, by design, incapable of giving full expression to any radical mood within the working class. Workers turn up to the polling booth as millions of scattered individuals. Unlike a union meeting, where workers can debate the issues and decide through a collective and open vote, a process that encourages a sense of solidarity, workers voting in parliamentary elections are isolated from each other and are more prone to influence by media and corporate campaigns supporting conservative candidates and slamming radicals. Parliamentary constituencies, further, are social hotchpotches, bringing together people based on their place of residence, not their class. So, the voice of workers can be affected by the middle and capitalist classes who also get to vote but who have far more opportunities to set the political agenda in their localities by their influence over local media and civic affairs. And so, while parliament is meant to represent the people's voice, it only provides democratic legitimation for the rule of one class, the capitalists.

Any reformist parliamentarian who gets elected would quickly experience a hostile and insistent media campaign demanding that they renege on their promises. Counter-pressure from their working-class constituency is only episodic and infrequent; politicians are free from any democratic accountability other than at three- or four-yearly elections. In addition, there are the spoils of office – the high salaries, the expense allowances, the government cars, the first-class travel, the respect afforded them by official society and the opportunities for plum government or corporate jobs on retirement from politics – that temper any enthusiasm for radical measures. Most reformist politicians who have gone into parliament to pursue a left-wing agenda have capitulated and become loyal defenders of the status quo. Those intent on reforming the state end up being reformed by it, and not for the better. The rare minority who have not given in to these pressures have either been expelled or relegated to the party's margins as eccentrics. Parliamentarians who aren't part of a revolutionary movement, not disciplined by a revolutionary party, are prone to succumb to all these pressures.

These are all important obstacles to any reforming government with a mandate for radical change coming to office, drafting the requisite legislation, passing it in both houses of parliament and implementing it through the machinery of the state. Further, and it's important to be clear on this point, whatever such a government might be capable of doing, this would not constitute socialism. Administering the capitalist state machinery in such a way as to redistribute resources to workers is not socialism, the rule of the working class. We would have a more generous welfare state and more public ownership. But it would still be a capitalist economy and a capitalist state. The working class would not be running society. The prison that is capitalism would be more comfortably appointed, but the working class would still be the objects of action by the state, not its masters. Or, as Polish-German revolutionary Rosa Luxemburg put it in 1908, the result would be that:

> Our program becomes not the realisation of socialism but the reform of capitalism; not the suppression of the wage labour system but the diminution of exploitation, that is, the suppression of the abuses of capitalism instead of suppression of capitalism itself.[14]

Suppressing capitalism requires a whole different strategy, whose aim would be to smash the state, not to run it.

If the state machinery is unsuited to allowing radical reform, still less socialism, an equally important obstacle, and one that buttresses the obstructive resistance of the state, is the power of the capitalist class outside the state. The likes of Gina Rinehart, Andrew Forrest and Frank Lowy will not sit back and allow their property and assets to be taken from them because a majority of the electorate voted for a big tax hike on the rich or nationalisation of their companies without compensation. The capitalists can pull their money from the country, cancel investment projects, push down the dollar and stock market, shut down business enterprises, throw thousands out of work, hoard supplies and disrupt production to cause economic turmoil.

The capitalists can also urge the conservative parties to block supply of funds to the government in the upper house (if the Senate is sympathetic) and sponsor gangs of hoodlums and elements of the security state to cause trouble. They can mobilise support from the US government, the IMF and international capital. The capitalists also have the wherewithal to mobilise crowds of middle-class supporters and more backward workers in street demonstrations to intimidate the government and its supporters. Their ultimate recourse is to team up with conservative opponents in the state machine to launch a military coup or fascist takeover.

Two Labor governments have been driven out of office by a range of these measures. The first was the NSW government led by Jack Lang, who was sacked by the state governor at the height of the Great Depression in 1932 after threatening to delay paying interest on British loans. The second was the Whitlam government, which was sacked in 1975 by the governor-general after the conservative-dominated Senate blocked supply. In the months running up to Whitlam's dismissal, the media ran a vicious propaganda campaign against his government. Demonstrations against unions and "socialism" were organised in some regional centres, while insurance companies and the Australian Medical Association denounced government reforms such as Medibank. Finally, once supply was blocked, the private banks refused to lend money to the government. The dismissal was the last step in a nearly year-long campaign of capitalist sabotage. Once it was announced, the army was placed on grey alert – one step from red alert – as the ruling class prepared to put down any mass resistance that might escape the control of the Labor Party.

The Whitlam sacking tells us not only of the willingness of the capitalist class to jettison norms of parliamentary democracy to get its way but also the character of the ALP. As news of Whitlam's dismissal spread, many workers struck in protest. But Whitlam, afraid of unleashing a storm of political protest that might slip out of Labor's control, discouraged mass demonstrations and strikes and steered working-class anger into a mainstream election campaign led by Labor's most conservative ministers. Whitlam was keen to appeal to the capitalist class and preferred his own government's defeat to the prospect of being re-elected on a radical platform off the back of a militant working-class campaign of self-defence.

The ALP drew the conclusion from Whitlam's sacking that his government had moved "too far, too fast" and that future Labor governments must proceed no further and no faster than what was acceptable to the capitalists. The result has been nearly five decades of Labor governments at state and federal levels that have pursued political programs barely different from those of their conservative opponents. The party has been predisposed to do so because it has never been part of its agenda to mount a vigorous attack on the capitalists. The ALP was founded in 1891 with high hopes among some socialists that it could be a vehicle to introduce socialism, but within a decade, the party had become completely committed to governing in the interests of Australian capitalism in the name of advancing the so-called national interest. It understood the power of the capitalist class and was determined to eke out a program of modest and gradual reform that would not antagonise the bosses. And so by the time of federation in 1901, the ALP had become a champion of White Australia, industrial arbitration and tariffs to develop infant industries: none of these had anything to do with socialism but everything to do with Labor's program to advance Australian capitalism. Labor governments have come and gone since then, some more conservative, some a little more reform-inclined, but they have never used the state as a battering ram against capitalist interests. Any reforms that have been passed, such as the abolition of university fees or the introduction of Medibank by the Whitlam government, have been made to improve the profitability of the capitalists based on a better educated, healthier and therefore more productive working class.

Disgusted by Labor's right-wing policies in office, some have looked to the Greens as an alternative party of reform in recent years. The Greens often pose to the left of the ALP, but they have never pursued a frontal challenge to the capitalist class. They share with Labor a project of minor reforms within the system while leaving the class structure intact. This means that the party fails on two basic fronts. It claims to be a party that relates to social movements and people power, but there is little evidence of this – parliament takes precedence. The Greens' strategy is to win seats in parliament, gain the balance of power and use it to force the government to pass reforms. They have no orientation to recruiting and organising the working class, the one class with the power to fight the capitalists, nor even to mobilise big demonstrations. But the Greens fail even on the terrain of working within parliament to win genuine reforms. On the two occasions when they have held the balance of power federally – during the 2010–13 Gillard government and the Albanese government today – they have achieved no meaningful reforms and instead rubber-stamped Labor's agenda while claiming great victories for extracting some minor concessions. Invariably, they maintain they will keep fighting for more, but by passing Labor's bills, they have lost all leverage. Neither the Greens nor the ALP is the answer for anyone looking to challenge the horrors of capitalism.

Not that socialist organisations should not try to get representatives in parliament. As long as we live under capitalism, parliament is an important institution that people look to, and so socialists should attempt to have a presence where it's viable to do so, to advance the struggle and make radical arguments. The Bolsheviks successfully contested parliamentary elections, and their elected deputies used the chamber to make revolutionary propaganda, organise strikes and campaign for the rights of workers and the oppressed. They did this alongside organising in the factories and the barracks as part of their overall project of winning the working class to socialism. Today, Socialist Alternative runs candidates in Victorian elections through the Victorian Socialists. The problem lies not in having members of parliament but in believing you can use these to reform the capitalist state. That is the root cause of the problems described above.

In summary

The various arms of the state appear neutral but serve capitalism. Parliament appears to represent the interests of the entire population but just represents the rich. Public services provide important services for the benefit of all but disproportionately work in the interests of business. The police say they protect and serve the citizenry but repress the working class and Indigenous people. The armed forces say that their role is to defend the country and undertake humanitarian interventions overseas, but they actually protect the interests of the Australian ruling class. Welfare state bureaucracies are supposed to look after the needy but only reproduce existing inequalities while indoctrinating and disciplining the working class and the poor.

The state, therefore, is a weapon in the hands of the capitalist class and rules in its interests. In moments of peril, the state machine and the capitalists outside the state join forces to repel the threat, up to and including the suspension of parliament and the abrogation of all democratic rights.

Labor governments can introduce reforms, as indeed can conservative governments, if they are pushed to do so by working-class agitation and if such reforms are also deemed to have some benefits for the capitalist class. But they can never use parliament as a mechanism to introduce socialism, the expropriation of the capitalists' property and the rule of the working class. We cannot take the state into our hands and wield it in our interests; we must smash it and create a workers' state. For that, we need a revolutionary party that represents a clean break from the right-wing reformism that characterises the ALP.

Notes

1.   This chapter includes extensive extracts from Rick Kuhn, "Illusions of equality: the capitalist state" in Rick Kuhn (ed.), *Class and Struggle in Australia*, Pearson Longman, 2005; Sam Pietsch, "To have and to hold on to: wealth, power and the capitalist class", in Kuhn, *Class and Struggle in Australia*.

2.   Thomas Hobbes, *Leviathan*, Touchstone Books, 1997, p.100.

3.   Friedrich Engels, *The Origins of the Family, Private Property and the State*, 1884.

4.   V.I. Lenin, *The Proletarian Revolution and the Renegade Kautsky*, 1918.

5.   Karl Marx and Friedrich Engels, *The Communist Manifesto*, 1848.

6.   The following account draws on Ben Hillier and Tom O'Lincoln, "Five hundred lashes and double irons: the origins of Australian capitalism", *Marxist Left Review*, 5, Summer 2013.

7.   Raymond Evans, "The country has another past: Queensland and the History Wars", in Frances Peters-Little, Ann Curthoys and John Docker (eds), *Passionate Histories: Myth, memory and Indigenous Australia*, ANU Press, 2014, p.31.

8.   Royal Commission into Misconduct in the Banking, Superannuation and Financial Services Industry, *Interim Report*, 2018, p.281.

9.   Amina Khan, "In New York, major crime complaints fell when cops took a break from 'proactive policing'", *Los Angeles Times*, 26 September 2017.

10. Maria Cramer, "What happened when a Brooklyn neighborhood policed itself for five days?", *New York Times*, 4 June 2023.

11. Hassan Kanu, "Police are not primarily crime fighters, according to the data", Reuters, 3 November 2022.

12. Audrey Farrell, *Crime, Class and Corruption: Politics of the Police*, Bookmarks, 1992.

13. Australian Institute of Health and Welfare (AIHW), *The Health of Australia's Prisoners 2015*, 2016; Productivity Commission, *Report on Government Services 2023*.

14. Rosa Luxemburg, *Reform or Revolution*, 1908.

Chapter three

Workers' struggle and revolution[1]

The history of all hitherto existing society is the history of class struggles. Freeman and slave, patrician and plebeian, lord and serf, guild-master and journeyman, in a word, oppressor and oppressed, stood in constant opposition to one another, carried on an uninterrupted, now hidden, now open fight, a fight that each time ended, either in a revolutionary reconstitution of society at large, or in the common ruin of the contending classes.

—Marx and Engels, *The Communist Manifesto*

CAPITALISM IS A CRUEL AND EXPLOITATIVE SYSTEM that is driving the world towards war and environmental collapse. But the working class is not only a victim of capitalism. Because of their strategic position in society, workers also have power. By stopping work, the working class can bring the profit-driven system and all the horror it produces to a halt. Workers can use this power positively to create the organs of a new society that puts human need before profit. In this chapter, we will examine how workers can move into struggle and how, from a simple strike or demonstration, workers' struggle can be transformed into revolution.

Workers' struggle

In Australia today, strikes are at an all-time low. In chapter five, we will look at some of the specific reasons for the current situation. That workers are not on strike and challenging the bosses most of the time, however, should not surprise us. Nothing in our society teaches workers it is right to fight for their rights. No current affairs program or news bulletin argues workers should strike for higher wages. The opposite is true. Every day, we hear how "the economy" cannot bear the "burden" of higher wages; far from it, economic prosperity demands that we accept less. From the day we're born, we are trained to obey our elders and "betters". We hear this from the employers, the media, the education system, politicians and bankers. The result is, as Marx wrote in 1845:

> The ideas of the ruling class are in every epoch the ruling ideas, i.e. the class which is the ruling material force of society is at the same time its ruling intellectual force… The class which has the means of material production at its disposal, has control at the same time over the means of mental production, so that thereby, generally speaking, the ideas of those who lack the means of mental production are subject to it.[2]

The problem with leaving our explanation here, though, is that it cannot explain why workers almost always hold some radical or oppositional ideas in their heads as well as conservative ideas, or how working-class consciousness changes.

The biggest block to workers developing class consciousness is the fact that they are alienated. That is, they lack control over the production process, which appears to be operating completely independently of them. This profoundly affects how workers see and understand society. Under capitalism, workers' labour power is converted into a commodity like everything else. It appears that no coercion is involved, but coercion is at the heart of the relationship between capitalists and workers, what Marx called "the dull compulsion of economic relations".[3] If we are to survive under capitalism, we must go to work every day. We cannot tell the boss to take a running jump if we are to keep our jobs. When the boss says, "If you don't like the job, there's plenty of others who will do it," they're right. The idea that the bosses should run the show and our job is simply to obey is based on material reality – that's what happens most of the time. We can't imagine our way to a different reality. This experience encourages passivity, a sense of powerlessness and an inability to grasp the overall nature of the process of production in which workers are involved.

The illusory sense that reality somehow happens to us, that we cannot influence it, is the fundamental secret to the capitalists' survival. It is the soil in which the individualistic ideas of the ruling class can take root. If workers accept the ideas of the status quo, the more likely they are to absorb its poisonous and divisive ideology – that immigrants are responsible for the housing crisis or that strikes harm the economy. In isolation from each other, workers are more easily prone to turn their suffering and bitterness on each other or on scapegoats.

History, however, has also shown workers time and again fighting the bosses, sometimes in individual workplaces, sometimes across an industry, sometimes across a nation and occasionally across national borders. How does this come about?

Workers hold many mixed ideas about the world they live in. Some of those ideas express a rejection of the status quo; others express acceptance of it. To quote the Italian revolutionary Antonio Gramsci, most workers actually carry in their heads two contradictory consciousnesses:

> [O]ne which is implicit in his activity and which in reality unites him with all his fellow workers in the practical transformation of the real world; and one, superficially explicit or verbal, which he has inherited from the past and uncritically absorbed.[4]

This contradiction reflects the fact that capitalism both divides and unites workers; it brings them together in large numbers while fostering competition between them. "Competition separates individuals from one another, not only the bourgeois but still more the workers in spite of the fact that it brings them together," wrote Marx.[5] But workers know also that if they are to improve their lot, they need to organise collectively. Sometimes, typically during an economic boom, they may fight for shorter hours and better pay; this was the case in Australia during the 1960s and 1970s when the strike rate soared. At other times, they are fighting defensively – to stop a wage or benefit cut or to resist anti-union laws. Necessity drives them to act in this way, not because Marxists have educated them in the doctrine of class struggle. As US socialist Hal Draper wrote:

> To engage in class struggle, it is not necessary to "believe in" the class struggle

any more than it is necessary to believe in Newton in order to fall from an airplane... The working class moves toward class struggle insofar as capitalism fails to satisfy its economic and social needs and aspirations, not insofar as it is told about struggle by Marxists.[6]

Workers first engage in strikes because they are the only means to secure immediate redress from their employer. However, the significance of strikes cannot simply be measured by their immediate results but by how they build workers' confidence in themselves and increase their fighting spirit. Struggle, even on a small scale, can challenge the sense of powerlessness and the under-confidence that the system fosters. Fighting against any aspect of this situation is a way to challenge the common sense ideas of subordination and acceptance. Through fighting, workers gain confidence and get a taste of our collective strength. "Every strike," wrote Lenin, "reminds the workers that their position is not hopeless, that they are not alone".[7] Lenin continued:

See what a tremendous effect strikes have both on the strikers themselves and on the workers at neighbouring or nearby factories or at factories in the same industry. In normal, peaceful times, the worker does his job without a murmur, does not contradict the employer, and does not discuss his condition. In times of strikes, he states his demands in a loud voice, he reminds the employers of all their abuses, he claims his rights, he does not think of himself and his wages alone, he thinks of all his workmates who have downed tools together with him and who stand up for the workers' cause, fearing no privations.[8]

This sense of class consciousness becomes more developed as workers see they have a common interest not only with workers in their own workplace or industry but also with workers across the entire country and indeed the entire world.

In struggle, the gap between workers' own experience and the ideas that dominate society widens to the point where workers can start to reject the latter – the ruling ideas begin to break down. In big struggles, these ideas break down quickly. "A strike," wrote Lenin, "opens the eyes of the workers to the nature, not only of the capitalists but of the government and the laws as well".[9] The important thing is that a group of workers decides to act. When they do, their experience opens their eyes to the truth, which gives them more confidence to fight. Workers who strike learn that the police and courts are set up against them and for the employers – and also that the press defends employers and tries to present workers' interests in a poor light.

The experience of struggle teaches solidarity to workers, calling into question divisions of race, caste, sex, gender identity, sexual orientation, language and nationality that are deliberately fostered between them by the ruling class. They learn that whenever the employers or the state can pit them against each other, they are weak, and when they unite, they are strong. They learn that if any part of the working class or oppressed is held down, it makes it easier for the bosses to hold all workers down. The more organised the struggle, and the more it involves wider layers of workers in struggle, the more likely workers are to develop internationalist class consciousness. It was in the late 1960s and early 1970s when strikes in Australia were a daily occurrence that the rights of women and Indigenous people and the anti-war campaign advanced the most, with trade unionists, women and men, Indigenous and non-Indigenous, at the forefront of the struggle.

As workers organise on a wider scale, they start to see that their interests lie not only in organising one workplace or one industry for self-defence, but in organising politically to secure better laws and, beyond that, to challenge the power of the state that serves the interests of the employing class. Lenin put it this way:

> The real education of the masses can never be separated from their independent political, and especially revolutionary, struggle. Only struggle educates the exploited class. Only struggle discloses to it the magnitude of its own power, widens its horizon, enhances its abilities, clarifies its mind, forges its will.[10]

That is why in periods of relative calm, when there is little struggle, the possibility of fundamental change seems remote. But behind the façade of calm, molecular processes are always creating the conditions in which a spark can set off an explosion of workers' struggle.

Workers' struggle has a dual aspect. On the one hand, the working class can paralyse the existing order by going on strike. On the other, this very fact creates the conditions for a new society based on democratic control of the workplace. Workers can encroach on the bosses' "right to manage". In 2011, 600 health workers at the Kilkis hospital in northern Greece joined together in an emergency mass general assembly and took over their hospital in response to savage wage cuts. They announced it to the world like this:

> The workers at the General Hospital of Kilkis answer to this totalitarianism with democracy. We occupy the public hospital and put it under our direct and absolute control. The General Hospital of Kilkis will henceforth be self-governed and the only legitimate means of administrative decision-making will be the general assembly of its workers...

> Keeping in mind our social mission and the moral character of our profession, we will protect the citizens' health, providing free care to people who need it...

The workers held daily meetings and regular general assemblies to decide things collectively and democratically. Their action was illegal, so they knew they had to spread their struggle to other hospitals and other sectors. They declared:

> We call upon our fellow citizens to show solidarity in supporting our effort, we call upon every mistreated citizen of this country to actively stand up against their oppressors, we urge...our colleagues in other hospitals to make similar decisions and we also call employees in all fields of public and private sectors, members of labour unions and other progressive organisations to do the same, until our mobilisation becomes a mass popular and labour movement of resistance and uprising, until the final victory against the economic and political elites that today rob our country and destroy the whole world.[11]

The government eventually wrested back control of the hospital from the workers, but in that brief period, they showed to the whole of Europe how workers could resist the continent-wide austerity offensive then underway.

This experience of workers taking the first steps to assert their right to control their workplaces and make decisions of wider social significance is apparent in Australia too. In the early 1970s, the NSW Builders Labourers Federation refused to allow property developers to tear down working-class housing to make way for expensive office buildings. A construction worker recalled the democratic way these decisions were made:

> The membership [would] hear a description of the proposal at a meeting, and [decide] to ratify it or not... At the height, when the radicalisation was at its strongest...we'd have had 250 to 300 people, probably about half of who would have been shop stewards... And then at the mass meetings, there would be many thousands... You really did feel a sense of pride, that you were a guardian, to some extent, of our culture, and you weren't going to let some things happen... Collectively you had that power.[12]

What do we mean by revolution?

Many people can see the benefit of strikes for immediate gains or to fend off bosses' attacks. But revolution is a whole extra step that opens up the possibility of a complete transformation of society. We need a revolution for two simple reasons: first, because the ruling class will not give us the changes we want to see in the world peacefully, we must disarm our rulers and build a new world with our own hands; second, because only by going through the experience of a mass revolution does the working class become fit to become the architects of the new and just society that is socialism.

Revolution is the ultimate social leap – a period when the gradual accumulation of mass bitterness and anger of the exploited and oppressed coalesces and bursts forth into a mass movement to overturn existing social relations and replace them with new ones. A few days of revolutionary upheaval bring more change than decades of "normal" development. Rulers and systems that seemed invincible and immovable are suddenly unceremoniously toppled. One need only think of the Tunisian and Egyptian revolutions of 2011, when long-standing dictators were toppled in a matter of a few days or weeks, to gain some understanding of their explosive quality.

A list of only some of these upsurges gives us an idea of revolutionary upheavals since the dawn of modern capitalism – the French Revolution (1789–94), the US Civil War (1861–65), the European revolutions of 1848, the Russian Revolutions (1905 and 1917), the German Revolution (1918–23), China (1925–27), the Spanish Civil War (1936–39), the Hungarian Revolution (1956), France (1968), Chile (1973), Portugal (1974–75), Iran (1979), Poland's Solidarność uprising (1980–81), the Arab revolutions (2011) and the 2019 wave of mass anti-government protests that occurred in 114 countries, ranging from Colombia to Iran and from Sudan to Hong Kong, the broadest wave of protests yet seen. This partial list is enough to put to rest the notion that such social upheavals are rare occurrences. Revolution, therefore, is not an aberration in an otherwise smoothly functioning society, any more than crisis is an aberration in an otherwise smoothly functioning economy.[13]

But what, to be more exact, is a revolution? More precisely, what did Marx mean by it?[14] Like the terms "democracy" and "freedom", the meaning of revolution is not always clear. Broadly speaking, revolution refers to sweeping social, political, and economic transformations that happen over a longer or shorter period. Hence, we talk about the "industrial revolution" which ushered in the system of factory production in Britain and the era of modern capitalism. More commonly, revolution refers to a forceful transfer of governmental power. This type of revolution can be purely political – in the sense that it simply transfers power from one section of the ruling class to another or from military to a democratic form of government (or the reverse) while leaving the social structure intact. A social revolution is much more far-reaching. It is not a military coup by a handful of plotters, nor is it simply a change of personnel at the top as a result of mass protests such as we have seen many times in Latin America. A social revolution occurs when a political revolution transfers power to a new rising class and puts it in a position to begin a restructuring of society. In today's world, that means a workers' revolution to smash the capitalist class and start the process of constituting socialism. Russian revolutionary Leon Trotsky described the essential content of a socialist revolution as "the direct interference of the masses in historic events… the forcible entrance of the masses into the realm of rulership over their own destiny".[15]

There is no wall between political and social revolutions. Political revolutions often involve a social element or, sometimes, are transitional to a more thoroughgoing social revolution involving a transfer of power to a new class.

How do revolutions happen?

Revolutions take place under particular circumstances. It is not the case that they only occur when people are driven down to the depths of misery and poverty; otherwise, the most wretched peasants of the poorest countries of the world would be in a state of constant revolt, whereas the poor peasantry are known worldwide and historically for their passivity and stoic tolerance of hardship.

Nor do revolutions occur because socialists have educated workers in the benefits of rising up in this way; if that were true, there would never be revolutions as there are so few committed socialists compared to the size of the working class, and revolutions would never occur in countries with no socialist traditions, whereas they frequently do. Nor do revolutions occur because revolutionaries hoodwink the working class into following them blindly. Any union delegate knows that hard and honest arguments are needed for workers to embark on even the simplest strike. And nor do revolutions occur because the working class wakes up one morning and decides to embark on a revolution. No revolution starts with the mass of participants convinced of the need for one. Revolutions invariably start as a demand or series of demands around immediate reforms or in response to a vicious ruling class attack. The realisation of the necessity of revolution only comes upon many participants during the struggle.

So, how do revolutions happen? It is worth quoting Lenin at length here:

To the Marxist, it is indisputable that a revolution is impossible without a revolutionary situation; furthermore, it is not every revolutionary situation that leads to revolution. What, generally speaking, are the symptoms of a revolutionary situation?... (1) when it is impossible for the ruling classes to maintain their rule without any change; when there is a crisis, in one form or another, among the "upper classes", a crisis in the policy of the ruling class, leading to a fissure through which the discontent and indignation of the oppressed classes burst forth. For a revolution to take place, it is usually insufficient for "the lower classes not to want" to live in the old way; it is also necessary that "the upper classes should be unable" to live in the old way; (2) when the suffering and want of the oppressed classes have grown more acute than usual; (3) when, as a consequence of the above causes, there is a considerable increase in the activity of the masses, who uncomplainingly allow themselves to be robbed in "peacetime," but, in turbulent times, are drawn both by all the circumstances of the crisis and by the "upper classes" themselves into independent historical action.[16]

In short, revolutionary situations arise when millions of ordinary people become convinced that society cannot continue in the old way, when there are splits and confusion at the top over how to restore order and overcome the crisis, and when the working class seizes the opportunity to take advantage of these splits and confusions in the ranks of their rulers.

Such circumstances arise because of the very workings of the capitalist system, which is in a constant state of disturbance. Capitalism is itself a revolutionary system that regularly transforms people's lives, the way production is organised and the technologies used to produce the means of our subsistence. The boom-bust character of capitalism means that everything is regularly thrown up in the air. Competition between capitalists throws entire countries into war with hugely disruptive consequences. Struggle between the capitalist and working classes often follows. Such struggle is often of a modest scale – a strike here, a demonstration there.

But when the struggle escalates beyond a single workplace or industry or beyond a single partial demand, the class divisions in society open up. When the class struggle is particularly intense, the long-term interests of the fundamental classes of capitalism can become apparent to many people. It becomes more obvious that capitalism is an exploitative system and that working-class interests lie not only in winning short-term improvements in living standards or by forcing governments to withdraw from wars, but ultimately in overthrowing capitalism.

Many things can be the straw that breaks the camel's back. In 1871, the workers of Paris seized their city after the government moved to disarm its defence in the face of an advancing Prussian army. In October 1905, the general strike in St Petersburg in Russia was set in motion by a strike by typesetters who were demanding pay to set punctuation marks. In Madrid in 1936, it was an attempted fascist coup by an army general that inspired the city's workers to seize the city, sparking off a national revolt against the attempted putsch. In Poland in 1980, it was a protest against the dismissal of a crane driver in the Gdansk shipyards that started the national wave of strikes and factory occupations. And in Tunisia in 2011, it was the self-immolation of a street vendor in a dusty provincial town in protest at constant police harassment that sparked off the revolution. No one can predict what the occasion or incident will be, and it is fruitless to try.

Lenin refers in the quote above to the requirement that "the suffering and want of the oppressed classes have grown more acute than usual". It is worth adding a qualifier here. Revolutionary situations are often nurtured out of desperation, but revolts can also grow out of unmet expectations. Ten million French workers staged a general strike in 1968, which escalated into a challenge to the French state, not because they were being driven into poverty but because the French economy had grown strongly for over two decades, the bourgeoisie had become wealthier than ever before, and the working class was seeing none of it. They were out to get their share. And further, the entire French political structure was authoritarian, and students and workers alike chafed against its restrictions.

Revolution changes the working class

Revolutions transform the working class by demonstrating to workers their power and the importance of solidarity and give us a glimpse of the human potential that is buried under the weight of capitalist oppression.

Italian revolutionary Antonio Gramsci reflected on the changes marking the workers of Turin when they occupied their factories in 1920:

> It was really necessary to see with one's eyes old workers, who seemed broken down by decades upon decades of oppression and exploitation, stand upright

even in a physical sense during the period of the occupation – see them develop creative activities; suggesting, helping, always active day and night. It was necessary to see these and other sights, in order to be convinced how limitless the latent powers of the masses are, and how they are revealed and develop swiftly as soon as the conviction takes root among the masses that they are arbiters and masters of their own destinies.[17]

The experience of Tahrir Square in Cairo during the Egyptian revolution of 2011 provides a more recent example.[18] Even though industrial workers were only a minority of those sitting in, the masses of those involved in the 18-day occupation went through the same experience recognised by Gramsci a century earlier.

There was an elation born from defiance of decades of stifling authoritarianism. People helped each other, cleaned up after themselves, talking, laughing, dancing, sharing food and water, and just enjoying the enormity of what they had achieved. Words and music suffused the square. As the protesters sat out the nights, they sang banned nationalist songs or read poetry from the last wave of struggle in the 1960s and 1970s. Political debates raged inside the square. How should the revolution progress? What attitude should the rebellion take to particular political leaders? Is the army really out to support the people? Arguments mattered – the life of the revolution depended on it. Different organisations produced leaflets to hand around to bolster their positions.

Although Egypt was much less developed, the scenes in Tahrir were reminiscent of the heady atmosphere of mass workers' democracy in the Russian Revolution of 1917. US journalist John Reed described the scene in Petrograd:

In all the barracks meetings every night and all day long, interminable, hot arguments raged. On the streets, the crowds thickened towards gloomy evenings, pouring in slow voluble tides up and down the Nevsky [the main thoroughfare], fighting for newspapers... At Smolny [the HQ of the workers' council] the committee rooms buzzed and hummed all day and all night, hundreds of soldiers and workers slept on the floor, wherever they could find room. Upstairs in the great hall, a thousand people crowded to the uproarious sessions of the Petrograd Soviet.[19]

Revolutions give the voiceless a voice. In Russia in 1905, the "dress rehearsal" for 1917, it was a young Jewish man, Leon Trotsky, who was elected chairman of the workers' council in St Petersburg when antisemitism was rife in the country. In Poland in 1980, one of the initial leaders of the rebellion against the repressive Stalinist government was a woman, Anna Walentynowicz. In Egypt in 2011, young women gave the lead on the megaphone to middle-aged men, to whom they would normally be expected to defer, while in Sudan in 2019, it was 22-year-old student Alaa Saleh whose image became a global symbol of the revolution as she stood atop a car to urge the crowds to defy violent repression.

As workers struggle together against the old order, divisions begin to break down as the need for solidarity comes to the fore. Despite a history of tensions between Coptic Christians and Muslims, in Tahrir Square they stood arm in arm, defending the square and each other's prayer sessions. Thousands of women visited the square each day, and there was none of the catcalling and grabbing that they were often forced to endure in public. To maintain the revolution, unity across racial, ethnic, religious, gender and sexuality lines was required.

The protesters gathered in Tahrir Square and set up their own self-contained community. Food, water and medical supplies were organised and dispensed by committees. Another committee produced a bulletin providing the latest updates on the conditions in the square and what was happening outside. Doctors and nurses provided medical care for protesters who had been injured in attacks by the police or hired thugs from the regime. Everyone came together to keep the streets clean. People wanted to show their neighbours – and the world – that they could make their city and their lives far better if they had real control.

In Spain in 1936, the working class effectively took over the running of Barcelona in the face of the fascist threat. English writer George Orwell wrote:

It was the first time that I had ever been in a town where the working class was in the saddle. Practically every building of any size had been seized by the workers and was draped with red flags or with the red and black flag of the Anarchists; every wall was scrawled with the hammer and sickle and with the initials of the revolutionary parties... Every shop and cafe had an inscription saying that it had been collectivised; even the bootblacks had been collectivised and their boxes painted red and black. Waiters and shop-walkers looked you in the face and treated you as an equal... There were no private motorcars, they had all been commandeered, and the trams and taxis and much of the other transport were painted red and black... And it was the aspect of the crowds that was the queerest thing of all. In outward appearance, it was a town in which the wealthy classes had practically ceased to exist... Practically everyone wore rough working-class clothes, or blue overalls or some variant of militia uniform. All this was queer and moving. There was much in this that I did not understand, in some ways I did not even like it, but I recognised it immediately as a state of affairs worth fighting for.[20]

The transformation of popular consciousness that sweeps through everyone involved in these mass revolts is exactly what Marx had in mind when he wrote that revolution allows the working class to "rid itself of the muck of ages and become fitted to found society anew".[21] The experience of revolution, of shared struggle, transforms the participants and creates a new collective consciousness. This is why revolution must be made by mass of workers and not by others "on their behalf".

The working class must lead

Workers have repeatedly used their power to bring down unpopular, oppressive regimes, whether in Iran in 1979, South Africa in the 1980s and '90s, South Korea in 1987, Bolivia in 2003, Egypt in 2011 or Sudan in 2019. In Sudan, for example, in the weeks after mass protests forced out the despotic regime of President al-Bashir, general strikes spread across the country, accounting for 90 percent or more of the country's high schools, public road transport, domestic flights, sea freight, railway traffic, oil and gas industries and engineering sector.[22] The strikes gave workers an enormous sense of confidence in their own power and laid bare the state's powerlessness in the face of a complete shutdown of society. One Sudanese activist recalled: "The reactionary forces hate the strike, the sectarians hate it, the army hates it; they hate this weapon capable of not only overthrowing some of them but also overthrowing the exact reasons for their existence and their privileges".[23] But unless workers seize the leadership of the struggle, they will never reap the rewards; others will jump in and steer the revolt to suit their own needs, sometimes carrying out a bloody counter-revolution.

The anti-apartheid struggle in South Africa provides an example of what happens if the working class cedes the ground to others. There, a combination of mass protests and strikes finally brought an end to apartheid – the system of racial separation and white supremacy. But the African National Congress (ANC), which led the struggle, was not prepared to go beyond what capitalism would permit, which was little more than a change of faces at the top of the state machine and the admission of a few Black faces to the boards of directors.[24] The ANC's commitment to capitalism meant that many of the issues that brought the masses of Black South Africans to rebel – lack of housing and basic services, unemployment, landlessness and severe exploitation at the hands of multinationals – continue today under a Black majority government.

Workers have an interest in taking the fight for a better society further than middle-class forces like the ANC, which are keen to restrict the struggle to a set of more or less limited reforms while leaving the economic system of exploitation intact. If they are not to be pushed into a secondary role – providing the muscle while other classes reap most of the rewards – then workers must be organised politically to assert their independent class interests. For the working class to come together in such a way and to assert its independent interests, those who are leading the struggle in the workplaces, on the streets and on the campuses need to be organised into a mass revolutionary party capable of pushing the struggle forward. Without such an organisation, workers will be pushed to the sidelines, their demands ignored.

When the working class rises up, it must not restrict itself only to demands for the betterment of their economic condition but must present itself as the only class capable of leading the *whole* of society, minus the minority of exploiters and its defenders, toward total human emancipation. As they organise, workers must therefore present a social and political program of change capable of leading *all* the oppressed in society, including women, racial, religious and national minorities, students, LGBTI people and sections of the middle class who are being crushed by the big capitalists.

The contest for power

Revolutions unfold not according to plan but for reasons of necessity. If one factory or office goes on strike, nothing much changes in the roles of the workers and the boss. But once hundreds of thousands or millions of workers are on strike, and not for one day but for a week, then it quickly becomes obvious that things need to be organised. Evidently, in any strike, things like a picket roster, publicity, financial support and solidarity action have to be sorted out. But with society grinding to a halt, as industry after industry comes to a stop, the workers have to step into the breach. Who will organise the provision of food? Of transport? Of healthcare? Of fuel and heating? Of security? What to do when the boss flees and tries to sabotage the machinery rather than see it fall into the hands of the workers?

In such circumstances, the workers have to take over, first in one workplace or another, then in several, and then across an entire industry. They need to occupy their workplaces and start to run them under workers' control. But it's not enough for one industry to act on its own. Committees and workers' councils need to be organised citywide, linking representatives from every significant workplace and industry to work out answers to the problems confronted by the movement. These then have to appeal to workers in other cities and regions, laying open the prospect of a national uprising. The workers can only advance by uniting; divisions within their ranks based on sex, race, religion and sexual identity have to be stamped out, failing which their solidarity will disintegrate, and the capitalists will seize back control. As the insurrectionary movement unfolds, therefore, it may draw behind it other groups of the oppressed – women, students, national minorities and others – and not only in one factory or office, but more generally, because the workers have shown a way forward to all those suffering oppression by the capitalist system. None of this is automatic; many factors can interrupt this sequence of events, but there is a logic to a revolutionary working-class movement that pushes developments in this direction.

The Russian Revolution of 1917 demonstrates this process most completely. We will explore this more fully in chapter nine, but here, we can sketch some basics. The February Revolution, which smashed the old tsarist order, saw a massive outburst of popular struggle and popular democracy in Petrograd.[25] Workers flocked to institutions both old and new. Unions were formed from scratch, others were revived, and trade union membership exploded. Factory committees sprang up in all the big workplaces and decided what would be produced and how. The factory committees were immediately accountable institutions and, over the course of 1917, most readily drew revolutionary conclusions. In the barracks and in the naval bases, soldiers' and sailors' committees started to agitate against brutal treatment by their officers. Then there were the workers' councils, or soviets, composed of deputies elected from the big workplaces, but also including representatives of soldiers and sailors, peasants and other layers. The Petrograd Soviet could form the basis of an entirely new way of organising society without capitalists, landlords or generals. Quickly, workers in other cities and regions followed Petrograd's example and set up soviets and factory committees of their own.

The Russian soviets and even the most democratic parliamentary systems embody two entirely different forms of rule. Soviet democracy is not merely an alternative to parliament; it is its antithesis, combining as it does power at the point of production with the battle for class dominance. The soviets in Russia unified political and economic power, whereas parliament leaves the most important power of the bourgeoisie, its economic strength, untouched. The soviets brought under democratic control the administrative and legislative functions of government – unlike parliament, which leaves the public service, army and police in unelected hands.

The soviets were an organ of struggle responsive to the will of the workers and capable of organising strikes and protests, whereas parliament is an organ dominated by the bourgeoisie and far removed from democratic accountability. Deputies to the soviet were immediately accountable to their workmates and enjoyed no special privileges, while parliamentarians enjoy far superior conditions of life to their constituents and only have to answer to them once every three or four years. Obviously, not every soviet in Russia met these standards, but their formation created the potential to bring workers' power into being, whereas parliament only entrenches the power of the capitalists. Workers' councils have been a feature of many uprisings since – in Spain in 1936, Hungary in 1956, Chile in 1973 and Iran in 1979, to name a few.

For a period, a rising movement of this nature can throw the state and the ruling class it represents onto the defensive. Divisions develop at the top over how to restore order – should reforms be granted to mollify the movement, or should repression be used, or both? Reforms may be granted, but instead of stopping the movement and placating it, these reforms embolden it. In such circumstances, sections of the ruling class and the military may begin to debate the possibility of restoring order by force, i.e. by physically crushing the rising. Reactionary forces begin testing the defences of the movement, probing for its weakest spots. Society balances on a knife's edge. Will the old order reimpose itself, or will new social forces seize power? This is the essence of all revolutionary situations.

Of course, if those leading the movement can channel the struggle into reforms that do not challenge the status quo, then the movement can be defused before it reaches revolutionary proportions. When this happens, as it did after the May 1968 general strike in France, the movement subsides, and the old order can restore itself without counter-revolutionary violence. Such an option is more likely if the system is booming, as it was in 1968, and the ruling class is not thrown into chaos and indecision by a severe economic or military crisis. But if workers are convinced they can and must move forward, then the only two choices are a dispersal of the old state power by the united working class, leading millions behind it, or the suppression of the movement.

A necessary feature of every revolutionary situation is "dual power" – the co-existence of workers' councils alongside the old state. But dual power cannot last. In all revolutionary situations, either society moves forward to the establishment of a new state based upon workers' councils (or some similar form of direct democracy) or backward to the destruction of the workers' organisations and the re-establishment of the capitalist order.

When workers take over their workplaces, the owners will call the police or hire thugs to have them removed. The question of the workers securing what they have won, therefore, quickly comes to the fore. That means the need for self-defence and, down the track, the formation of workers' militias under the control of the workers' committees to repel attacks by the police, thugs and army.

Revolutions are often equated with the use of violence and, for that reason, are rejected by some who want to see radical social change. But although all major revolutions involve violent clashes between contending social forces, revolution is not *equal* to violence, which is merely a means to an end, an end that is not by any means always aimed at social transformation. When harnessed to social aims and employed as a means by a mass social movement, however, violence can play a crucial role in shattering the repressive apparatus of the state.

Central to the victory of any thoroughgoing revolution is the fomenting of splits in the army. In mass upheavals, the weakest link of the ruling class is the armed forces. Repression can only work if soldiers are disciplined to carry out their orders. But in circumstances of great social upheaval, this isn't a foregone conclusion – because most soldiers are themselves workers. If this were not true, revolutions could never win. However, to give the soldiers the courage to break with their officers and refuse to fire on crowds of demonstrators, the working class has to show that it is serious about its fight. As Trotsky put it, "the revolutionaries can create a break in the soldiers' mood only if they themselves are actually ready to seize the victory at any price whatever, even the price of blood".[26] The supposedly all-powerful state then becomes temporarily paralysed because it cannot rely on its own armed forces.

This happened in the February 1917 revolution in Russia, as we shall see in chapter nine. During mass street demonstrations, the tsar's crack mounted soldiers (known as the Cossacks) gave a nod to the workers as they dived under their horses and regular soldiers turned their guns on the police when they attacked the crowds.[27] There are countless examples of this development throughout the history of class struggle.

Workers all over the world suffer the same system of oppression and exploitation. All workers feel the rhythms of capitalist booms and crises, wars and breakdowns similarly. And so when one group of workers rises up in revolutionary struggle, it gives hope to millions of others. Workers do not labour and fight for the capitalists every day because they love the system but because they can't see any way out. When some workers point out by their actions that there is an alternative, others follow their lead. This was true in Europe in 1848, in the period 1917–23, and again in the late 1960s and early 1970s. It has been many years since such an outburst of workers' struggle, but the Arab revolutions of 2011 and the international wave of protest in 2019 give us a taste of what is possible. And, thanks to the globally coordinated supply chains and networked information technology that the bosses use to organise production globally today, the potential for workers to coordinate their actions across national borders is immeasurably greater than ever before.

Capitalism throws workers into struggle, encouraging a basic sense of "us versus them" in workers' ranks. But for a revolution to succeed, workers need to be armed with a lot more than that basic understanding. The hold of old ideas does not vanish overnight. Workers do not all advance at the same pace in their political consciousness, and the leaders of the established trade unions and reformist political parties will do their best to hold them back. A workers' revolution requires its own organisation and leadership, in other words, a revolutionary party, specifically focused on the problems and challenges raised by the task of fundamental social change. Such a party holds onto and develops the insights gained by the most class-conscious workers at the height of struggles, to generalise them as widely as possible and to overcome sectional divisions and reformist tendencies within the working class. This is not only a question of technically preparing a revolution or of spreading socialist propaganda and ideas, however important these things may be. Revolutionary parties must intervene in events as they unfold, to push the struggle as far as it will go, to bring to the fore the revolutionary tendencies that are developing within the working class and to unite workers in an active assault on the system.

Could there be a revolution in Australia?

Many people might agree that revolutions can happen overseas and that it would be good if one happened in Australia. But the prospect of revolution in Australia seems remote. Such scepticism is hardly surprising. It's not just that Australia, unlike, say, France, Germany or England, has never had a revolution. It's also that the entire history of class struggle is deliberately omitted from most school textbooks and popular conceptions of Australian history. And so you hear people often argue that Australians are "apathetic" or "too well off" to mount a revolutionary challenge to capitalism.

And yet, class struggle and resistance to oppression is as old as Australia itself. From the Aboriginal resistance to invasion to trade union protests against attacks on workers' rights in more recent times, the country has experienced the full range of mobilisation by workers and the oppressed short of an insurrection. These upsurges have been around both political and economic issues. We might cite the Castle Hill rebellion by 600 predominantly Irish convicts in 1804, the Eureka rebellion of 1854 and the surge of union organising in the shearing sheds in the 1880s. The great strikes and lockouts in the shearing and maritime industries in the early 1890s saw class struggle in Australia take on a bloody and bitter dimension. Such episodes continued into the twentieth century, and it's worth looking at them briefly.

During World War I, Australia was rocked by a great wave of upheavals that were to continue into 1920. The high points were the 1917 NSW general strike and the massive campaigns that defeated two conscription referenda. The Labor Party split in the face of mass insurgent demonstrations, armed street clashes, the formation of Labor Volunteer Armies to defend anti-conscription rallies, and a string of strikes outside the control of the union leaders. Many, both on the left and the right of the political spectrum, came to see revolution as inevitable and looked, respectively, with hope or horror at the revolution unfolding in Russia. Meat workers in Townsville sported jerseys with the word "Revolution" emblazoned on them, such was their enthusiasm for the revolution taking place thousands of kilometres away.

In the early 1930s, fresh opportunities for revolutionaries opened up in Australia. The immediate circumstances did not look promising. Some of the strongest unions – the coal miners, waterside workers, and timber workers – suffered crushing defeats in 1928–29, weakening the rest of the union movement. Strikes collapsed, and things looked bleak for the left. But the Depression conditions radicalised tens of thousands, as unemployment skyrocketed to 25 percent, wages were slashed and food in storage was eaten by rats while people starved. Capitalism was exposed as bankrupt, unable to feed its wage slaves. This gave rise to a radical political movement in NSW around the socialisation units in the ALP. These units campaigned for the party to adopt a plan to bring in socialism within three years, involving workers' control over industry and nationalisation of the economy. The ALP conference over Easter 1931 adopted their program, and even Premier Jack Lang, by no means left-wing, was forced to give lip service to it. By 1932, membership of the units was outstripping Labor membership in branches around Sydney. Meanwhile, the hard right was also on the move, with the New Guard, a mass fascist movement, threatening to stage a coup. Workers formed a Labor Defence Army to defend workers' gatherings from fascist attacks.

The sacking of Lang by the NSW governor in May 1932 brought everything to a head and was the impetus towards further radicalisation and militancy – hundreds of thousands suddenly saw that their democratic rights were of no concern to capitalists determined to reduce workers' living standards. Sydney was swamped by the biggest demonstration in Australian history until then. The atmosphere was of pending revolution. Only two things saved the governor. One was Lang's determination to go quietly. The other was the sectarian stance adopted by the Communist Party (CPA), which regarded the ALP as no different from the fascists, rendering the party incapable of responding to the surge of opposition to Lang's sacking.

Over four decades later, the sacking of Gough Whitlam in 1975, referred to in chapter two, brought on another crisis that could have developed into an enormous social and political upheaval.[28] The Communist Party newspaper *Tribune* reported that debates raged on blue-collar worksites nationwide. Mike Jackson, secretary of the union committee at the Garden Island Dockyard in Sydney, reported that:

Announcement of the Kerr business hit like a bombshell. There was spontaneous hostility and amazement... people wanted action. The call went up straight away for a nation-wide stoppage. It was not whether we were going to take action, but how quickly.

Jackson described the demonstration that was rapidly organised:

As we marched into Pitt Street, we caught sight of the workers from Cockatoo Dock, who had also stopped work. You could hear the roar that went up from both groups all over town! The two marches joined...together with seamen and office workers who swelled our ranks as we went. At Liberal Headquarters, officials refused to see a deputation from the march, so workers decided to march on the citadel of Australian high finance and power, the Sydney Stock Exchange.

In Melbourne, about 400,000 workers went on strike. All public transport was closed down. Forty thousand people rallied in Melbourne's City Square. A student march to the main rally opposite Melbourne's Town Hall converged with two other marches, one from the waterfront and one of clothing trade workers. "It was like the convergence of three mighty rivers," reported *Tribune*. In Queensland, 100,000 workers struck, and 20,000 people jammed King George Square and surrounding streets to hear Gough Whitlam speak.

Working class resistance to the Kerr coup did not come out of the blue. Over the preceding ten years, tens of thousands had been radicalised by the struggle against the Vietnam War and the student movement, and strikes had increased in number and militancy. Proportionately, Australia had one of the largest anti-Vietnam War movements in the world.

The movement to defend the Whitlam government was ultimately shunted into a straightforward electoral contest in which the Labor Party was thrashed. But this was not the result of any congenital conservatism of the Australian working class; rather, it reflected the absence of a revolutionary party that could have directed the resistance into a general strike and potentially much further.

So what about today? In some respects, the situation looks dire. Australia has not seen a wave of serious workers' struggle since the 1970s, and the union movement is a shadow of its former self. In chapter five, we will look at the responsibility of the trade union leaders for the current poor state of the labour movement. But this weakness of our side does not alter the fact that capitalism in Australia, like everywhere in the world, is characterised by a yawning class division between the exploiters and the exploited, the accumulation of wealth at one pole, of misery at the other. This basic reality means that there is a significant section of the population in Australia that, under the right circumstances, can become open to radical, revolutionary politics. While Australia has not experienced a deep recession and high unemployment since the early 1990s, inevitably, at some stage, these will return. Although most may try to keep their heads down, at least a minority of workers may be prepared to fight.

It is not just austerity that might jolt Australian politics out of its current passivity. War has often been a catalyst. Australia's enthusiastic support for the United States in its preparations for war with China is already leading to ever-larger arms budgets, money stolen from civilian needs. A major inter-imperialist war, with Australia fighting alongside the US, is a real prospect. War is, as Marx and Engels argued, a potential midwife of revolution. This has been the case on several occasions, such as with World War I, which led to the Russian and German revolutions in 1917 and 1918.

Capitalism is a world system of integrated production and exchange. Economic and political crises are usually contagious. Political movements, and revolutions in particular, spread not only because the economy and capitalism's institutions are integrated globally but because people naturally follow other people's attempts to change the world for the better. The Russian Revolution of 1917 spread first into Europe before inspiring the formation of Communist parties worldwide. The Arab revolutions of 2011 started in Tunisia but soon swept North Africa and the Middle East. The Black Lives Matter protests in the United States inspired solidarity demonstrations worldwide.

This tendency of events to spread is actually one of the most important things to consider. Because Australia is one of the most stable capitalist democracies in the world, it is unlikely that a revolution will break out here first, even with all the obvious problems in our society. It is much more likely that revolution will wash onto our shores only after major revolutionary waves appear in other parts of the world and global capitalism is beginning to falter, throwing our own society into turmoil – making existing problems worse, exposing new ones, while inspiring people to do something about them by following the lead of people overseas. Australia is far from insulated from such trends. Indeed, demonstrations in Australia taking up international issues, such as those opposing wars in Vietnam, Iraq and Palestine or the Black Lives Matter protests, have been among the largest in the world relative to population.

In any new period of world revolution, the Australian ruling class will most likely be at the forefront of the counter-revolution, contributing militarily to every reactionary government or helping to overthrow new revolutionary governments. You only have to look at Australian imperialism's record of intervening in Asia and the Pacific. Yet military intervention entails risks, as the Vietnam War illustrates. The US government invaded the country in the 1960s. Unable to put down the Vietnamese resistance, and with the war dragging on, the main result was a radicalisation among its own soldiers and a mass anti-war movement at home. Hundreds of thousands of young people in the US identified as revolutionaries and supported the Vietnamese. While this didn't end up in a revolution, it created a huge crisis – and this was when the US was at the peak of its power and prosperity. In Australia, too, there was a radicalisation as domestic resources were diverted to the war, which fed into a rising tide of workers' struggles for better wages and even workers' control of industry.

There is already a gap between people's hopes for a decent life and the reality of living under Australian capitalism. There is also a lack of enthusiasm for, even hatred of, the main political parties and a lack of trust in the media and other capitalist institutions. This is true even without an acute economic or political crisis in Australia and without an international revolutionary movement yet developing. It is not a question of if but when these crises occur. When they do, the situation will change quickly. When it does, the question will not be, "Can it happen here?" – the question will be, "How can we win?" The answer to that will depend to a large degree on how many people have already been trained as activists and know how to organise people, how many people have studied other revolutions and their dynamics and can apply the lessons learned by millions of people in previous attempts to change the world, how many people understand the ways different social classes mobilise to defend their interests. In short, it will depend on how organised our side is.

Don't all revolutions end in tyranny?

Perhaps the most insistent criticism of revolutionary socialism is that "revolutions always end in tyranny". Such attacks from the mouths of defenders of the capitalist system can easily be shown to be hypocrisy. Capitalism has no objection to tyranny if it serves its needs. Capitalists have repeatedly promoted fascists, dictators and military rule and will do so again when parliamentary democracy will not guarantee their control. The growing surveillance and detention powers in the hands of the police and the security agencies ensure that even during times of parliamentary rule, our rights are more and more taken away from us. More than this, the capitalist workplace is a dictatorship – unless they are well unionised, workers are subjected to the tyranny of the employer. Tyranny in the workplace is mirrored by tyranny in the distribution of goods and services that we produce: we get no say in who gets what – the most the capitalists will allow us is to argue over a few crumbs. No, socialists will take no lectures on "tyranny" from those who defend capitalism.

The same is true when defenders of the system warn of the inevitability of violence during revolutions. Coming from people who constantly promote the accumulation of more and more weapons and who never fail to cheer imperialist wars, such warnings are impossible to take seriously. The violence of the capitalist system is of a vast scale and built into the competitive logic of the system whereby the minority have to maintain their rule over the majority and where rival ruling classes fight each other, or more accurately, have us fight each other on their behalf, to secure the biggest share of the resources of the world.

The violence of the system is also manifested in mass starvation, as people die because capitalism cannot make a profit by selling them food, or in factory collapses, such as the 2012 Rana Plaza collapse in Bangladesh, where over

1,000 textile workers perished because the owner refused to pay the money to make the building safe.

But you do not have to be an apologist for capitalism to have concerns over the prospect of violence or a new tyranny arising from a revolution. After all, how often have we seen fine words about universal brotherhood, liberty and equality thrown around during revolutions, only for these to give way to a repressive crackdown as one group or individual seizes the moment to grab power for themselves? George Orwell, by no means a right-winger, made this the theme of *Animal Farm*, a staple item on high school syllabuses.

There can be several responses to this argument. First, the tyranny that often follows revolutions is not the product of the revolution but of the counter-revolution. Egypt in the years after the 2011 revolt is perhaps the best recent example. A popular revolution had overthrown President Hosni Mubarak, but failing to weaken the repressive state machinery for which Mubarak only served as front man, the revolutionary forces allowed the army to push the revolution back. In the months and years that followed, the army and police carried out mass arrests, torture and killing of student radicals, socialists and civil liberties activists. Four decades earlier, in Chile in 1973, the armed forces massacred tens of thousands as they crushed the government of Salvador Allende, whose election in 1970 had spurred a mass left-wing working-class, student and peasant movement in the factories, universities, city slums and villages. In both cases, the state was determined to smash the democratic impulse that had blossomed and to intimidate the oppressed from ever trying to repeat the experience.

The only way to prevent such an outcome is not to forswear revolution but to make the revolution more thoroughgoing, to purge the state machinery completely and to build new organs of democratic power. Unless the state machine is smashed, the ruling class can bide its time and then strike back. As the French revolutionary Louis de Saint-Just put it in 1793, in words whose wisdom has been repeatedly confirmed, "Those who make a revolution halfway merely dig their own graves".

Then there are those revolutions that are pushed to a successful conclusion, but which are not working class or which never aimed to put power into the hands of the working class. The English and French revolutions of 1641–49 and 1789–93, for example, were revolutions in which the representatives of the rising bourgeoisie sought to settle accounts with the old aristocratic order. In both cases, having executed the king, these revolutions gave way to dictatorships under Oliver Cromwell and Napoleon Bonaparte respectively. Even though radical democrats won a wide audience among the soldiers in Cromwell's New Model Army and the urban poor who drove the French Revolution in its first years, it was the bourgeoisie that took advantage of the momentum provided by such mass involvement. The working class was still too small, and the world capitalist system was too much in its infancy, for there to be any other outcome. Once the masses had played their role in bringing down the old system, they were forced back by the bourgeoisie that now sought to make the world in its image.

In neither England nor France were the masses set in motion under their own banners and for their own demands. The new ruling classes that emerged following these revolutions did not need mass democracy; indeed, they were petrified by it, and thus, a new tyranny was an inevitable outcome. The details differ, but the same essential logic was played out repeatedly in many anti-colonial revolutions in the twentieth century.

In only one case has there been a revolution carried out by the working class in its own name and which destroyed the old state machine. This was Russia in 1917. We will deal with Russia in much more detail in chapters 9 and 10, but here it is enough to say that tyranny was not the inevitable outcome. A working-class revolution differs from all others because it is the only type of revolution that can open the way to eliminating class society. As we saw in chapter one, the working class, as the majority class around the world today, has no other class to exploit when it takes power, and therefore, the basis of class division can fade away once the threat of counter-revolution by the old dominant classes has been eliminated. The problem that befell the Russian working class was its international isolation in the context of famine, disease and imperialist military intervention. The entire economy, already flattened by World War I, was hit further. The working class was atomised as a political force and could, therefore, no longer rule. The peasants would support the revolution so long as they feared the return of the landlords, but once the threat of a restoration of the landlords was over, they saw no need to cooperate with the urban working class in the absence of the plentiful supply of industrial goods. Only a revolution in an advanced country such as Germany could save the Russian workers' revolution. Without such support, the state bureaucracy took over with Stalin at the helm of the counter-revolution. The subsequent tyranny was "necessary" – that is, the gains of the revolution had to be smashed – if the new Russian ruling class was to compete with its rivals in the West. This was not a continuation or logical extension of 1917 but its reversal and extinguishment. The lesson from Russia is not the futility of revolution but the need for revolution to spread to other countries if it is to be successful and for the gains to be sustained.

Looking to the future, there is no reason that a new working-class revolution needs to submit to tyranny. If workers are to carry out such a revolution, they will have to undergo tremendous struggle and sacrifice and will transform themselves in the process. Having done this, why would they willingly surrender their power to some new autocrat? We would expect them to fight tooth and nail to defend their new, democratic ways of running their lives. So long as they can link up with other revolutions in neighbouring countries, we might expect them to consolidate the gains resulting from the revolution in their fight for a better world.

In summary

The last two centuries have seen revolutions in almost every continent of the world. Revolutions, which can be defined as the forceful transfer of government power, can be grouped into two types: political, which only change the political complexion of the existing state structure, and social, which usher in a new class order. Elements of the two can often intermingle, with now one element dominant, now another.

Revolutions are not caused simply by the accumulation of misery and hardship, nor by the working class just spontaneously deciding to make a revolution, and definitely not by socialists educating or fooling the working class into revolution. The precondition for a revolution is that millions of ordinary people become convinced that society can't continue in the old way, there are splits and confusion at the top over how to restore order and overcome the crisis, and the workers seize the opportunity to push their demands. Revolutionary situations can also grow out of raised expectations that are not being met. What sparks off a revolution is impossible to predict in advance. It can often seem purely accidental, but this should not disguise the underlying class tensions that transform a seemingly trivial incident into an insurrection.

The working class does not go into struggle as fully fledged revolutionaries. Revolutions are needed not only because the ruling class will not surrender power through constitutional and peaceful means but also because they make the working class fit to rule. Through engaging in revolutionary struggle, all the backward ideas and prejudices of the working class, ingrained by centuries of capitalism, can be challenged. As workers fight, they tend to eliminate the divisions in their ranks. Further, they begin to learn and use the skills needed to take over the running of society.

The working class must lead the revolution because other social forces that may take part in the early stages of any great upsurge have different ultimate goals. Only the working class has the interest and capacity to smash the status quo and institute a whole new form of egalitarian rule. This does not preclude alliances with other forces, including elements of the middle class, whether urban or rural, but it does mean that the working class has to insist on its own organisation and demands and not dilute them to what is acceptable to forces inclined to prevarication.

As mass working-class struggle develops, workers become more aware of their collective power. The action of workers in taking over their workplaces and then moving from there, by force of circumstance, to take over the distribution of food, the movement of goods and people, the organisation of power supply, health and education, begins to throw up a form of power, the workers' council, which runs parallel and in conflict with capitalist authorities. This is known as dual power and is inherently unstable: either the working class go forward and smash the power of the capitalist state, or the capitalists crush the insurgency.

The working class can only advance by resolute action – to solidify their ranks, push the capitalists back, split the armed forces and win them over to the side of the revolution, and give confidence to other social layers that a successful working-class revolution will resolve their grievances. The capitalist class will try to prevent the working class from advancing through concessions and repression. In such circumstances, a revolutionary party, tens or hundreds of thousands strong, made up of the advanced sections of the working class, is needed to argue for the way forward and to defeat attempts to send the revolution into a cul-de-sac.

Revolution can occur in Australia. The country has a rich history of class struggle, and on several occasions, the polarisation between the capitalists and the working class has created a politically volatile situation. Australia is integrated into a world system, and there is no reason to expect Australia to be immune from a revolutionary wave elsewhere, particularly if it embraces other developed countries.

Working-class revolutions are not doomed to end in tyranny. This is much more likely when the working class is not resolute enough to smash the capitalist state but seeks to compromise with it. A successful outcome requires the utmost "extremism", that is, the deepest and most profound dismantling of the old order, lest the ruling class catch its breath, rally its forces and unleash a savage counter-attack.

Notes

1. This chapter includes extensive extracts from Paul D'Amato, *The Meaning of Marxism*, Haymarket Books, 2014, Vashti Kenway, "Revolutionary democracy from Russia 1917 to Egypt today", *Socialist Alternative*, February 2011, and Ben Hillier, "Could there be a revolution in Australia?", *Red Flag*, 14 August 2022.

2. Karl Marx, *The German Ideology*, 1845.

3. Karl Marx, *Capital*, Vol. I, chapter 28, 1867.

4. Antonio Gramsci, *Selections from the Prison Notebooks*, International Publishers, 1980, p.333.

5. Marx, *The German Ideology*.

6. Hal Draper, *Karl Marx's Theory of Revolution*, Vol. 2, *Monthly Review Press*, 1978, p.42.

7. V.I. Lenin, *On Strikes*, 1899.

8. Lenin, *On Strikes*.

9. Lenin, *On Strikes*.

10. V.I. Lenin, *Lecture on the 1905 Revolution*, 1917.

11. "Greek hospital now under workers' control", 5 February 2012, https://libcom.org/article/greek-hospital-now-under-workers-control.

12. Dave Kerin, quoted in Jeff Sparrow, "The workers' flag is deepest green", in Rick Kuhn (ed.), *Class and Struggle in Australia*, Pearson Longman, 2005, p.209.

13.   Samuel J. Brannen, Christian S. Haig and Katherine Schmidt, *The Age of Mass Protests: Understanding an Escalating Global Trend*, Center for Strategic and International Studies, Washington, 2020. One academic study identified 345 "revolutionary episodes" between 1900 and 2014. Mark Beissinger, *The Revolutionary City: Urbanization and the Global Transformation of Rebellion*, Princeton University Press, 2022.

14.   The following draws on Draper, *Karl Marx's Theory of Revolution*, Vol. 2, pp.17–48.

15.   Leon Trotsky, *History of the Russian Revolution*, Pluto Press, 1977 [1933], p.17.

16.   V.I. Lenin, *The Collapse of the Second International*, 1915.

17.   Antonio Gramsci, "Once again on the organic capacities of the working class", *L'Unità*, 1 October 1926, republished in David Forgacs (ed.), *The Gramsci Reader: Selected Writings 1916-1935*, Schocken, 1988, pp.106–9.

18.   Sameh Naguib, "The tragedy of the Egyptian revolution", in Colin Barker and Gareth Dale (eds), *Revolutionary Rehearsals in the Neoliberal Age*, Haymarket Books, 2021.

19.   John Reed, *Ten Days that Shook the World*, 1919.

20.   George Orwell, *Homage to Catalonia*, Penguin Books, 2000 [1938], pp.3–4.

21.   Marx, *The German Ideology*, 1845.

22.   Sudanese Professionals Association, "Civil disobedience and general strike – field report", 13 June 2019.

23.   Muzan Alneel, "Strategies and tactics in the Sudanese revolution", *Spring magazine*, 23 January 2021.

24.   Claire Ceruti, "The end of apartheid in South Africa", in Barker and Dale (eds), *Revolutionary Rehearsals*.

25.   This was the name given to St Petersburg at the outbreak of World War I.

26.   Trotsky, *History*, p.141.

27.   Trotsky, *History*, p.125.

28.   The following account, including the quotes from *Tribune*, is drawn from Phil Griffiths, "Strike Fraser out! The labour movement campaign against the blocking of supply and the sacking of the Whitlam Government, October–December 1975", 1997, https://sa.org.au/interventions/sacked.htm

Chapter four

Socialism

You are horrified at our intending to do away with private property. But in your existing society, private property is already done away with for nine-tenths of the population; its existence for the few is solely due to its non-existence in the hands of those nine-tenths. You reproach us, therefore, with intending to do away with a form of property, the necessary condition for whose existence is the non-existence of any property for the immense majority of society.

In one word, you reproach us with intending to do away with your property. Precisely so; that is just what we intend.

—Marx and Engels, *The Communist Manifesto*

"WE KNOW WHAT YOU'RE AGAINST. WHAT ARE YOU FOR?" is a question often asked of socialists.[1] We can answer simply. We are for a classless society free of oppression and exploitation where people with different abilities or disabilities, parents taking time for children, the sick and the elderly would get what they need, eradicating some of the sources of egregious inequality and injustice in capitalist society. We envision a decent world for all and a sustainable society that cherishes rather than destroys our environment. Such a society would be a truly democratic society that does away with the centralisation of power in the hands of a small clique of capitalists and opens up decision-making to the masses. But precisely because it is based on mass democracy, we cannot come up with an exact blueprint for such a society; it will be created by millions who, in the process of bringing a new society into being, will transform themselves.

We cannot immediately leap straight into a completely communist society the day after a workers' revolution. As Marx stated:

> What we have to deal with here is a communist society, not as it has developed on its own foundations, but, on the contrary, just as it emerges from capitalist society; which is thus in every respect, economically, morally, and intellectually, still stamped with the birthmarks of the old society from whose womb it emerges.[2]

There must be a transition period in which the old is dissolved, broken apart and reshaped, and new social relations and habits of intercourse gradually emerge. "Between capitalist and communist society there lies the period of the revolutionary transformation of the one into the other," wrote Marx. "Corresponding to this is also a political transition period in which the state can be nothing but the revolutionary dictatorship [rule] of the proletariat."[3] So workers rise up, form new institutions of democratic rule, seize power and can now reshape society.

A workers' state

Marx and Lenin insisted that the working class could not construct socialism until it had first destroyed the old state based on bureaucratic chains of command and created a new state based on entirely different principles – Lenin called it "a commune state, a state which is not a state". Their ideas were drawn up not based on some utopian dream but on observations of the working class in action – in revolutions that swept Europe in 1848, the 1871 Paris Commune and the soviets (workers' councils) formed during the 1905 and 1917 Russian revolutions.[4]

Although it lasted only two months, the Paris Commune represented the first time workers took power. Marx had concluded after the 1848 revolutions that workers would need to smash the capitalist state to transform society. The Paris Commune taught him what workers would create in place of the old state. Lenin studied Marx's writings and drew on his own experience in the 1905 revolution when preparing his pamphlet *The State and Revolution*.

He also concluded that because the state exists as a repressive apparatus to maintain the power of the capitalists, it cannot simply be "seized" by workers but must be dismantled and replaced by direct workers' democracy based on recallable delegates elected by workers themselves. Whereas the capitalist state serves the interests of a small minority of society, the workers' state has to serve the interests of the overwhelming majority. It aims to democratise all of its institutions and functions. Where a minority of hired killers exercises force in the capitalist state, cut off from the rest of society and trained to obey upper-class officers, force would be needed by a workers' state only so that the majority could protect themselves against anti-social acts by the remnants of the old, privileged classes and their middle-class supporters. Force would be used by organisations staffed by workers and under workers' control.

I described the basic difference between workers' councils and parliaments in the last chapter, but I will reiterate the main points here since they illustrate how workers' power is so much more democratic than even the most liberal of democracies.

Parliamentary representatives in a capitalist state pass laws but leave it to full-time bureaucrats, police chiefs and judges to implement them. This setup allows MPs and councillors to wriggle out of any responsibility for enforcing their laws. The workers' representatives in a workers' state would have to see their laws implemented. They, not top bureaucrats, would have to explain how things should be done to the public service workers, the army, and so on. Elected workers' representatives would have to interpret the laws in the courts.

Politicians today are cut off from those who elect them by high salaries. In a workers' state, the representatives would get only the average worker's wage. The same goes for those who work full time in key posts implementing the decisions of the workers' representatives (the equivalent of present-day public servants). Unlike MPs today, workers' representatives and all those concerned with implementing workers' decisions would be subject to at least annual elections and immediate recall by those who elected them if they did not implement their wishes.

Where parliamentary representatives are elected by all the people living in a particular locality – capitalists, middle class and working class, slum landlords and tenants, stockbrokers and labourers – in a workers' state election would be by those who work or who depend on those who do, with voting only after an open discussion on the issues concerned. So, the core of the state would be workers' councils based on the factories, mines, docks and big offices, with groups such as pensioners and students having their own representatives. In this way, each section of the working class would have its representatives and be able to judge whether they were following its interests. The new state cannot become a force separate from and against the majority working class – as it was in the old Eastern Bloc countries, which called themselves "communist".

The workers' council system provides a means by which workers can coordinate their efforts in the running of industry according to a democratically decided national plan and not end up running their factories in competition with each other. It is easy to see how modern computer technology would enable all workers to be given information on the various economic options open to society and to direct their representatives to choose what most workers thought the best set of options – for example, whether to spend resources on toll-roads or a cheap and reliable public transport system, how to abolish nuclear bombs, whether to build anti-social casinos or kidney machines and so on.

Reorganising society

Socialism aims to do away with all class distinctions and create a society whereby the state – an instrument of class domination – gradually withers. But it cannot do this immediately. Having gained power through insurrectionary struggle, workers must first ensure that the old order cannot gain a foothold again. They must still use coercion, where necessary, to suppress those who would use violence to restore the old exploitative relations in society. But this task fades, as does the resistance of the old exploiters, giving way to the difficult but more rewarding task of social transformation. The new workers' state must implement a series of reforms that, step by step, abolish profit and the market and replace it with conscious, democratic planning.

Marx and Engels wrote in the *Manifesto:*

The proletariat will use its political supremacy to wrest, by degree, all capital from the bourgeoisie, to centralise all instruments of production in the hands of the state, i.e. of the proletariat organised as the ruling class; and to increase the total productive forces as rapidly as possible.[5]

Some of these measures might include: introducing steeply progressive income and wealth taxes on the rich; establishing free education at all levels; abolishing advertising and all other wasteful and costly diversions, with the funds going toward health, education and artistic needs; instituting free abortion on demand and free childcare provision; confiscating all empty houses and mansions of capitalist developers and the rich to house the poor and homeless; establishing free kitchens to feed the hungry; and immediately reducing the workday and providing jobs for the unemployed.

An immediate start could be made to dealing with the environmental disasters unfolding around us. The same scientific knowledge used to produce things in ways that recklessly pollute the earth could, under different circumstances, create a more harmonious balance between human beings and their environment. The aim of socialism is not unchecked growth for its own sake, as under capitalism, but the rational use of society's productive capacities, planned according to human need, as Engels writes, to reduce the hours of labour, "offering each individual the opportunity to develop all his faculties, physical and mental, in all directions and exercise them to the full – in which, therefore, productive labour will become a pleasure instead of being a burden".[6] Indeed, in a socialist society, there may be an increase in the production of some things – like healthy foods and shelter – to ensure that those deprived of the necessities of life under capitalism get them. But rational scientific planning will also entail the curtailment of growth in other areas – and its restructuring in all areas. Eliminating "inbuilt obsolescence" – like smartphones whose batteries only last one or two years – combined with efficient use of materials and energy to maximise the quality of life rather than profit is possible only in a rationally planned society.

Wealth would no longer be measured in how much profit could be amassed or in the obscene conspicuous consumption of a tiny minority but in our well-being, free time and creativity. Such a society would be antithetical to practices that degraded the natural basis upon which such a society could thrive. The point is not to leave nature alone like some pretty postcard, but to transform human social relations and, thereby, our relationship with nature.

We can adopt new technologies that use solar, wind, wave and geothermal energy. We can replace cars with efficient forms of public transportation. We can develop agricultural methods that are both environmentally sustainable and yet still capable of feeding billions of people in place of the large industrial farming model based on monoculture, mechanisation, chemical fertilisers, pesticides and genetic alteration of seeds.

There are also our sexual needs. Alienated and stunted sexuality prevents the full enjoyment by human beings of each other in this realm. There are also mental and spiritual needs that are closely associated with, but not reducible to, our physical needs. The lack of open and green space and attractive art and architecture designed to facilitate our comfort harms our sense of well-being. The lack of control over our work and its products – feeling chained to a job – converts work from a genuine need that satisfies us to merely a means to an end: a way to get money to buy our necessities. Lack of control over virtually every aspect of our life outside of work also engenders a sense of helplessness and alienation. Leisure time, direct participation in the important decisions of community and society, comprehensive education, the ability to move from one type of work to another, and from one creative endeavour (or whim) to another – these are human needs by any rational measure and are only luxuries mostly for a few in a capitalist world.

The market and money cannot be done away with in one stroke. But the workers' state can nationalise the banks and place them under workers' control and redirect funds into much-needed state projects, like building a better public transport system. Money can be transformed from a means of profit-making into a means of accounting for what is produced and how it is distributed. If, at first, workers' control at the workplace means exercising control over management, over time, it would develop into a system of workers' management.

Although inequality cannot be abolished immediately, several measures could be implemented to uproot it. Special measures could be taken to wipe out inequalities in the education system and to provide opportunities for education and equal participation in society for all, regardless of race, nationality, gender, language or other differences. Education could be provided in all languages and could be designed to allow individuals to switch jobs, moving from intellectual to manual work with ease. At first, workers may need to exercise joint control over technicians, engineers, and planners, some (but not all) of whom may still hanker for the privileges they received under capitalism. However, the extensive reorganisation of education and the production process would allow everyone to pursue a variety of jobs, gradually weakening the barrier between mental and manual labour and providing an environment in which the full potential of every individual was given the means to develop.

In a socialist society, improvements in labour productivity would be a means to shorten the workday to a minimum to free people up as much as possible to devote their energies to other pursuits, including taking part in the running of society. There is no reason we could not shift to a working week of 15–20 hours. Since workers would own and control the labour process and its results, work would no longer have the sense of emptiness it possesses today. Instead of workers dreaming of the weekend and working only to pay the landlord or bank, work would be a source of fulfilment. The boundaries between work and leisure would dramatically diminish.

All of this depends on the existence of material abundance. Socialists are sometimes accused of being interested only in want or privation: everyone might be equal, but living in a cramped apartment on a daily diet of two slices of bread and half a can of processed meat. Or maybe we advocate everyone growing their own food, spinning their own yarn and making their own clothes. These arguments are right-wing tropes aimed at discrediting the idea of socialism. Socialism is not about sharing poverty around equally, nor is it about deindustrialisation and going back to the land. It is about everyone having access to the plenty that our society can provide. As Marx and Engels so brilliantly summarised in the *Communist Manifesto*, the rise of capitalism has created a world market, where each part of the world depends on the other; it has concentrated populations in large cities, subordinating the country to the town; it has, by the development of centralised and expanded machine-based mass production, created productive forces that far surpass all previous societies. Abundance is the first material premise that makes socialism more than just a utopian dream and makes its achievement possible. This abundance, on a world scale, makes international revolution so imperative. Cooped up in a single country, a revolution that lacks the necessary resources will fall back in on itself. As people struggle to survive on resources that are in short supply, all the evils of capitalist competition will return. This abundance has removed every excuse for the existence of a handful of exploiters or for any kind of privation. Indeed, the existence of a ruling class has long been an absolute hindrance to human development.

When the resistance of the old ruling classes is gone, so too is the need for the state. With the abolition of class distinctions comes what Engels called "the withering away of the state", leaving only purely administrative tasks such as the postal service, transportation and maintaining the power grid.

What replaces the state is the free association of people – communism. Society is administered according to a plan, but there is no need for organised coercion because everyone gives what he or she can and takes what they need. Society might freely choose volunteers to handle small-scale conflicts. But because society is not divided into classes, coercion would be largely unnecessary, at most incidental rather than systematic, and could be handled with no "special bodies" of armed people. As the remnants of the old society against which it was directed became resigned to the success of the revolution, and as revolutions elsewhere removed the threat of invasion or strangulation by foreign ruling classes, there would be less and less need for coercion, until eventually workers need never take time off from work to staff the "police" and the "army".

Only in such a consciously and democratically planned and administered society can the potentialities slumbering in the millions of people now oppressed and stunted by capitalism flourish. Marx wrote of this higher phase of communist society:

[A]fter the enslaving subordination of the individual to the division of labour, and therewith also the antithesis between mental and physical labour, has vanished; after labour has become not only a means of life but life's prime want; after the productive forces have also increased with the all-around development of the individual, and all the springs of co-operative wealth flow more abundantly – only then can the narrow horizon of bourgeois right be crossed in its entirety and society inscribe on its banners: From each according to his ability, to each according to his needs![7]

Against human nature?

Plenty of people can have criticisms of the way capitalism destroys the world, but are sceptical that the working class can run the world in an egalitarian fashion. Alongside the idea that revolutions always end in tyranny, dealt with in chapter three, the notion that socialism is against human nature because people are naturally greedy and lazy is probably the most widely held criticism of the socialist project.

The notion of an unchanging human nature is deeply conservative and wrong. If there is a fixed human nature, then how can it be that human societies have differed so much between different regions and historical times? How is it that some societies were egalitarian, sharing societies, while today they are all competitive and class-divided? How is it that some were warlike and violent, while others were relatively peaceful? How did some accord women an influential position and others a subordinate one? How is it that some societies proscribed same-sex intimacy while others embraced it?

The French Jesuit missionary Le Jeune lived among the Montagnais-Naskapi Indigenous peoples on the Labrador coast of Canada in the early 1630s. "Alas!," he lamented, "if someone could stop the wanderings of the Savages, and give authority to one of them to rule the others, we would see them converted and civilised in a short time". He observed:

They have neither political organisation, nor offices, nor dignities, nor any authority, for they only obey their chief through the goodwill toward him, therefore they never kill each other to acquire these honours. Also, as they are contented with a mere living, not one of them gives himself to the Devil to acquire wealth.[8]

It was not just on the question of authority and hierarchy that the non-European societies differed from those of the missionaries. Family customs differed dramatically. Jesuits who proselytised in Canada considered it healthy to beat children into submission, while the Montagnais-Naskapi considered the practice barbaric. And when a French missionary tried to tell a Montagnais-Naskapi man that women should love only their husbands so that men could be sure of who their children were, he responded: "Thou hast no sense. You French people love only your own children, but we all love all the children of our tribe".[9] New archaeological evidence regularly sheds new light on the past. In the Anatolian community of Çatalhöyük (in today's Turkey), ruins dating from 7000 BCE show that women and men did similar work; men did not do all the hunting, nor were women confined to the home. Ian Hodder, the chief archaeologist at Çatalhöyük, argues:

> [O]verall, there is little evidence that gender was very significant in the allocation of roles... There must have been differences of lifestyle in relation to childbirth, but these differences do not seem to be related to major social distinctions.

Nor did differences in dress or lives mean that "one gender was privileged above the other in terms of the transmission of rules and resources or in terms of social status and lifestyle".[10]

The "human nature" view of the world assumes that humans have a built-in nature – shaped genetically by their physical attributes – in the same way that other animals have a nature that determines their behaviour. The wolf has sharp teeth to tear raw meat, the bear has fur to keep warm, and fish have gills to breathe underwater and special muscles adapted for swimming. But we humans have none of these special adaptations.

Our brains are not hard-wired for certain behaviours and not others; we possess a great deal of neuroplasticity. Human beings shape their environment through labour, and the environment shapes our brains. It is this that explains our infinite adaptability. Our peculiar genetic inheritance – in particular, our upright gait, larger brain size, opposable thumbs and the capacity for language – gave us the ability to make tools to manipulate our environment cooperatively and to pass those skills on to our offspring. Humans can make fur coats, build shelter, and catch, grow and cook food, i.e. we can create the things nature did not physically endow us with, which allows us to work with virtually every environment on the planet.

Our social nature and our ability to reproduce our means of existence artificially make humans distinct from other animals, even though we are still animals. This creates a plasticity of behaviour that other animals do not have. In short, we adapt culturally.

Humans have changed relatively little genetically or biologically over the last 40,000 years. Yet our social forms of organisation – how we organise ourselves to procure food, shelter, clothing and other necessities – have changed tremendously, and in recent centuries, at an accelerating rate. It is this that accounts for the changing "nature" of humans – our morals, our ideas about the world and about ourselves – from one society to the next. This is a fundamental point. As Marx argued: "In acquiring new productive forces…in changing their way of earning a living, [humans] change all their social relations".[11]

Basing his argument on the work of early anthropologist Louis Henry Morgan, Engels argued that humans had lived for tens of thousands of years in societies "without soldiers, gendarmes or police; without nobles, kings, governors, prefects, or judges; without prisons; without trials".[12] All things beyond personal possessions were communally owned and shared in what some have called "primitive communism". This is because work was of necessity cooperative, and productivity was not sufficient to generate a surplus that a minority could seize and use to establish itself as a new ruling class exploiting others.

Subsequent research has backed up most of Engels's arguments. Anthropologist Richard Lee wrote in 1988:

> Before the rise of the state and the entrenchment of social inequality, people lived for millennia in small-scale, kin-based social groups, in which the core institutions of economic life included collective or common ownership of land and resources, generalised reciprocity in the distribution of food and relatively egalitarian political relations.[13]

The economic structure of society shaped the role of women. Among the Iroquois, women were accorded equal status in part because women did most of the labour in the fields (having been the gatherers and therefore knowing the most about edible plants), which accounted for more of the group's food than did hunting. It was only as women were edged out of production that their social status sank, a phenomenon we explore more in chapter eight.

In pre-capitalist class societies, the surplus over immediate needs was small. To keep on developing the means of production and technology, that small surplus needed to be managed by a minority who gained power and prestige by so doing (see chapter eight for more about how this happened). This power meant that they put their control and their ability to increase their own wealth above the needs of the rest of society. This was the basis for class society to emerge, leading to hunger and deprivation existing side by side with obscene wealth and the waste of resources on useless and destructive things.

The findings from hunter-gatherer and early horticultural societies tell us that in a society based around cooperative production, social relations will adopt non-hierarchical forms. The productive potential inherited from capitalism could be utilised under socialism to benefit all, not only the tiny ruling class. Abundance will mean that people will not need to fight over resources – such conflicts emerge only when there is not enough to go around for everyone. Under socialism, society's surplus wealth would collectively enhance the welfare of all rather than that of a small group. Why would people steal what was freely available?

Marx and Engels dealt with the question of our alleged predisposition to laziness in the *Communist Manifesto*. "It has been objected," they wrote, "that upon the abolition of private property, all work will cease, and universal laziness will overtake us". Their answer is as simple as it is devastating: "According to this, bourgeois society ought long ago to have gone to the dogs through sheer idleness; for those of its members who work, acquire nothing, and those who acquire anything do not work."[14] Any casual observation of the life of the likes of Gina Rinehart would confirm this.

Hard work is simply not rewarded in our society. Many millions of workers work hard, produce more, see more clients, serve more customers, drive more kilometres, teach more students, or nurse more patients, and still, their wages remain the same. The bosses pocket the fruits of their labour. Workers' only incentive is that without work, they cannot survive, so they buckle down but try to find ways of quietly resisting the drive to work harder and longer. In other circumstances, people put in hours of hard work for no financial gain. Anyone involved in community theatre or sports can attest to the satisfaction of pouring hours of time after work into making a theatrical production or sports team come to life. Or there were the thousands who put everything aside to help their communities during the 2011 Brisbane floods and the 2020 bushfires in NSW and Victoria.

Nor can the argument be levelled that socialism takes incentive away because it doesn't allow for personal possessions. It is only property used to exploit others that socialism prohibits. Socialism will allow people to have more, not less, of the things that enhance their lives, like leisure time, good quality food and shelter, access to art and culture and so on. The incentive to invent better technology will remain and be enhanced without the profit motive because such inventions will improve everyone's quality of life.

But "Who will do the shit jobs?" many right-wing opponents of socialism ask: someone's got to empty the bins, sweep the streets and clean the public toilets. But many of today's unappealing jobs can be easily automated, as indeed they are even under capitalism – self-cleaning toilets are now common in many European cities. The number of people involved in collecting rubbish or sweeping streets has been dramatically reduced because of the improved design of garbage trucks and the introduction of mechanised street sweepers. The problem in our society is that those who used to do these backbreaking jobs are tossed aside with no care for their future. And if there are unpleasant jobs that are impossible to mechanise, such jobs could be rotated so that people do not have to spend a large part of a working week or their working lives doing this kind of work.

People performing such work in capitalism are low in the pecking order. But why should they be? Their work is much more valuable than that of hundreds of thousands of advertising and finance professionals who destroy more than they create, or human resource managers whose careers are spent humiliating workers. In our society, the more useless and parasitic the work you do, the more you are held up and admired; the more valuable it is, the more degraded you are. Under a socialist society that valued meeting human needs rather than the accumulation of money in the hands of a few, people doing dirty jobs would have much shorter working weeks and would be treated with dignity. It's the way the workers are treated, not anything inherently distasteful about the job itself, which is the most "shit" thing about many such jobs. Further, people would take much more responsibility for their environment, as the occupiers of Tahrir Square in 2011 did: everyone chipped in and helped clean up during and after the 18-day occupation, because they now had pride in their city and saw it as belonging to them, rather than as something alien and oppressive.

Can workers run society?

Another common objection to socialism is that workers can't possibly run society because they do not have the skills to do so. Given the "complex" nature of society today, the critics argue, we need experts to run things. The legendary stupidity of former US president George W. Bush, whose rich parents and crony friends bought him passing grades and much more, is a strong argument against this view. There are many other examples that could be cited of ministers, industrialists and bureaucrats with limited, if not non-existent, abilities. Switch off their autocues and remove them from their minders, and their veneer of competence crumbles.

Most people at the very top of society, the multimillionaires and billionaires, play no direct function in society's running – they merely collect the rewards of ownership. The ruling class today has become entirely parasitic, siphoning wealth but serving no useful social function. Bankers and investors don't make steel or wash hospital patients. It hardly takes intellectual brilliance for someone who inherits $50 million to double or triple it. Society could do away with the ruling class and suffer no more than when an appendix is removed from a human body. But do workers possess the capacity to rule? Won't they still depend on experts?

Often, it is workers' own hard-won, first-hand knowledge that engineers and managers use to figure out how to improve production, that is, to squeeze as much out of workers as possible. Much of what is now called science originated with the people closest to nature: hunter-gatherers, peasant farmers, sailors, miners, blacksmiths, folk healers and others forced by the conditions of their lives to wrest the means of their survival from daily encounters with nature.

There are many examples of workers demonstrating admirably their ability to run their workplaces under their direct control and supervision. From the Paris Commune to the Russian Revolution, from the Spanish Revolution of 1936 to the Argentinian uprising of 2001, workers in struggle have, for various reasons and under various guises, seized control of their workplaces and have attempted to run them and sometimes, link them together with workers in other concerns. In 2001, a deep economic crisis in Argentina led to factories shutting en masse, with hundreds of thousands of workers sacked. Most times, the bosses just locked up and abandoned the premises. Rather than rot at home, many of the workers broke open the factories and assumed control over them, restarting production. In doing so, they achieved things they had never dreamed possible. One worker explained in 2002:

> Without workers a factory does not function. But without bosses, yes, it functions – and very well indeed! With all the other comrades, we are going to demonstrate that the nation functions with the hands of working people and not with the thieving hands of the politicians.[15]

Of course, creating a new society does not mean making immediate administrators and planners out of waiters and nurses. But given the opportunity, everyone can learn the scientific, administrative, and mathematical skills necessary to play a direct role in running society, just as in pre-class society, knowledge of terrain, plants and animals, or of tool-making, was shared by the group, and not treated as the monopoly of a minority.

Experts and scientists would still be needed for a time, even under socialism, until the education system was improved so that the majority received an education that today is only reserved for the privileged few. For a time, workers would have to exercise democratic control over the accountants, managers and engineers. But with society's vast resources diverted toward education, the distinctions between mental and manual work would break down, and the majority would be capable of doing many different jobs, from manual to scientific to administrative work.

When all is said and done, the idea that workers are incapable of running things is elitism. The ruling class and their ideological supporters believe they are indispensable and that workers are idiots. History tells us the opposite: they need us, we do not need them.

In summary

Socialism is not a brilliant idea dreamed up by clever individuals and then imposed on the working class. It is the creation of the working class in struggle who must smash the capitalist state, establish a new form of government based on mass democracy and mass participation, and then use this new workers' state to reshape society.

A capitalist state and a workers' state have nothing in common. The most fundamental difference is that the former aims to perpetuate the rule of a minority ruling class of exploiters; the latter seeks to defend and advance the rule of the formerly exploited majority in the transition between capitalism and full communism. Its primary goal is to crush the threat of counter-revolution by the former ruling classes and to oversee the steps necessary to create abundance and the extinction of class differences over a long period.

Using the political weapon of the workers' state, the working class must expropriate the wealth of the capitalists, in particular by taking the means of production from them and redirecting resources based on public need, not private profit. A workers' state is the working class in control and is a democratic instrument for imposing the will of the working class (and its allies) on society.

After a lengthy period, with the threat of counter-revolution eliminated and abundance in place, there will be no more need for the state to impose the will of the working class on a recalcitrant minority, nor to oversee a giant plan to ensure that resources go to those who need it – if there is plenty to go around, everyone can help themselves from the common store.

The existence of classless societies for most human existence shows that inequality and the domination of rulers are not hard-wired into human society.

The need for a minority to manage that surplus for the needs of society as at first has long been obsolete. Socialism and equality are no longer a utopia dreamed up by dreamers and philosophers because of the plenty created by capitalism.

The various arguments that are used to convince us that socialism is impossible – the alleged laziness, greed and ignorance of humanity – are easily disposed of. The working class, even in this dog-eat-dog society, demonstrates its capacity for human solidarity all the time. They are the largest donors to flood, fire and earthquake appeals and other charities. They have a long history of donating to strike funds for other workers out of meagre wages. And frequently, well short of socialism, they have demonstrated their capacity to organise the basics of production and provide social order and security effectively and democratically. There is every reason to expect we can do this again, not just in a given workplace, town or city, but on a national and global basis.

Notes

1. This chapter includes extensive extracts from Paul D'Amato, *The Meaning of Marxism*, Haymarket Books, 2014, and Chris Harman, *How Marxism Works*, Bookmarks, 1984.

2. Karl Marx, *Critique of the Gotha Program*, 1875.

3. Marx, *Critique of the Gotha Program*.

4. The relevant works were Karl Marx's *The Civil War in France*, 1871, and Vladimir Lenin's *The State and Revolution*, 1917.

5. Karl Marx and Friedrich Engels, *The Communist Manifesto*, 1848.

6. Friedrich Engels, *Anti-Dühring*, 1878.

7. Marx, *Critique of the Gotha Program*, 1875.

8. Quoted in Eleanor Burke Leacock, *Myths of Male Dominance*, Haymarket Books, 2008 [1981], p.35.

9. Leacock, *Myths of Male Dominance*, p.50.

10. Ian Hodder, *The Leopard's Tale: Revealing the Mysteries of Çatalhöyük*, Thames and Hudson, 2006, p.211.

11. Karl Marx, *The Poverty of Philosophy*, 1847.

12. Friedrich Engels, *The Origin of the Family, Private Property and the State*, 1884.

13. Richard Lee, "Reflections on primitive communism", in T. Ingold, D. Riches and J. Woodburn (eds), *Hunters and Gatherers*, Vol. 1, Berg, 1988.

14. Marx and Engels, *The Communist Manifesto*.

15. Quoted in James Cockcroft, "Argentina: Workers' control and the crisis, part I," *Against the Current*, 103, March–April 2003.

Chapter five

Trade unions

When the union's inspiration through the workers' blood shall run
There can be no power greater anywhere beneath the sun
Yet what force on earth is weaker than the feeble strength of one
For the Union makes us strong.

—Ralph Chaplin, *Solidarity Forever*, 1915

C LASS STRUGGLE TAKES PLACE IN EVERY COUNTRY OF THE WORLD.
Workers' unity in struggle is critical in determining whether they
are victorious or defeated in such battles. The capitalist class does
all it can to break workers up, set us against each other, to help them cut
wages and speed up work. Our side, the working class, must fight for unity
in our ranks. By uniting rather than competing, workers can gain more from
their employers and start seeing themselves as a class. The best tool to do this
is the trade union, the basic combat organisation of the working class. As
early as 1844, Engels wrote, "as schools of war, the unions are unexcelled".
Even though union action may be over seemingly narrow issues of wages and
conditions, Engels wrote, "their real importance is this, that they are the first
attempt of the workers to abolish competition".[1]

Trade unions' very existence indicates class antagonism. Employers oppose
effective trade unions for two simple reasons: by boosting wages, union
struggle eats into the bosses' profits, and by bringing workers together in
opposition to the bosses, unions infringe on the employers' self-appointed
right to run workers' lives.

Everything that the working class in Australia has won has come about
through union struggle – the five-day week and weekends, the eight-hour day,
paid holidays, sick leave, penalty rates, lunch breaks, overtime pay, child labour

laws and health and safety provisions, equal pay for women, redundancy pay and unemployment benefit, age pensions, Medicare and the right to some, albeit limited, consultation over significant changes at work. None of these has come from the generosity of the bosses or governments. Where it has been legislated or enshrined in awards (standard conditions laid out by the industrial tribunals), this has always followed a union struggle. At every step of the way, the employers have dug their heels in, crying poor and threatening to sack workers. And, if workers are given any rights in non-union workplaces, it is only because the bosses have been forced to do so by legislation or awards that have resulted from union campaigns or because they fear losing their workforce to unionised companies where the conditions are better. Take away trade unions, and Australia would be like the US, with its poverty-line minimum wages and two weeks' paid annual leave.

The strike is the workers' chief weapon in their fight with the bosses. Where unions are strong and willing to strike, as they were in the 1970s, they can have some real say over what goes on at work. Graeme Haynes, a militant working at Robe River, a remote mining town in the Pilbara, explained the impact of strong trade unionism. Organised and willing to down tools, the workers at Robe River won a series of concessions from the bosses, who desperately needed their labour and to keep them at work:

> We got proper housing and set up a housing committee to stop "queue jumping"; we'd threaten a strike if they put a boss in ahead of the workers on the list. We got a childcare centre built, a workers' club and cyclone committees that could override a boss's decision [whether or not to evacuate the site]. If you didn't like how things were, you withdrew your labour and you got the things you wanted, the things you needed.[2]

Strikes do not only advance the wages and conditions of the working class; they also build unions, because it is only when unions strike that workers see the purpose of them. Workers learn that by acting collectively in a united and determined fashion, they have power, and the boss must bend before them. Industrial action answers the basic question "Why should I join the union?" and provides a response to the objection "I can't afford to join the union".

Without strikes, workers suffer, and unions die. Workers also develop their confidence to speak up, write leaflets and organise pickets, skills that can be used in broader political struggles outside the workplace.

Take, for example, a strike in 2023 by meat-processing workers at the Ingham's plant in Adelaide.[3] The company, the biggest of its kind in the southern hemisphere and making money hand over fist, had offered the 1,000-strong workforce wage "rises" that were well below inflation. The workers, members of the United Workers Union, rejected the insulting offer and went out on strike for a decent pay rise, more breaks and job security for casuals. Many were paid little more than the minimum wage. Most were migrant workers, many refugees, and all were feeling the bite of the cost-of-living crisis as they struggled to support themselves and their families overseas with their meagre wages. The workers were not experienced militants; for most, this was their first-ever strike and Ingham's had played on the workers' lack of industrial confidence. One worker explained to *Red Flag* newspaper: "They are very vulnerable because they think they are alone, and for this reason, the company uses these people, they take maximum advantage, slavery".[4] The workers, though, now decided to take a stand. They did not sit at home hoping the boss would give in. They mounted a solid picket line at the factory gates.

The first night was the biggest test at the Ingham's strike. At 2.00 am, the early morning shift workers arrived – most of them wearing union shirts and ready to join the picket. Some came to scab but were soon surrounded by strikers who fiercely argued with them. The crowd cheered whenever one of these workers was won over and donned a red union shirt. Hardened scabs lingered angrily outside the gates, unable to spot an opening to sneak in. By morning, the site was bustling with activity. When decisions had to be made, workers argued passionately with each other, discussing the best tactics to win the strike. If they saw scabs trying to get in, or trucks with produce trying to get out, they jumped into action on the picket line, chanting "Nothing in and nothing out!". At the end of the first day, the workers decided to extend the strike indefinitely until the company met their demands. The company's dominant position in the market now became its liability, as chicken began to disappear from the shelves in major supermarkets across South Australia.

The strike was putting a serious dent in Ingham's profits. The company finally gave in after six days of the strike, substantially lifting its pay offer, a victory for the workers who won more by striking for a few days than through months of negotiations.

Socialists fight for working class unity in struggle, which means combating the corrosive divide-and-rule tactics employers use to keep us divided. We reject the capitalist lie that "we are all individuals" and must engage in the competitive dog-eat-dog fight to get ahead at work. The working class can only advance collectively or not at all. Every socialist in a job needs to join the appropriate union and must be the most principled union member and staunchest defender of workers' rights. We support 100 percent union membership in every workplace. Anything less strengthens the bosses' hand by giving them a potential scab workforce.

The state of unions today

Unions can play a vital role in fostering working-class consciousness and power. Unfortunately, any review of the state of unions in Australia today would reveal that they are in poor shape. One indicator is the decline in union coverage. For decades, Australian workers were some of the most unionised in the world, with one-half of all workers signed up as union members.[5] Now, the figure is down to one in eight. Not coincidentally, strikes, too, have dropped dramatically since the early 1980s. Publications and commentary anticipating the demise of the union movement are commonplace.

The dramatic decline of trade unionism is a big problem for everyone keen to push back against the capitalist class. A range of arguments have been advanced to explain it. One is that unions as working-class institutions have been sidelined because the working class is disappearing, even that "we are all middle-class now". Such commentators point to the increasing number of workers who take annual overseas holidays or who hold university degrees, supposedly indicating that they are no longer working class.

This notion that the working class is vanishing is entirely mistaken. Yes, the children of working-class families are more likely to go to university than 50 years ago, but for what? An enormous debt, ever more crowded lecture theatres, a piece of paper enabling them, perhaps, to get an interview for a job that their grandparents could have got with a school certificate, and a salary that is not much more than the average wage. And yes, as overseas tourism has become cheaper, it has become more accessible to many workers, but this does nothing to change their fate when back at work – the continued struggle, the exploitation, the bullying and harassment by supervisors. Then there are things where working-class life has evidently become much tougher in recent decades, access to secure housing most obviously.

Others point to the decline of the blue-collar workforce – those working in mining, manufacturing, railways, the waterfront and power generation, many historically important bases of unionism – to explain union decline.[6] The working class has indeed changed substantially in recent decades. Workers in blue-collar industries have fallen from 55 percent of the workforce in 1971 to 29 percent in 2021, led by a dramatic drop in manufacturing from 23 percent to 6 percent.[7] Those in blue-collar occupations – tradespersons, labourers, process workers, rural workers – have shrunk from one-half of all non-managerial workers in 1971 to one-third in 2021. Workers in white-collar industries have increased their share from 41 percent to 67 percent, with finance, insurance, real estate and business services, health, education and welfare services and entertainment, recreation, hospitality and personal services all more than doubling their share of employment. White-collar occupations, such as professional and technical workers and community and personal service workers, have likewise grown from 44 percent to 65 percent of all non-managerial workers. Construction, however, has held up as a bastion of blue-collar work, standing at a record high of 9 percent of the workforce.

None of the structural changes, however, explains declining union coverage. For a start, union coverage has fallen in every sector, blue-collar and white-collar, factory and office, so we must look at why this is so. Nor is the growth of white-collar work a reason for union decline. Two major employers of white-collar workers, education and healthcare, have among the highest union membership rates. They are hardly cossetted workers with no reason to join unions. Teachers in public schools are subjected to increasing regulation about what and how they teach in schools starved of government funding. Other white-collar occupations, such as workers in call centres and large retail stores, are non-union for the most part, but they too are treated badly, with their time strictly monitored, like factory workers on an assembly line. There is no reason these workers should not join unions.

The working class is not disappearing, only being restructured. The Australian working class has always been in the process of recomposition, as old unionised mass industries such as the railways or shearing sheds fade or become more capital intensive and new industries, almost inevitably non-union in the early years, emerge. Many of these new industries, however, were subsequently unionised and became union strongholds. The problem today is that no one is having a serious go at organising new industries.

Another explanation that has been advanced for union decline is that workers in the growth industries and occupations lack leverage and thus find it difficult to organise. When wharfies strike, they can halt the nation's trade; that has been the secret of their strength for decades. But office and other white-collar workers, it is said, lack the power to disrupt production in the way that wharfies and railway workers once could. Others suggest that the working class is becoming atomised, broken up, dispersed across millions of small workplaces like bars, cafes and professional offices. Others argue that growing casualisation and part-time and agency work have rendered the working class powerless – workers are "here today, gone tomorrow" – or that the ability of the bosses to shift production overseas or replace workers using artificial intelligence technologies means workers are impotent.[8]

These arguments miss the crucial point: *all* workers are exploited, and workers' labour remains the wellspring of profits for the bosses. That is the source of workers' misfortune. It is also the source of workers' power – if they stop work, they can halt production and end the flow of profits to the bosses. The bosses are ultimately at the mercy of workers, whether white-collar or blue-collar. Cleaners, caterers, security staff and maintenance workers in corporate office buildings, call centres, government buildings, universities and hospitals are essential to the accumulation of profits or at least the daily functioning of these institutions. In the first year of the COVID-19 pandemic in 2020, a wide swathe of workers, including healthcare workers, utility workers and public servants disbursing emergency social welfare and Medicare payments, were deemed "essential workers". So, too, were others whose work was needed to keep the system ticking over, including supermarket shelf stackers, food processing workers, delivery and garbage truck drivers, warehouse workers, wharfies, postal workers, journalists and teachers. Suddenly, it was revealed who keeps society ticking over, and it was not those who are normally held up for acclaim by the media and politicians. These workers have leverage and, if organised collectively, could exercise tremendous power at work. The same too with banking and IT workers who would only need to mount a solid strike for a few hours for the entire economy to grind to a halt.

While blue-collar workers may be fewer today, each worker is more powerful now because they use more expensive equipment than their forebears. Construction workers whose great-grandfathers used to work with a pick and shovel now work with big excavators. Wharfies who used to lift heavy bags on their backs now hoist huge containers with cranes. Warehouse workers work in critical nodes for the national economy. It only takes small numbers of such workers walking off the job to cause huge losses for the bosses because they idle so much capital equipment or gum up entire sales and production networks.

The idea that workers are all employed in small workplaces that militate against the kind of "us and them" outlook that is conducive to union membership is also false. There are still plenty of workers in large workplaces: over three million work in workplaces of over 100. Every multi-storey office block in the Melbourne and Sydney CBD brings together hundreds, if not thousands, of white-collar workers, and the same is true of shopping malls, hospitals, airports and universities. Any strike in such a workplace has a massive impact if carried through effectively.

What of the growing "precariousness" of Australian workers, which is supposedly robbing them of their power? This is much exaggerated. Sixty-three percent of employees are employed on a permanent full-time basis, and the figure is much higher once we take out students. The same proportion of employees work a five-day week, and in any given year less than 10 percent of workers change their jobs, including those still at school or university. Even many "precarious" workers have relatively stable jobs. Nearly one-half of casual employees work five or more days a week, and 83 percent expect to be in the same job in 12 months' time. These are no fly-by-night workers, and there is no reason they cannot be drawn into unions.[9]

All workers can be organised into unions and can fight for their rights. Consider another group of "precarious" workers from an earlier generation: the wharfies. If these workers – unskilled mostly, some with criminal records, a life only one step up from desperate poverty and confronting a plentiful supply of potential scabs – could be forged into a militant union in the first half of the twentieth century, so too can young schoolteachers or nurses who are employed on short-term contracts today.

Finally, the notion that Australian workers lack power because their jobs may be easily shipped abroad or replaced by artificial intelligence is misleading. There is a wide range of services – from hairdressing to physiotherapy – that simply cannot be easily moved or replaced by AI but must be performed in person and on-site. Then there are industries that are literally fixed in the ground, such as the mines, supermarkets or construction. Even manufacturing companies are usually loath to uproot themselves because of the costs and inconvenience – far more jobs have been lost due to new technology.

When bosses shift jobs overseas, they still must face a battalion of the international working class. Bosses can move where they like in the search for cheaper wages, but for every pair of hands they employ, they must also hire a brain and a heart, and workers worldwide have proven their capacity to fight, no matter how adverse the circumstances.

Explaining the rot

If the potential power of the working class has not atrophied because of workforce and industry restructuring, how can we explain the dramatic decline in coverage since the 1980s? The answer is politics, specifically the rotten politics of the trade union leaders who have held back working-class struggle for decades.

The decision in the early 1980s by Australia's trade union leaders to embrace open class collaboration with employers and the Hawke Labor government and to sacrifice working-class living standards to boost business profits was the start of the rot. Not that the trade union leaders were reliable defenders of working-class interests before then. They have long sought compromises with the bosses and to sell workers short. But the 1983 ALP-ACTU Prices and Incomes Accord, by which the union leaders agreed to abandon strikes for higher wages and better working conditions in return for six-monthly wage indexation by the Arbitration Commission (the forerunner of the Fair Work Commission), marked a notable degeneration in the union bureaucracy. By signing this agreement, the union leaders threw away the workers' chief weapon at their disposal, the strike, and left them at the mercy of the industrial tribunal and ALP government. The Accord was sold to trade unionists as a way to protect living standards and strengthen trade unions and, according to some union leaders, as the first step towards socialism. These were lies. The Accord cut wages and strangled union activism where it is needed most – at the workplace or shop floor.

To understand why the ACTU signed up to the Accord and continues to defend it to this day, even though it was scrapped by the Howard government when it took office in 1996, we need to look at the role of the trade union leaders. They occupy a contradictory role. They are under pressure from the bosses with whom they negotiate and who value industrial "partners", who can deliver "reasonable" outcomes that do not jeopardise their profits and who can ensure any deal struck will stick with the rank-and-file membership. Outside the workplace or enterprise, union leaders are also subjected to pressure by the courts, government ministers and the media to be "reasonable"; nothing must be done that jeopardises the ability of business to make money.

The union leaders are also, however, under pressure from rank-and-file members who join unions in the belief that by coming together, workers can go on strike to improve their wages, working conditions and treatment by supervisors, to defend their jobs and, sometimes, to make political demands on governments. Such pressure may not be constant, but it is sufficiently common to ensure union leaders cannot ignore it. Union leaders who demonstrate no capacity to lead such fights may be shunned by members and replaced by more militant contenders for the leadership, or their unions may simply lose out to others who demonstrate these fighting qualities. To buttress their bargaining power with recalcitrant employers, the union leaders may sometimes try to galvanise rank-and-file workers for industrial action.

The job of union leaders is to manage these conflicting pressures rooted in their social position as a buffer between labour and capital. They are, as the US radical sociologist C. Wright Mills called them in the 1940s, the "managers of discontent".[10]

But the union leaders do not merely compare the contrasting force of the pressure from above (the employers, state, media) and below (the members) and follow whichever seems the stronger. Ultimately, the full-time union official is a creation of capitalism; their role depends on the continued existence of wage labour. Unlike the working class, they have no interest as a social layer in fighting to overthrow the capitalist system. Indeed, union leaders have repeatedly proven themselves to be the last line of defence for the capitalist order when all else has failed. Even short of a revolution, which hardly impinges on their consciousness on a daily basis, an active, militant, rank-and-file membership means more work for them, puts them under more pressure, forces them to stand up more to the boss, and, if they will not do so, makes it much more likely they will be thrown out of office at the next union election. Union leaders want to control the membership, urging members to fight at one point, dampening them down at another, but whether up or down, they want to ensure rank-and-file workers do not take control out of their hands. Hence the appeal of arbitration for union leaders, because it provides a perfect mechanism for directing class conflict away from the hurly-burly of strikes and lockouts and towards the serenity of the courtroom. In the former, they are subjected to the indignity of workers poking them in the chest, wanting answers; in the latter, they reign supreme as the embodiment of the union's collective will. Hence, the appeal also of Labor governments as an avenue to pursue workers' demands: quiet lobbying by union delegations in ministerial offices is less irksome and onerous than the hard work involved in a strike.

The union leaders enjoy various material benefits that go with their role. For those who used to work on the shop floor or construction site, taking a job in a union office is a definite social and economic advance in terms of pay and conditions of work – apart from anything else, they are unlikely to suffer any serious injury at work. Union leaders are commonly paid three times average weekly earnings. And none of these benefits are affected by any deals they strike. If they sign off on a deal to cut jobs or hold down pay, they do not face the dole queue or cuts to their living standards. If they agree to reduce staffing or speed up work, they do not have to work any harder themselves. They are not workers but functionaries of the union. And if they rise through the ranks, they become figures of note, interviewed by the media and treated with respect by government officials and politicians. More rewards wait for those who do not make waves: the prospect of a position in parliament, appointment to the Fair Work Commission, the offer of an HR position at a big company, or a well-paid job in the public service. Few full-time officials happily return to the workplace from such a position. If social being determines consciousness, as Marx argued, the pressures on trade union leaders towards conformism with the capitalist system are obvious. All these factors combine to mould the union officialdom into a bureaucracy, a conservative social layer in the labour movement.

The union leaders are not one undifferentiated mass. Some openly suck up to the bosses, some put on militant rhetoric at times. But the history of unionism is that it has been the left officials, with their greater credibility among the militants, who have the greatest capacity to save the capitalists' skins. So it was with the ALP-ACTU Accord, which the left officials invented, something that was central to its success because only these leaders had the credibility to convince worker militants to accept it. The left officials promoted the Accord even as workers' living standards fell year after year.

The Accord was not only responsible for cutting wages. Unions became identified as organisations that fought not for improved living standards but for "national competitiveness", meaning profits came first. This was clear in their role in promoting "industry restructuring" and "workplace reform", which involved thousands of redundancies in blue- and white-collar industries. Union delegates who had once organised strikes now told workmates they had to accept lower wages and accept the elimination of established work practices that had once given workers some control over the workplace. Those unions that did not buckle under were destroyed with the full support of the ACTU. Hallowed traditions, like respecting picket lines, were trashed.

In the early 1990s, the bosses, the Keating government and ACTU ganged up to introduce enterprise bargaining, which broke up industry wage campaigns and isolated each group of workers to fight alone, company by company, government agency by government agency. Any notion of solidarity was abandoned. The ACTU again heralded this as a step forward for "productivity" and "competitiveness". Those workers who did not negotiate enterprise agreements had to accept whatever pay rise the industrial tribunal would decide. New industrial laws made striking more difficult – Australia now has some of the harshest anti-strike laws in the West. The union leaders were doing the bosses' job for them.

By the time the Keating government was defeated in 1996, union coverage had fallen dramatically, from 48 percent to 31 percent. The incoming Howard government simply took over much of the legal framework it had inherited from Labor and made it even more repressive and anti-worker. But the union movement still would not fight. It was not that workers would not rally behind a call for action. In 1998, Patrick Stevedores sacked all 1,400 of its unionised workers and replaced them with scabs. Thousands of workers heeded the call to attend pickets and rallies on docks around the country. There was momentum for a general strike to beat Patrick and the Howard government and its anti-union laws. It could have been a rerun of a general strike in 1969, which smashed anti-union laws. But the leaders of the maritime union and the broader union movement refused to make that call. They told workers to trust the courts to get the workers their jobs back. The presence of picket lines at every port swayed the Federal Court to order the wharfies' reinstatement, but the court also gave the company the go-ahead to smash union conditions and to casualise the workforce. The maritime union leaders went along with this.

In place of strikes, the union leaders now told workers their salvation in the face of increasingly aggressive bosses and Liberal governments lay with lodging court cases and waging electoral campaigns to get Labor back into office. Starting with the campaign to defeat the Howard government's anti-union WorkChoices laws in 2005, union leaders have simply thrown the machinery of the unions, money and personnel into expensive public relations campaigns for the ALP and phone-banking for ALP candidates. Early campaign slogans such as "Your Rights at Work, Worth Fighting For" became "Your Rights at Work, Worth Voting For".

None of this has done the unions any good. Labor governments have come and gone, and workers still lack the right to strike. Solidarity action is still banned. The Fair Work Commission still has the power to terminate strikes and "modernise" awards, stripping away many established conditions. The Fair Work Commission is allowing the minimum wage to fall further and further behind going rates and has savaged penalty rates with no resistance from trade unions.

The union leaders continue to issue press releases heaping praise on Labor governments despite their failure to deliver genuine reforms. While they may sometimes slam Liberal governments, they refuse to fight them seriously. The ACTU acts as little more than a non-government organisation or lobby group, not as a peak body of worker organisations with the power to stop production and squeeze the bosses.

Class collaboration is the union leaders' default position. As the COVID pandemic hit Australia in 2020, they rushed to offer their services to the Morrison government and went out of their way to keep businesses open, endangering workers even as the virus spread through the workforce. In recent years, with unemployment at the lowest level for five decades, labour shortages reported in sector after sector and inflation rising, union leaders have been given the perfect opportunity and incentive to organise strikes for higher wages. They have failed to do so. Public sector unions hold strike ballots, win overwhelming endorsement for action and then their leaders refuse to organise strikes beyond a token day or two, and frequently not even that. Unions settle for new enterprise agreements that cut wages. It is this dismal retreat of trade unions since the 1980s that explains why today, 88 percent of the workforce are not members. What have union leaders done to make union membership compelling for young workers starting their first jobs? Why would workers join organisations that won't lift a finger to fight for workers' rights? Never in Australian history have strikes remained so low for so long, and unions have never declined for such a sustained period. Class collaboration is destroying trade unionism in Australia. We need a radical change of direction to rebuild our trade unions and make them once again appeal to workers and frighten the bosses.

Fighting back

That the unions are mostly led by cowards more interested in settling for rotten deals is nothing new. For much of the twentieth century, however, this was challenged by another tradition – a willingness by workers to fight for wages and conditions regardless of who was in government. Labor governments came and went, but it was workers fighting on the job that delivered the victories or pressured governments or industrial tribunals to introduce the reforms that workers were demanding. This was the case in the decade before World War I, with Broken Hill miners, Queensland sugar workers and Sydney rock choppers mounting significant strikes and enduring savage lockouts. The unions did not win all these fights, but in every case, these battles fostered a culture of working-class solidarity. The successful fights for shorter working hours and paid annual leave in the 1940s are another example where militant unionists led the way, breaking things open for the entire working class and building trade union organisation.

If history is any guide, it will be those workers who are today regarded as "industrially backward" or unorganisable who will play a leading role in the next labour upsurge. And it is through the process of struggle that so-called "precarious" workers will establish themselves as a new bastion of unionism. In 2023, dozens of workers at Mint My Desk, a chain of stationery stores in Brisbane, struck twice to demand their award rate of pay and other legal entitlements. The workers were all students in their late teens or early 20s, many from migrant backgrounds and only one was a union member before the strike, a Socialist Alternative member who was pivotal in bringing these industrial novices together to decide on strategy and tactics. After the bosses at Mint My Desk rejected their log of claims, offering them only sham contracts that continued to breach the award, the workers voted to strike for three hours at the company's three Brisbane stores. After stopping work at 9am, refusing to open their stores, they held a rally in the city centre, calling themselves "Mint My Desk Workers United". Young women workers grabbed megaphones and spoke up confidently about their situation to passers-by. They then marched into the city mall and held an impromptu (and illegal) speak-out close to one of the stores, with dozens of supporters gathered around them. In the space of only one hour on strike, these women, who had never engaged in public speaking in their lives, were filled with new confidence and boldly aired their grievances and lambasted their bosses. One of the workers led the chant, "The workers united will never be defeated", which was soon adopted by the workers as their favourite line.

The bosses responded to the strike by shutting two of the three city stores, effectively a lock-out. The workers held a second strike four days later and again marched into the mall and spoke out about their demands. They backed up their action with a string of social media posts, which quickly went viral and made their campaign a *cause célèbre* among young people in Brisbane. The company then suspended the main organisers but had to lift their suspension within 24 hours under pressure from the workers' anger. The workers chalked up some immediate gains, winning payslips, correct penalty rates and superannuation. To head off the prospect of the company's Sydney workers walking off the job, the company offered all staff part-time contracts with entitlements. The outcome was not a complete victory – the bosses are still refusing to pay them on the right classification and are holding out on hundreds of thousands of dollars of back pay – but this small action by workers demonstrated that most basic union adage: "If you don't fight, you lose".

We see the same phenomenon of workers with little or no industrial experience leaping ahead throughout history – in the dockers' struggle in London in 1889, in the sit-down strikes in the US car industry in 1934–36 and in the explosion of strikes in France and Italy in 1968–69. Precisely the fact that such workers are so oppressed can fuel their explosive qualities when they fight. We cannot predict today which groups will move first when the next upsurge takes place in Australia, but we do know that workers retain their role as capitalism's gravediggers – the bosses need us, we don't need them.

In every case of trade union advance, political radicals have played a role. In Queensland and NSW in the period around World War I, radicals or militants such as Ted Theodore, Bill McCormack, Ernie Lane, Emma Miller, Tom Mann, Con Hogan, Henrietta Greville, Minnie Lalor and Peter Bowling organised the unorganised into a fighting force. In Victoria, members of the

Victorian Socialist Party played an important role in building the railways union, while militants agitated among women workers in the Flinders Lane rag trade in Melbourne. During the Great Depression, facing savage wage cuts, mass unemployment, state repression and union leaders who refused to fight, the Communist-led Minority Movement rebuilt unions in the Victorian and NSW coal mines, the Queensland sugar industry, Victorian textiles, NSW railway workshops and public works projects in Melbourne and Sydney. In Sydney and North Queensland, they organised unions on the waterfront despite blacklisting, police thuggery and bashings. In the 1960s, left-wing militants built the Builders Labourers Federation among labourers on the construction sites of Sydney and Melbourne in the face of threats from organised crime and Liberal governments. Within a few years, the new leadership had won big gains for builders' labourers – on pay, on job security, on protection from victimisation, on health and safety on the job – using aggressive industrial tactics, snap strikes to halt concrete pours, "guerrilla action" to sabotage the work of scabs and marches to the offices of the big employers, courts and government departments. Building on the confidence that BLF members had developed through such struggles, the union took action to support Aboriginal land rights and oppose the Vietnam War and the tour by the racist South African rugby team. The NSW BLF also imposed green bans to halt the destruction of working-class housing by developers in inner Sydney.

The fight to build unionism inevitably involves a fight not only against the bosses, but within the union movement itself, against those union leaders favouring class collaboration. These leaders fear what is needed to rebuild unions – industrial militancy, democracy, solidarity and class struggle politics. In this fight, socialists can play a vital role. To revive trade unions, we need more socialists active in their workplaces, organising their fellow workers and pushing back against the do-nothing trade union leaders. This is a central responsibility for worker members of Socialist Alternative today. Wherever members find themselves, they do what they can to build class confidence and organisation. Sometimes, the first step is cultivating a sense of "us against them" at work, turning the many individual grievances workers express, sometimes expressed as grievances against other workers, into a sense of collective grievance aimed at the boss. That might mean testing the waters to find out what the issues that most irk your workmates are and working out some potential solutions that get them to do something about the situation rather than ringing the union office to solve the problem. It means signing up fellow workers to the relevant union and encouraging the more confident ones to take on some tasks themselves. It means familiarising yourself with the relevant award or industrial agreement for your work so you can become the person others turn to when trying to assert their rights or deal with a problem. Sometimes, socialists can get an initial hearing by discussing broader social and political questions rather than the specific work conditions. This might involve taking a photo of a group of workmates holding up a sign expressing solidarity with striking workers somewhere, or maybe showing support for Palestine or refugees and then posting that on social media. Selling *Red Flag* newspaper and inviting workmates to Socialist Alternative public meetings or conferences can be another way to test and build relations with trustworthy workmates.

Sometimes, Socialist Alternative members are in a position where having established themselves as trustworthy and courageous, they can lead industrial campaigns in their workplace. In 2022, a Socialist Alternative member was a lead delegate in a six-week strike at the Knauf plasterboard factory in Melbourne, which defeated management attacks on job security and won significant gains in pay and conditions. In 2023, Socialist Alternative members played a significant role in two unprecedented week-long strikes for job security and better pay at Melbourne University.

Revolutionaries work with the union leaders when they are prepared to lead workers' struggles, but we oppose them and must work around them when they get in the way or try to sabotage workers' rights. In 2020, as the COVID-19 pandemic set in and the university vice-chancellors circulated stories of impending financial disaster as international students were barred from entering the country, Socialist Alternative members in the National Tertiary Education Union led the most significant rank-and-file revolt in a union in Australia for many years, defeating a planned 15 percent wage cut for university workers that the union and employers were proposing to implement.

On a much smaller scale, the Mint My Desk strike in Brisbane demonstrated the important role revolutionaries can play in the face of bureaucratic obstruction. On the face of it, the union movement should have rallied behind these young workers. For decades, the union leaders have been proclaiming the importance of recruiting young workers to revive the union movement and halt its downward spiral. They have offered discounted membership and cheap movie tickets, set up TikTok accounts, and appointed youth committees. But when it comes to young workers going on strike without jumping through the legal hoops that Labor governments have introduced to squash strikes, they run a mile. Not a single union, left or right, backed the strike. Lack of union support was a serious hindrance to the workers as it cut them off from legal assistance and solidarity from the union movement – if transport unions had refused to make deliveries to the company, the bosses would have had no choice but to capitulate. It was only because a Socialist Alternative member was leading the workers that they could withstand the intimidation they faced from the company and the absence of support from the unions.

Socialist Alternative wants to build a revolutionary socialist organisation where every member can learn how to inject socialist politics into the working-class struggle. This might involve taking members and supporters of socialist clubs on campus to picket lines during strikes, even where we have no members to show our support. We try to identify the most left-wing workers to invite them to meetings, to sell *Red Flag* and so forth and to gather information that can be used to write articles about the dispute to carry in *Red Flag* to let others know of their fight. Students and workers can raise motions of support and donations for the strike in our own workplaces and student unions.

The revival of trade unionism will undoubtedly come as part of a broader radicalisation in society, and not only in Australia. This has been the case in every previous such recovery. But this does not mean socialists simply fold our arms and wait for that day. We build our organisation now, in workplaces and on the campuses, so we can do what we can even in the smaller disputes typical of today while steeling our ranks for the battles that are to come.

Notes

1. Friedrich Engels, *The Condition of the Working Class in England in 1844*, 1845.

2. Liz Ross, "Rank and file rebellion at Robe River", *Red Flag*, 4 November 2014.

3. The following account is drawn from Harvey Menadue, Kalesh Govender and Danica Scott, "Ingham's workers win higher wages", *Red Flag*, 1 October 2023.

4. Menadue et al, "Ingham's workers".

5. The few countries with higher membership were for the most part in Scandinavia, where union membership was tied to the welfare system, or so-called Communist societies where workers were automatically enrolled in state-run unions that operated as an extension of the government.

6. Mark Wooden, *The Transformation of Australian Industrial Relations*, Federation Press, 2000.

7. Source: *Census of Population and Housing, 30 June 1971, Bulletin 1: Summary of Population, Part 9: Australia*. Australian Bureau of Statistics, Census of Population and Housing: *Income and work data summary*, 2021.

8. See, for example, David Harvey, *A Brief History of Neoliberalism*, Oxford University Press, 2005; Guy Standing, *The Precariat: The New Dangerous Class*, Bloomsbury, 2011.

9. Australian Bureau of Statistics, *Working Arrangements*, August 2023, cat. No. 6336.0; Australian Bureau of Statistics, *Participation, Job Search and Mobility*, February 2023, cat. No. 6226.0.

10. C. Wright Mills, *The New Men of Power: America's labor leaders*, Harcourt Brace, 1948, pp.8–9.

Chapter six

Imperialism[1]

Shamed, dishonoured, wading in blood and dripping with filth, thus capitalist society stands. Not as we usually see it, playing the roles of peace and righteousness, of order, of philosophy, of ethics – but as a roaring beast, as an orgy of anarchy, as a pestilential breath, devastating culture and humanity – so it appears in all its hideous nakedness.

—Rosa Luxemburg, *The Junius Pamphlet*, 1915

WAR EXPOSES THE BARBARIC, BLOOD-SOAKED TRUTH at the heart of the system. Capitalism is not peace and progress for all. Capitalism is the millions of workers sacrificed in World War I in the contest by European powers for world supremacy. Capitalism is the 200,000 Japanese killed by the US atomic bombing of Hiroshima and Nagasaki, motivated by America's desire to demonstrate its overwhelming power to its rivals. It is the so-called War on Terror that destroyed hundreds of thousands of lives in the Middle East while seeding violent racism at home. It is Russia's 2022 invasion of Ukraine, which brought artillery war and trenches back into Europe for the first time in decades. Capitalism is the tens of thousands of Palestinians murdered by Israel in its genocidal war on Gaza in 2023–24, carried out with the permission of the Western powers, including Australia. It is the trillions of dollars spent on armaments every year while essential public services are stripped of funds. The depravity of the system is beyond words. The US, which promotes itself as a champion of peace and democracy, is the world's leading terrorist nation. Its military interventions have brought only misery to its victims.

The socialist movement has a rich history of opposition to war and imperialism. Russian and German workers, sailors and soldiers rose in revolt to end the bloodbath that was World War I. Australian workers were in the thick of the anti-war agitation as well, twice halting the government's attempt to introduce conscription for the front lines. Five decades later, US and Australian socialists helped lead a movement against the Vietnam War, bringing tens of thousands of workers and students onto the streets and contributing to the withdrawal of Western forces from Indochina. Socialists also campaigned against the US-led and Australian-backed invasion of Iraq in 2003, with nearly one million demonstrating across the country. In more recent times, socialists have been at the forefront of mass demonstrations against Israeli barbarism in Palestine.

Every imperialist power, including Australia, claims that it is motivated by humanitarian ideals or a desire to halt aggression by some other power. They lie. Every one of them is led by a murderous government that sees human life as expendable in the contest for domination of the region or the world. The US may be the most aggressive, but socialists do not distinguish between them. In a world where every big imperialist power tries to assert itself against its opponents, where supposedly "peaceful" competition frequently gives way to war, our slogan is "Neither Washington nor Moscow nor Beijing, but socialist revolution".

What is imperialism?

Two great separations characterise capitalism: first, the separation of the direct producers, the workers, from ownership and control over the means of production. This is the basis for exploitation. The second is separation, or competition, between rival capitalist enterprises, which is the basis for economic crisis. But competition between rival capitalists is not restricted to peaceful means, nor is it only a matter of individual enterprises. Imperialism describes the condition of modern capitalism in which advanced capitalist states compete both peacefully and by military means to dominate the world market on behalf of the capitalists in their territory.

This definition is in contrast to several common understandings of imperialism. One is that imperialism is merely the domination of small countries by the large – typical of the colonial period in the late nineteenth and early twentieth centuries. But imperialism continues today when colonies are few. Indeed, countries such as China and India, which were once the victims of colonialism, are now imperialist powers in their own right. Imperialism does not require the physical occupation of oppressed countries; it is better to see colonialism as a feature of a particular phase in the rise of the imperialist world order. Nor is imperialism simply the domination of the world by the United States. All the major advanced countries are imperialist rivals. Today, that means not only the United States but also China, Russia, Japan, Britain, Germany, France and Canada, with others such as South Africa, India, Saudi Arabia, Brazil, Iran, Nigeria and Mexico aspiring to rise up the pecking order. Australia, too, is an imperialist power, although a modest-sized one. And nor is imperialism simply a policy pursued by right-wing governments like that of former US president George W. Bush, who ordered the invasions of Afghanistan and Iraq in the early 2000s. The US has been an imperialist power for more than a century, whether under Republican or Democrat administrations, whether under "hawks" or "doves"; imperialism is not just a policy that can be switched on or off.

Imperialism is the form that advanced capitalism has taken since the late nineteenth century. It emerged from the Long Depression from 1873 to 1896, when the industrial economies experienced a long period of slow growth, deflation and unemployment.[2]

Capitalism was restructured during the Long Depression in three ways. First, by monopolisation. Small and medium firms went to the wall and giant corporations organised themselves into cartels to fix prices and protect their profits. The industrial giants relied heavily on government contracts and bank loans, creating a tight nexus between the state, finance capital and industrial capital. This process was most advanced in Germany and the US, which overtook Britain as the leading industrial powers by 1914. A key feature of the new capitalism was protectionism: all governments other than the British imposed high import tariffs to encourage their infant industries.

The second trend was colonialism. In pursuit of cheap raw materials, captive markets and new investment outlets, the great powers raced to grab colonies in China, Central Asia, the Middle East, Africa and the Balkans. In 1876, only 10 percent of Africa was under European rule; by 1900, the figure had grown to 90 percent. Local resistance was put down brutally. Historians estimate that Belgium's allegedly humanitarian colonial enterprise in the Congo led to the deaths of roughly six to ten million Africans between 1885 and 1908. This genocide was highly profitable. The Anglo-Belgian India Rubber and Exploration Company made a profit of over 700 percent in the country in these years. The impact of British rule on India was no less atrocious. On the eve of its conquest by the British in the 1750s, India was as wealthy as Europe. But forced labour, the wrecking of India's textile industry with cheap British manufactures, and the destruction of India's traditional irrigation and granary systems all combined to drain India's economy for two centuries. Tens of millions of people died of starvation in a series of devastating famines even while food was exported.

Protectionism and colonialism were competitive strategies, which explain the third aspect of capitalist restructuring during and after the Long Depression – an arms race between the established and emerging Western powers. British military spending more than doubled between 1887 and 1914, while German naval expenditure more than quadrupled as the German government sought to close the gap with Britain. The result was that governments, generals and arms manufacturers became inextricably linked.

While Germany, the US and Britain may have been the leading world powers in the late nineteenth century, every European country responded in kind.

World capitalism was now entering its imperialist phase. Competition between individual companies was no longer fought based on "free competition" over prices but in monopoly battles for domination over entire markets. Lenin wrote: "If it were necessary to give the briefest possible definition of imperialism, we should have to say that imperialism is the monopoly stage of capitalism".[3]

In this new era, state assistance, both economic and military, played an increasingly important role in determining the success of these monopolies. Without such aid, even relatively large companies were incapable of breaking open new markets or forcing rivals out of old ones. More and more, success in the marketplace depended on the accumulation of military force.

Capitalist restructuring created the conditions in which the slightest spark – the revolver shot that rang out in Sarajevo in June 1914 – would ignite World War I. Contests for supremacy on the fringes of the world system, whether in Asia, Africa or the Balkans, were now brought into the heartland of Western and Central Europe.

World War I was the first total war and involved the mobilisation of entire societies and economies. Conscript armies of hundreds of thousands or even millions took to the field. The cost in human life escalated as the destructive power of weaponry multiplied. By the war's end, Germany and Russia had each suffered 2 million dead, Austria-Hungary and France 1.4 million each, and Britain 800,000.

World War I was supposed to be "the war to end all wars". But capitalism recognises no such notion. The 1919 Treaty of Versailles confirmed the rise of the United States and Japan, the weakening of France and Britain and a temporary halt to Germany's ascendancy. But no sooner was the new world order established than it was challenged again. Germany could not be held down indefinitely, and nor could Russia, which under Stalin's dictatorship had re-emerged as an imperialist power. Both sought to expand. Former allies, the US and Japan, also came to vie for influence over the Pacific. Japan lacked an empire, and its big industrial corporations and the military needed oil: this brought it into conflict with the US and the Dutch and British, who dominated East and Southeast Asia. In 1939, the temporary peace gave way to another world war, even bloodier than the first. The world was again up for grabs.

Ruling class ideologists in the US, Britain, Russia and Australia argue that World War II was a "good war", a "war against fascism and for democracy". This is a lie. It was a war between the big imperialist powers to dominate the world, just as much as World War I was. It was not a war for democracy. Britain and France possessed vast empires whose subjects had few or no democratic rights, including, most obviously, the right to decide who governed their country. Australia, too, had a small Pacific empire. The US propped up dictatorships and regularly invaded countries in its sphere of influence. Russia, which joined the Allies in 1941, was run by a bloody dictatorship.

Nor was it an anti-fascist war. Senior figures in the British and Australian ruling establishments expressed sympathy for Hitler and Mussolini during the 1930s and following the German invasion in 1940, many in the French ruling class were happy to serve under the collaborationist Vichy regime. If the Allies were seriously motivated by anti-fascism, they would have backed Republican Spain against a fascist uprising in 1936 led by General Franco; instead, they let Franco take power, resulting in four decades of dictatorship. For the first two years of the war, Russia was allied with Nazi Germany and the two countries carved up Poland between them. The US was happy to allow Germany to seize territory in Europe, but when it became obvious that a German conquest of Europe would eventually lead to a German advance into Africa, Asia and Latin America and, ultimately, to an attack on the US itself, the US prepared to fight. The cold calculations devoid of any moral scruple were in plain sight in the closing stages of the war when the victorious powers, Britain, the US and the USSR, sat around a table and drew lines on a world map to confirm their new spheres of influence, completely ignoring the wishes of the people.

The "good war" argument does not stand up to scrutiny but is perpetuated because it provides cover for imperialists launching new wars today. Every enemy of the US is labelled "a new Hitler" even if, like Iraq's Saddam Hussein, they were close allies a year or two previously.

The vanquishing of Germany and Japan in 1945 quickly saw the alliance between the US and the USSR give way to military rivalry. A new Cold War – a permanent state of military distrust and rivalry – broke out. The same logic that brought Germany and Britain to war in 1914 and 1939 now ruled in relations between the two new superpowers, held back from the brink only by the threat of mutually assured nuclear destruction. This did not prevent murderous proxy wars from breaking out across the world, in which the two powers backed opposite sides, or wars of national liberation in which one side supported the insurgent revolt to help spread its influence and undermine the other.

US, terrorist state

The United States claims that "American leadership is what holds the world together".[4] In reality, the story of US intervention since 1945 has been one of death and destruction. Barely a day has gone by without the US causing carnage somewhere in the world. In the Korean War in the early 1950s, the contest between the US and its superpower rival Russia for domination over the peninsula resulted in the deaths of 3 million Koreans. The US backed the military government of South Korea for decades afterwards. The US war in Vietnam was just as bloody. The US blanket bombed the whole country, massacred peasants and burned their villages, starved the people, dropped chemical weapons to poison farmland, buried millions of land mines and tortured prisoners, whether combatants or not. Before it was done with Vietnam, the US widened the war to Cambodia. The US was responsible for three million deaths in Indochina. Dr Martin Luther King rightly described the US in a 1967 speech as "the greatest purveyor of violence in the world today".

Korea and Vietnam were the US's main battlegrounds in the postwar decades, but the US spread terror across the world. In 1954, it overthrew the Arbenz government in Guatemala at the behest of the United Fruit Company. In 1958, it invaded Lebanon to prop up the right-wing Christian minority government. In 1961, the US sent 1,500 Cuban exiles to overthrow the Castro government, which had nationalised US sugar interests. In 1965, the US deployed 25,000 troops to the Dominican Republic to put down an anti-military revolt. In 1965–66, the US supported Indonesian general Suharto as he launched a military coup, resulting in the massacre of a half-million Indonesians. The US also backed Philippines dictator Ferdinand Marcos for two decades until his overthrow in a 1986 popular revolt. In the 1970s, the US supported military coups in Argentina and Chile that killed tens of thousands and backed El Salvadoran government death squads that killed 75,000. In the following decade, the US-funded and trained right-wing resistance forces ("Contras") fought the Sandinista government in Nicaragua, resulting in thousands of deaths. Washington armed right-wing forces fighting the Angolan government, extending a 20-year civil war that resulted in 750,000 deaths. The US backed Israel's 1982 invasion and occupation of Lebanon and supported right-wing Lebanese forces, which massacred 2,000 Palestinians in refugee camps. The 1980s also saw US forces attack Grenada, Libya and Panama, shoot down an Iranian airliner over the Mediterranean, killing 300, and provide Iraqi leader Saddam Hussein with weapons for his war with Iran.

The 1990s were even more bloody, with the US turning on Hussein and massacring 200,000 Iraqi conscript soldiers and civilians in 1991 on the pretext of "liberating Kuwait" and "protecting Kurds". Following the Gulf War, the US maintained sanctions on Iraq, resulting in half a million deaths over the decade. The US continued to support right-wing forces in Central America and the Caribbean, backing a military coup against the reformist government in Haiti. US forces invaded Somalia in 1992, killing thousands, before they were driven out in the following year. In 1999, the US bombed Serbia for 11 weeks, killing hundreds of Serbs and Kosovars on whose behalf the US was supposedly fighting.

Al-Qaeda's 2001 attack on the United States unleashed a fresh round of US aggression. The collapse of the Soviet Union ten years earlier had placed the US in an unchallenged position, and President George W. Bush and his advisers believed they could use the 9/11 attack as an opportunity to secure US primacy against rivals. Afghanistan was the first to suffer in the US's so-called War on Terror. President Bush said that the US would liberate Afghans from the oppressive Taliban government. Far from bringing peace and stability, the US-led invasion brought catastrophe. US forces in Afghanistan committed atrocities against combatants and civilians, with Australian special forces joining in. Over 200,000, including 50,000 civilians, died during the war and subsequent occupation, with still more perishing from disease, loss of access to food and water and the devastation of infrastructure that resulted from the war. The US's 2003 invasion of Iraq unleashed yet more terror on the country that had already been devastated by years of sanctions. The US defeated Saddam Hussein's army in weeks, but peace did not follow. When resistance inevitably emerged, the US lashed out, destroying the city of Fallujah and killing thousands of resistance fighters and civilians alike. Iraqi fighters taken captive were imprisoned in the notorious Abu Ghraib prison where the US military committed what a 2004 inquiry by the US itself called "numerous incidents of sadistic, blatant, and wanton criminal abuses" on detainees. The US could only maintain its occupation by stoking divisions in the Iraqi population, resulting in sectarian violence that led to tens of thousands of deaths – with the US now backing one side, now another. The US was eventually forced out of Iraq, but its eight-year occupation had cost around half a million lives.

Special mention must be made of US support for Israel. The US has backed despotic governments in the Middle East for decades, but Israel has long stood out as America's chief ally and recipient of favours. Since Israel emerged triumphant against its Arab neighbours after the Six Day War in 1967, the US has donated more than $100 billion in economic and military aid to the Zionist state. The US rightly regards Israel as a bastion of Western imperialism in a region that is home to both the world's biggest oil supplies and a string of Arab governments sitting atop a volcano of popular discontent. The US supplies Israel with the most advanced military equipment in the world; it protects Israel from censure in international forums like the United Nations; and its military and security agencies work closely with Israel, including in joint military drills. When Israel wages war on its neighbours or the Palestinian people, slaughtering them in their thousands, Israel can always rely on the White House to defend its supposed "right to self-defence" and to condemn Palestine supporters as antisemites. In late 2023, when Israeli bombardment was levelling Gaza, President Biden pledged another $14 billion in military aid, much of which will come back to the US arms industry, satisfying the interests of both the military and financial elements of American imperialism.

Australia's role

Australia has been one of the US's chief allies throughout its long and bloody reign as the number 1 terrorist state. It has backed every single US war since World War II. Why this is so is a subject of longstanding debate. It is common to hear on the left and in liberal circles that Australia is a mere lackey of the United States, and its prime ministers only await orders from the White House before getting dragged into American wars that are none of our concern. This is often associated with the demand that Australia pursue an "independent foreign policy" in the belief that an "independent Australia" would be less inclined to go to war.

This is a serious misreading of Australia's standing. Australia is an imperialist power in its own right. It is not anyone's puppet. The Australian military is the most powerful in Southeast Asia and the South Pacific and is fourth only to China, Japan and South Korea in the broader region. Successive governments have not failed to use this military to assert Australian power offshore. Australia goes to war alongside the US not unwillingly but as an enthusiastic junior partner.

Australian imperialism operates on two fronts. First, in what the Gillard government's 2013 Defence White Paper called "our maritime territory, our offshore territories and the critical sea lanes in our approaches".[5] Throughout its history, the prospect that a power hostile to Australia might come to control the sea lanes around the continent has been regarded as the primary threat. These sea lanes have been the vital artery through which military supplies and trade to and from the country's most important markets in Britain and, more recently the US and Asia, have flowed. They have also been significant in allowing Australia's burgeoning capitalist class to loot countries in its immediate neighbourhood, including Papua New Guinea, Nauru and Fiji. Ensuring stability in this region, the pacification of any threat has, therefore, always been the country's most immediate challenge.

Given the sheer size of this task, the Australian state has sought a major imperialist power, a "great and powerful friend", to assist it and under whose wings its own imperialist tendencies could grow. Initially, Britain was the ally on whom the emerging Australian ruling class depended for both the finance and military protection. Later, the US came to the fore. The ruling class's primary fear was abandonment by its military protector, laying it open to threats by a hostile imperialist power, at different times France, Russia and Japan. This fear of abandonment has prompted the Australian ruling class to continually pressure its patrons to deploy their military in the region, even to the point of pushing them into wars.

This reliance on a great imperialist power has led to the second front for Australian imperialism: the despatch of sometimes significant, sometimes token forces to far-flung wars and occupations to assist first Britain and then the US in its efforts to dominate the world. The two fronts are mutually reinforcing: the Australian ruling class hopes that by supporting the US in distant imperialist wars and occupations today, it can call on it for support for its own defence if directly threatened or to help extend its power in the region. Sending troops to US-led wars and occupations and backing US allies like Israel in the United Nations is equivalent to payment of a premium on an insurance policy that can be called upon at a time of threat. Whether the US would actually deliver at a time of threat is not predetermined – the ANZUS Treaty, unlike the NATO treaty, has no obligation that partners go to each other's defence if they are attacked. However, far from encouraging Australian governments to exercise a more cautious strategy towards the US, this uncertainty only encourages them to double down on supporting Washington.

This is the basis on which we can understand Australia's most significant contribution to US wars – the establishment of US spy and communications bases at Pine Gap, Nurrungar and Northwest Cape, without which the US and allies such as the UK would be fighting blind in the vast expanse of the globe from the Middle East to Southeast Asia. These bases are also a conspicuous statement of long-term US involvement in Australia, something keenly sought by successive Australian governments. Australian support for the US also explains why Australian governments have enthusiastically supported Israel. Australia no more wants to see Israel weaken or fall than it does the US. All three are part of an imperialist alliance with global reach.

Australia backs the US not because it is a lackey but because the alliance with the US suits its own imperialist interests. It is not only that the US provides Australia's security umbrella in the Asia-Pacific, securing the sea lanes around the continent. As a trusted US ally, doors open for Australia in Asia that might otherwise be closed. This constitutes a significant advantage to Australian diplomatic leverage in trade and strategic negotiations. The alliance also gives the Australian ruling class access to the highest echelons of the US ruling class, and close relations also attract significant foreign investment: many US multinational companies use Australia as their Asia-Pacific base. Further, Australia does not have to pay for armed forces of a scale that would be required to support its regional ambitions if it were forced to fend for itself. While the Australian ruling class does not skimp on military spending, which at $2,000 per head every year is higher than most other comparable countries, including Britain and France, the military pact with the US has meant it has not had to build its own nuclear program, and has given Australia access to vital intelligence gathered by the US and its close allies, the UK, Canada and Israel.

These considerations help explain why Australia sent tens of thousands of troops to help the US wage war on Vietnam in the 1960s, something regarded by many on the Australian left as a sure sign of the country's subservience. Far from simply following slavishly behind the US, Australia aggressively pushed the US deeper into Vietnam and arm-twisted the South Vietnamese government to extend an "invitation" to Australia to send troops. The Menzies Liberal government was determined not to miss an opportunity to lock the US firmly in Asia, to secure what it perceived as Australia's strategic interests.

Because the US alliance underpins the strategic power of Australian capitalism in our region, it is a bedrock commitment of the ruling class and is supported by any party that aspires to rule. The Labor Party has disagreed with Australian involvement in some of the US-led wars in the past 50 years, including Vietnam and, initially, the second Iraq war of 2003, but it has never questioned the alliance itself. As a party that wishes to run the Australian state, it understands the important role that the US alliance plays in assisting Australian power in the region and enthusiastically defends it.

Imperialist competition today

The US is the world's biggest superpower. It accounts for 40 percent of the world's military spending and, boasting hundreds of overseas military bases, is the only state with a truly global military reach. It is the world's largest economy, the biggest oil producer and the centre of international finance and information technology. Its multinationals dominate the list of the world's biggest companies measured by market capitalisation. The US also plays an outsized role in the International Monetary Fund (IMF) and the World Bank, both based in Washington. IMF structural adjustment policies, under which loans are advanced to poor countries on condition that they privatise, cut public spending and open up their economy to foreign investment, are examples of the US state intervening to enhance the interests of US companies.

Despite US domination, other countries have emerged to challenge its ability to dictate terms to the world. Chief among these is China. Although it remains weaker, the gap between the two has shrunk substantially in recent decades. Russia's invasion of Ukraine in 2022 also served notice that it, too, has ambitions beyond its borders. Iran has taken advantage of American failures in the Middle East to extend its reach. Then there are regional powers such as Turkey, Saudi Arabia and India, which are aligned with the US but are not always compliant with Washington. We are now entering an era like that before 1914 as contestation in the world system between several powers, old and new, becomes the chief characteristic.

Both world wars were fought over which powers were to dominate in Europe. Today, the Asia-Pacific is the main prize. The region is a vital hub for the world economy. Sixty percent of maritime trade passes through it, one-third through the South China Sea alone. Since 1945, when the US crushed Japan's bid for Pacific dominance, the US has been the paramount power. The US Pacific Fleet is the most formidable mobilisation of naval and aerial weaponry. The US has military facilities across Asia and the Western Pacific, with tens of thousands of military personnel stationed in Japan and South Korea and naval bases in Guam and Diego Garcia. American banks and multinationals play an important role in the region, and the US dollar still dominates trade and investment.

China is now contesting US supremacy in the Asia-Pacific. The Chinese ruling class cannot tolerate a situation in which it is prevented from exercising what it regards as its proper role in the region. Washington, however, cannot afford to see its Pacific Fleet pushed out of the area because this would signal to allies and adversaries alike that it is no longer "the world's indispensable nation", as Hillary Clinton once described the US. Each side is developing a multi-pronged strategy against the other.

The US is aggressively targeting China across all domains. Its military budget is rapidly increasing, and it is deepening alliances in the region. Joint naval drills, euphemistically called "freedom of navigation exercises", involve the US carrying out hostile patrols close to the coast of China and through the

Taiwan Strait with longstanding allies Japan, South Korea, Thailand, Australia and Singapore, and new partners, India, Vietnam and the Philippines. These are designed to intimidate China. US allies are following its lead in boosting military outlays. Japan is doubling military spending as a share of GDP, while South Korea has announced 7 percent annual increases over the next five years.

Australia is joining the US in its bid to contain China. Both Labor and the Coalition are committed to substantial new military expenditures, most notably hundreds of billions on a fleet of nuclear-powered submarines. New ships, fighter jets, missiles, drones and tanks are also coming into service by the end of this decade. The US is also investing hundreds of millions of dollars in new facilities in the Northern Territory and Western Australia for US Marines, Air Force and Navy operations, allowing it to wage war with China even if a Chinese attack wipes out its bases in Guam and Okinawa.

Australia is not being dragged unwillingly into playing this aggressive role. The AUKUS pact with the US and UK, by which Australia gets access to US nuclear propulsion technology, was the initiative of the Morrison government, not the Biden administration. The ALP has been as enthusiastic about the nuclear submarines as the Coalition, and the Albanese government is working to extend US military operations on Australian soil.

The war planning and the billions spent on it are justified to the Australian public on the grounds of "national security" and the threat of disruption to "the rules-based international order", a thinly veiled reference to China. But China poses no territorial threat to Australia. The only reason China might threaten Australia directly is if Australia joins the US in an attack on China. Everything Australian governments are doing now makes this more likely. Australian imperialism regards US supremacy in the world system as a precondition for its own success and is willing to risk the lives not just of hundreds of thousands, even millions, of Chinese civilians but Australians too and also those of any other country drawn into the conflict.

If China poses no direct threat to the Australian mainland, it does, however, challenge Australian imperialism in what the ruling class has long regarded as its "backyard", the vast Pacific region to the country's north and east. In the first two decades of this century, Australia regularly despatched troops, federal police and senior public service administrators to the Solomon Islands,

Papua New Guinea, Tonga, Nauru, Fiji and East Timor to restore "stability".[6] China was not the primary motivation; these were policing missions to affirm Australia's role as top dog and to quash anything that might threaten this. In more recent years, China's growing presence in the region has become Canberra's chief concern. Australia has responded by pushing through security deals of its own with impoverished South Pacific islands, increasing repression of their domestic populations and drawing them into US military plans for the region.

If the US and its allies are building their military arsenals, China, too, is modernising and enhancing its fighting capacity as it prepares to push the US far from its shores. According to the 2020 US Defense Department report to Congress, "China has already achieved parity with – or even exceeded – the United States in several military modernisation areas", including shipbuilding, land-based conventional ballistic and cruise missiles, and integrated air defence systems. Like the US and its allies, China regularly conducts threatening offshore naval and aerial manoeuvres in the East and South China Seas and the Western Pacific. Both sides are sharpening their swords in preparation for war.

Imperialist competition is now reshaping the world economy as both the US and China try to reduce their economic entanglement with the other. For years, China has been trying to foster greater self-reliance in core military-related industries, particularly in computing, semiconductors, and satellite technology. The US is playing catch-up. "Made in America" is now replacing globalisation as the guiding principle in select industries of strategic importance. Economic policy as a weapon of war was, in the early years of the twentieth century, a precursor to hot war; it is now being used in the same way with equally disastrous prospects.

We are witnessing a prolonged period of escalating tensions, shoring up of alliances and military build-ups by the big imperialist rivals that make a showdown inevitable at some point. The US and Russian governments are now abandoning treaties that once limited the proliferation of nuclear weapons. The doomsday clock, which measures how close the world is to destruction, now stands at 90 seconds to midnight, the closest to global catastrophe it has ever been.[7]

Some miscalculation or entirely unpredicted event could easily unleash a showdown between the big powers. That happened with World War I. In the Spring of 1914, few would have imagined that one of the deadliest wars in human history, with a death toll of 20 million, would break out by August. The capitalist world order has undoubtedly changed since 1914, but the underlying competitive logic of capitalism remains entrenched. The consequence is repeated outbreaks of war.

The US is attempting to frame the new global contest as one between "democrats" led by the US and "autocrats" led by China and Russia. The Chinese and Russian leaders claim only to be interested in self-defence and peaceful development. Some sections of the left are mistakenly picking a side. Russia's invasion of Ukraine in 2022, for example, saw social democratic and Green parties across Europe, whether in government or opposition, support the rapid militarisation of the Continent under NATO auspices. This was to be expected since these parties had backed US imperialism on many occasions – "social patriotism" has a long history stretching back to 1914, when the leaders of the European socialist movement threw their support behind their own governments as they marched workers off to war. But others, too, including some who have recently identified as Marxists, fell in line behind the White House.[8] But as US support for Israel demonstrates, its claims to be defending peace and democracy anywhere in the world are lies. The US will only do what suits its interests, which are not those of the world's workers.

On the other side of the coin are a smaller but still significant number of individuals and parties of the left who prefer to cheer on the other camp in big power politics – what Presidents Xi and Putin called the "no limits" partnership of China and Russia. Some of these, often from Maoist or Stalinist backgrounds, are open supporters of the Chinese and Russian governments because they believe there is something progressive about them. More common, though, is the belief that the US is the only imperialist power, and any other power ranged against it must be favoured, including not only Russia and China but Iran, North Korea, Venezuela, Cuba, Syria and sometimes Brazil, South Africa and Turkey as well.[9] In the West, these "campists" usually attack their own governments, but their politics have nothing to do with socialism. They have no connection with working-class politics, substituting for it geopolitics and the cynical slogan, "The enemy of my enemy is my friend". Regardless of the practice of the politically abhorrent regimes they promote, "campists" end up defending them against NATO and internal opposition simply because they oppose the US. They label as "stooges for US imperialism" any opposition movements organising for democracy or national rights in these countries.

The US has a long history of destabilising governments it opposes. Socialists in the West must oppose this while also defending the rights of the working class and national minorities to demand their rights as an elementary act of working-class solidarity in whatever country they may be doing so. Our slogan is not "The enemy of my enemy is my friend", which means picking one imperialist (or imperialist camp) over another, but "Down with all the imperialists!". We must condemn both the US and Australian governments for their support for Israeli war crimes and the Chinese government for its persecution of Uyghurs and Hong Kong democracy activists. Alongside our support for Black Lives Matter protests in the US, we stand by workers striking against the authoritarian regime in Iran. If the left does not support democratic movements everywhere, these movements will find other worldviews and, unable to challenge capitalism, never achieve their goals. Only revolutionary Marxism can explain how movements from Hong Kong to New York and Gaza struggle against a single global system.

The intense competition between the rival imperialist powers also means it is useless to look to the United Nations to secure peace in the world. In 2022, UN Secretary-General Antonio Guterres declared that "humanity is just one misunderstanding, one miscalculation away from nuclear annihilation".[10] But the UN cannot halt such a catastrophe because it is dominated by the imperialists which retain veto power on the Security Council. These vetoes mean that the United Nations was powerless to take action against Russia when it invaded Ukraine and against Israel when it carried out a genocide in Gaza. Nor are the other members of the General Assembly any guardians of peace or national liberation, as they oppress their own working class and peasantry and are, in many cases, entangled in local or regional conflicts themselves.

The right of nations to self-determination

Capitalist development does not proceed evenly around the world. The shape of imperialist conflict changes, but its principal features – competition between the biggest powers for hegemony and the subordination of weaker nations to stronger nations – will continue as long as world capitalism survives. It is this that underlies national oppression.

The ruling classes of every country play upon nationalist sentiments to solidify their rule. These poison workers' minds and turn them against their natural allies: workers from other countries. Socialists oppose such attempts to set workers of one nation against those of another or to elevate in workers' minds the claimed superiority of their nation, language or culture over those of another.

Genuine internationalism requires full equality between nations, i.e. that no nation or culture is privileged over another. It follows from this that Marxism does not lump all nationalisms together. There is a difference between the nationalism of the oppressor countries, such as Israel and China, and of those who are oppressed, such as the Palestinians and Tibetans. National equality can only be established if oppressed nations have the right to self-determination – not to be colonised, annexed, occupied or otherwise denied their own sovereignty.

This is an important consideration for the workers' movement. Lenin argued that workers in the oppressor countries – the dominant nations that forcibly held colonies all over the world – had to break any allegiance to their own ruling class. That meant socialists in countries that oppressed other nations had to support the oppressed nation's right to be free. Only then could there be unity between workers of both nations based on equality. Not that Lenin welcomed nationalism; his goal was to break down national boundaries between people. But this could only occur where workers and peoples came together based on free will, not at gunpoint. This means that for socialists to be consistent internationalists, it is not enough to preach the "brotherhood of man"; we must actively oppose all efforts by imperialist Australia to impose its will on other countries and peoples – whether in the South Pacific, Asia or the Middle East.

Socialists support the rights of nations to fight for self-determination where such struggles weaken imperialism and help to undercut imperialist sentiment in the minds of the working class of the oppressor nations. For this reason, we do not support any spurious claim by Zionists that Israel is the product of self-determination by oppressed Jews. Zionism was a colonial project whose success in displacing a million Palestinians in 1947–48 rested on its backing by the big imperialist powers. It stands strong today because the US and other Western powers, including Australia, see it as a guarantor of their interests in the Middle East.

Support for the right of self-determination is not conditional on whether those oppressed use violent or non-violent methods. Socialists distinguish between the armed uprising of the Vietnamese people in the 1960s and the aerial bombardment of Vietnamese villages by the US. One is the violence of the oppressed, which is completely justified; the other is the violence of the oppressor, which is always wrong. Socialists may have criticisms of particular tactics used – for example, the bombing of civilian targets by the Algerian national liberation movement in its war against French occupation in the 1950s – but this does not negate our support for their struggle. We unconditionally support their goal – national liberation – even if we retain the right to criticise their methods and the middle-class or capitalist figures who usually lead these movements.

While socialists support the right of oppressed nations to fight for their liberation from imperialist oppression, this does not mean positive support for nationalism in its own right. Every national struggle involves different classes, and each class strives, beyond national independence, for different things. The wealthy classes in the oppressed nation try to limit the national struggle, elevate the national project over the class interests of workers and stifle the aspirations of the most oppressed for complete liberation, lest their struggles threaten their own rule. Before independence, fear of mass mobilisation from below has often rendered bourgeois nationalists half-hearted and vacillating and willing to make deals with bigger powers to secure some advantage or another. Once independence is attained, class divisions come even more to the fore in the formerly oppressed nations. So it was that after winning independence, many governments in the former colonies in the Middle East,

Asia and Africa, whether identified with the left or the right, repressed their own working class, banning strikes and jailing trade unionists, and threw peasants off their land to foster industrialisation.

The bourgeois nationalists also have their own national aspirations as a ruling class that involve the oppression of other groups – for example, Indonesia's annexation of West Papua in 1969, only a few decades after it won independence from the Dutch. For these reasons, the working class in the oppressed country, while supporting the struggle for national liberation, must maintain its own independent organisation to ensure that its own class aims, which always go further than the bourgeois nationalist leaders, are not sidelined.

Nationalism cannot offer the working class a way out of its predicament. The material condition for socialism – abundance – exists on a world scale, but not within the confines of national borders. This is true because economic development is extremely uneven, with enormous wealth and productive power concentrated in some regions far more than others. Any country that attempts to fall back on its own resources quickly finds that its production system is too lopsided and incomplete to pull itself up by its own bootstraps. Having been shaped in connection with the world economy, one country finds it cannot produce enough agricultural products and must import them; another does not have enough machinery and spare parts. The *Communist Manifesto* ends with the resounding phrase, "Workers of the world, unite". This was not simply a moral appeal. Capitalism has created a world working class in the billions from whose labour the profits of the world's multinationals derive. Workers face the same essential conditions the world over. Whether their pay is high or low, all workers are exploited. They therefore have a common interest that spans national borders despite their national differences.

The fight against war

Imperialism throws the world into constant wars. Hundreds of millions have died in the past one and a half centuries because of wars of various kinds. Even more have been maimed. The financial cost has been catastrophic and has led to ruinous effects on the standard of living of workers on the home front. But it is the very shock of wars that can set in motion the forces that bring them to an end. Wars have been the catalyst for resistance and, sometimes, revolution around the world. World War I provides the best example.

The outbreak of World War I was greeted with rapture among the middle class and capitalists in Britain, Europe and countries like Australia. The working class and peasantry were not so easily swayed. Some went along with the war hysteria. A minority were resolutely opposed. As for the majority, only the rabid support for the war by the social democratic (labour) party and trade union leaders could win their consent for the first couple of years at least. Where that was not forthcoming, state repression drove opposition underground.

From early on, there were episodic outbreaks of resistance to the war among the soldiers. The 1914 Christmas truce between German and British soldiers is the best known. Less dramatic was the practice of "live and let live", by which soldiers in opposing trenches did their best to avoid actual engagement. By 1916, support for the war at home was cracking. The cost in lives at the front and the sacrifices at home were now taking their toll on war fever. The burden of taxation grew sharply, and inflation ravaged working-class living standards. Hundreds of thousands in Germany were dying from starvation.

If the working class and peasants in and out of uniform paid a heavy price in the war, the capitalist classes prospered. Huge contracts to supply the army offered every big capitalist, every senior officer and every high-up bureaucrat the chance to fill their pockets. Popular hatred of these war profiteers grew enormously. Soldiers could easily see the gross inequalities between the conditions of the generals, comfortably ensconced in mansions well behind the lines, and their own lot in the trenches, and the injustice rankled. The 1916 Easter Uprising in Ireland, which supplied 200,000 soldiers for the British Empire, was the most dramatic sign that imperial jingoism was breaking down. The successful battle against conscription in Australia in 1916 was another. But it was the February Revolution of 1917 in Russia, followed quickly by massive mutinies in the French and Italian armies, that signalled that the masses were turning against the war. In April 1917, 200,000 German engineering workers struck against reductions in the bread ration. Mass desertions and voluntary surrenders became more and more frequent.

In October 1917, Russian workers overthrew the Provisional Government that had taken power on the fall of the tsar and pulled their country out of the war. The Russian Revolution inspired rebellious workers and soldiers across the world. A big strike wave in Berlin and Vienna in January 1918 was crushed, but the continuing high rates of casualties and the ever-worsening conditions of life fed anti-war sentiment.

In October 1918, the Kaiser ordered the German fleet on a suicide mission to confront the British navy in the North Sea. Sailors at the Kiel naval base refused to sail and took over the town, sparking off a revolution that saw all the institutions of imperial Germany crumble in a matter of days.

The German revolt quickly spread, and by the war's end, three major empires – the Russian, the Austro-Hungarian and the Turkish – had collapsed. The war had transformed the entire continent into a cauldron of revolution.

If World War I is the best demonstration of how bloody wars can unleash revolution, there are plenty of others. Discontent among Portuguese soldiers serving in the colonial occupation of Angola and Mozambique in the early 1970s, along with resistance by the guerrilla armies in those countries, led to a full-blown mutiny and the crumbling of the occupation. The shock of the collapse in the colonies then reverberated in the streets, colleges and factories of Portugal, leading to a massive revolution against the fascist regime that had run the country for four decades.

American GIs revolted against the bloody war in Vietnam, both those on duty and those stationed in bases in the US and Europe. Many refused to engage in combat with the Vietnamese, went AWOL, or even joined the Vietnamese National Liberation Front. Others threw grenades into the tents of the more gung-ho officers. Anti-war newspapers circulated by the dozen in military bases. GI opposition to the war was inspired by and fed into the anti-war movement at home. By the end of the 1960s, demonstrations were drawing out millions across the US, and the issue was radicalising an entire generation, a significant number of whom were drawing explicitly revolutionary conclusions. The US top brass concluded by 1970 that the soldiers in Vietnam were so infected by anti-war sentiment that they were incapable of continuing the war. The US had to pull most of the troops out and was forced to conduct most military operations from the air from that point on. The defeat of the US in Vietnam was a stunning blow to the credibility of US imperialism and the ruling class at home.

We face a new situation today, with a potential World War III between the US and China. If this were to escalate into a nuclear war, which it might do within days if not hours, we would not have time to build an anti-war movement to prevent catastrophe in the way previous generations of socialists have done. Catastrophe would be upon us, the priority would be survival. Therefore, we must do what we can today to build a revolutionary socialist movement big enough to hold back war. In Australia, that means challenging the US war drive by preventing Australia's participation in it, including the use of Australia as a rearguard base of operations by the US. This means opposing escalating arms spending. It means cancelling the nuclear submarines. It means shutting down Pine Gap. It is inconceivable that any of the existing parliamentary parties would agree to these demands, since they threaten the vital interests of the Australian capitalist state. Preventing World War III, therefore, entails a revolutionary struggle to smash capitalism.

In summary

Imperialism is inherent in capitalism, not an optional add-on or a policy pursued by an aggressive government. It describes the condition of modern capitalism in which advanced capitalist states compete, both peacefully and by military means, for domination of the world market on behalf of the capitalists based in their territory. It is as much part of capitalism as competition for market share between the mining companies, the banks or the supermarkets. Imperialism cannot, therefore, be eliminated by the election of a more "peaceable" government.

The imperialist hierarchy changes over time, and it is the jostling for supremacy occasioned by these shifts that creates the potential for war. Currently, the United States is the top power, but China is challenging it. Various factors prevent the competition between them from breaking out into war in the next year or two, but the ground is being prepared for military conflict between them.

Imperialist powers often try to justify their wars as driven by humanitarian considerations. This is always a lie. Colonialism destroyed the economies and lives of hundreds of millions. Two world wars resulted in the deaths of tens of millions of people. Western interventions in Asia and the Middle East have resulted in widespread death and destruction. Even short of war, imperialist agencies such as the World Bank and the IMF hold back the economies of some of the poorer nations of the world. Foreign aid is designed not to enhance the lot of the downtrodden but to extend business opportunities and strategic influence for the donor. The United Nations is no solution; it is irrelevant or complicit in imperialist wars.

Australia is an imperialist power. It is one of the dominant economic and military powers in Asia, and it has never hesitated to use its power to bully smaller nations. It is not a pawn of the United States. Its alliance with the US helps the Australian ruling class to project its influence further than it could otherwise manage and to do so relatively cheaply. Australia's participation in distant wars in Europe and the Middle East alongside the US and Britain resulted from its desire to show to its senior imperialist partner its value as an ally, not its blind subservience. Now, Australia is fully committed to the US's war preparations with China.

Socialists in Australia stand in solidarity with those oppressed by "our" government, support the right of the oppressed to fight for their liberation and oppose every war waged by "our" armies. So long as the armed forces are those of the capitalist state, they cannot fight wars that benefit the Australian working class.

Imperialism is a threat not only to those on the receiving end of imperialist bombs and sanctions but also to the working class in the imperialist countries themselves. It is they who don the uniforms and face the brutality and constant threat of death that accompanies war. It is they who suffer hardship as money is spent on armaments that could be spent on health, education and social security. And it is they who, on returning home from battle, suffer neglect and are abandoned by those who sent them off to war with fanfare. For this reason, the working classes of the imperialist countries are allies of those oppressed by imperialism in a common struggle. The class struggle within the imperialist countries can fuse with the struggle of those oppressed by imperialism to shake the system to its foundations.

One era in world politics is ending, and a new era is unfolding. Imperialist rivalry is becoming more dangerous. Military budgets are on the rise. Nationalism is ascendant. The logic of developments is pushing toward all-out imperialist war. The terrible weapons the imperialists have at their disposal, and the consequences for each should it lose, warn us of the catastrophe that lies in store for the world's population if a new regional or world war breaks out. War is not inevitable, but we cannot rely on diplomacy or the good sense of our rulers. And we cannot sit back and wait to see what happens. We need to lay the basis for a mass anti-war movement with socialist politics at its core that challenges the powers that be and halts their preparations for war.

Notes

1. This chapter includes extracts from Tom O'Lincoln, "The neighbour from hell", in Rick Kuhn (ed.), *Class and Struggle in Australia*, Pearson Longman, 2005, and Paul D'Amato, *The Meaning of Marxism*, Haymarket Books, 2014.

2. The following account of restructuring during the Long Depression is drawn from Neil Faulkner, *A Marxist History of the World: From Neanderthals to Neoliberals*, Pluto Press, 2013.

3. V.I. Lenin, *Imperialism: the Highest Stage of Capitalism*, 1916.

4. "Full Transcript: Biden's Speech on Israel-Hamas and Russia-Ukraine Wars", *New York Times*, 19 October 2023.

5. Australian Government, *Defence White Paper 2013*, p.24.

6. Tom O'Lincoln, *The Neighbour from Hell: Two Centuries of Australian Imperialism*, Interventions, 2014, pp.61–7.

7. https://thebulletin.org/doomsday-clock/current-time/.

8. See Paul Mason, "Ukraine, NATO and a Zeitenwende", 11 April 2022, https://www.socialeurope.eu/ukraine-nato-and-a-zeitenwende

9. For example, the US website, https://thegrayzone.com/.

10. Edith M. Lederer, "UN chief warns world is one step from 'nuclear annihilation'", AP News, 2 August 2022.

Chapter seven

Class and racial oppression[1]

Every industrial and commercial centre in England now possesses a working
class divided into two hostile camps, English proletarians and Irish proletarians.
[...] This antagonism is artificially kept alive and intensified by the press, the
pulpit, the comic papers, in short, by all the means at the disposal of the
ruling classes.

This antagonism is the secret of the impotence of the English working class,
despite its organisation. It is the secret by which the capitalist class maintains
its power. And the latter is quite aware of this.

—Karl Marx, letter to Sigfrid Meyer and
August Vogt in New York, 1870

WE LIVE IN A SOCIETY RIFE NOT ONLY with capitalist exploitation
and economic inequality but also with myriad forms of oppression
– unequal treatment of various groups based on perceived racial,
sexual, national and other differences. Oppression is popularly understood as a
matter of derogatory language or pejorative attitudes held towards these groups,
particularly by religious zealots or those regarded as uneducated. However,
oppression is a structural phenomenon with roots in the underlying economic
functioning and social institutions of capitalism. Oppressed groups experience
not only abusive or patronising treatment from the media and politicians
but some or all of the following as well: lower wages, discrimination when
looking for work, fewer opportunities for training or promotion, inferior
housing, harassment or unjust treatment by the police, over-representation
in the prisons, worse health outcomes or shorter life expectancy and fewer
educational opportunities. These arise not primarily because of "bad attitudes"
but because of the operation of a series of capitalist institutions, including the

media, police, courts, and the health and education systems, and because of the underlying exploitative nature of relations of production.

It is essential to establish from the outset that oppression affects not only women or minorities. The entire working class, the majority of society, is both structurally oppressed and exploited, and one feeds into and shapes the other. Capitalism could not have come into being without terrible violence against the majority. "If money...'comes into the world with a congenital blood-stain on one cheek'", wrote Marx, "capital comes dripping from head to foot, from every pore, with blood and dirt".[2] It took the genocide of indigenous populations, the crushing of peasants, the formation of the constabulary to crack the skulls of rebellious workers, and an industrial prison system to lock away radicals and the poor.

Oppressive violence against the working class continues to this day. When riches in the hands of a few sit side by side with poverty and want for the many, an enormous amount of violence, or the threat of it, will always be needed to maintain and protect the status quo. The ruling class has an extensive apparatus of violence, including the police and legal system, charged with keeping "order" – i.e. maintaining the oppression and exploitation of workers, as we saw in chapter two. The justice system is irredeemably biased against the working class because it defends the rights and interests of those with property. In the military, it is working-class soldiers who die, not the generals in their cushy billets far from the fighting.

The oppression of the working class also takes some less obvious forms that I outlined in chapter one. The workplace is a bastion of authoritarianism, where the boss rules. Bosses may destroy people's lives by sacking them from jobs on which their whole livelihood, and that of their families, depends. Bosses also mobilise their economic power and influence to ensure governments pass and enforce laws that constrain the ability of workers to fight back or protect rights and safety at work.

Added to this, working-class people are derided in the media – witness the treatment of "bogans", while the rich are lauded as "job providers" or philanthropists. The working class suffer from substandard housing compared to the wealthy, and when they need healthcare, they have to wait in the queue while the rich jump to the front to be treated by the top specialists. The working class die younger than the middle and capitalist classes, their bodies worn out by the physical and mental stress of work. So far as the capitalist class is concerned, the working class are only "factors of production" to be used up and tossed aside when they can no longer make money for them.

Faced with oppression at every turn, many working-class people internalise the oppression that they suffer. This explains the widespread belief that only Important People can improve the lot of the working class. It is also the source of stresses and strains that play out in interpersonal violence and self-inflicted harm.

If the whole working class is oppressed, some groups of workers are subject to multiple oppressions. Not only their class but their gender, race, sexuality or physical traits also condemn them to second- or third-class status. In this chapter, we will focus on oppression based on race, and in chapter eight, we will focus on sex, gender identity and sexuality. But oppression reaches beyond these now widely accepted categories. People with disabilities, for instance, are often treated as burdens to be excluded from the labour force, segregated, institutionalised and managed at a minimum cost; when employed, super-exploited; and in the public sphere, often denied necessary facilities. As Australian disability rights advocate Stella Young explained:

> Half of all people with disabilities live near or below the poverty line. Less than 40 percent of us participate in the workforce, compared to almost 80 percent of people who don't have disabilities. Many people who need assistance with things such as showering can only access that kind of support twice a week. Australia ranks last among the OECD countries when measured on the quality of life for people with disabilities.[3]

People are also oppressed in Australia on the grounds of age. Children are still treated as the property of their parents, denied any say in their schooling and forced to endure an education system geared towards preparing the next generation for work rather than their emergence as fully rounded adults. The elderly are treated as a burden on society because they no longer contribute to capitalist enrichment. It would be best in the view of those at the top if workers died on the day of their retirement to avoid becoming a drain on society. One only has to see how little attention is paid to the thousands who have died in aged care homes during the COVID-19 pandemic to understand how little consideration is paid to the elderly.

Racism

Racism is endemic to capitalism. It exists in every country, from US police murdering African Americans to the Israeli genocide in Palestine and the oppression of Roma in Europe. It is an inevitable product of the political, economic and ideological imperatives of capitalism and has accompanied capitalism from its birth. The way racial oppression is manifested can vary between different groups, and this is true for all forms of oppression. The way that refugees are oppressed is different to migrants and to Indigenous people because of the specific way that their racial oppression fits into capitalism – whether they are an extremely exploited and profitable section of the working class or whether they are marginal to it, whether or not their oppression is bound up in imperialism.

The enslavement of millions of Africans, for example, was a necessary condition for the establishment of cotton plantations in the United States and the prosperity of the Lancashire cotton industry. The expansion of European empires exported capitalism around the world, bringing with it genocides and the dispossession and disenfranchisement of millions. Colonised peoples were cast as less than human, legitimately dominated by foreign powers and undeserving of dignity and rights. In *Capital*, Marx linked the economic and political conditions driving racism to the exploitation of the working class, one of the defining features of capitalism, writing of the US: "Labour in white skin cannot emancipate itself where the black skin is branded".

Racism was also a necessary condition for the "settlement" of Australia because Indigenous people constituted a barrier to capitalism's expansion into the continent and so were subjected to genocide. The settlers of the First Fleet did not immediately set out to exterminate the native population. But even if the British did not arrive with the idea of exterminating the Indigenous peoples, they had no intention of respecting them or their way of life. When the colony needed land for farming, the Aboriginal people had to make way. The most devastating conflict occurred with the penetration of sheep and cattle in the late 1830s and 1840s. Sheep especially required vast areas of land to graze, and so the squatters pushed relentlessly outwards, driving hundreds of thousands of Indigenous peoples from the fertile areas into harsh wastelands and killing all who resisted. As the frontier moved to northern and western Australia in the latter half of the nineteenth century and the early twentieth, the killings increased. At the most conservative estimate, over 10,000 Indigenous people were killed in 403 massacres in the Northern Territory and Western Australia between 1860 and 1930.[4] By 1901, the number of Aboriginal people in the entire continent had been reduced from perhaps a million to 67,000. The Australian nation was founded on the genocide of the Aboriginal people.

If the first impulse was to wipe out the Indigenous population, this changed in south-east Australia in the 1850s in the context of dramatic labour shortages facing the pastoralists, as thousands of free white settlers moved to Victoria to make their fortunes in the gold rush. Indigenous people were now recruited to work on cattle stations and sheep runs. Extermination, while it continued in some parts of the country, gave way to the new language of "protection". Aboriginal reserves or missions were established to herd Indigenous families together to provide a ready labour pool for the rural capitalists.

Missions and government settlement superintendents were given many restrictive and repressive powers. Indigenous people could not vote, control their own bank accounts, drink alcohol or enter or leave the reserve without permission. Their children were often forcibly taken away. Special laws were passed to prevent trade union organisers from approaching the downtrodden Aboriginal workers.

In the twentieth century, with the increasing urbanisation of Indigenous people and their successful struggle to gain some basic rights, official policy changed once again. During World War II, the shortage of labour on the home front meant that Indigenous people were drawn into the paid workforce in the cities in record numbers. In 1951, "assimilation" was announced. "Cultural genocide", replied the Aboriginal people. It was an attempt to forget about the rights of the Black population and to cover up what they had already suffered by trying to blend them into the general society. Again, the kidnapping of

Indigenous children was part of the policy. At the same time, an enormous edifice of segregation continued – schools, hospitals, toilets, cinemas, pools and tennis courts.

With the discovery of abundant mineral resources in the Northern Territory and Western Australia in the 1960s came a further round of dispossession of the Indigenous population. Much of this wealth was on previously waste and unproductive land that had been relegated to missions or government reserves because it was considered useless and, therefore, sufficient for the Indigenous peoples. More and more of this land was resumed by the government and leased to mining companies.

The government policy of assimilation was followed by "integration" (with or without consultation) and the "self-determination" and "self-management" of the 1970s and 1980s. What all these policies have had in common is that they were based on what capitalism was prepared to offer, not on the needs of Indigenous people themselves. And so when Eddie Mabo and the Mer people won the right to their land in the 1992 Mabo High Court decision, the Keating government and the Howard government that followed passed laws hemmed in with so many qualifications and entitlements for pastoralists and mining companies that few successful Indigenous land claims followed over the next couple of decades.

In the 2000s, self-determination was sent into sharp reverse as the Howard government introduced the Northern Territory Intervention, which aimed to shut down the outstations, push the Indigenous population into centres where they could be "managed" more efficiently and then steal their land on 99-year leases. "Income management", using the Basics Card to replace social security payments, added to the humiliation of the Aboriginal population. When the Northern Territory Intervention lapsed after five years in 2012, it was simply rolled into "Stronger Futures" by the Gillard Labor government, which maintained all its repressive elements. The Abbott government kept Stronger Futures in place and announced cuts of more than half a billion dollars to Aboriginal support services. In 2014, the West Australian Liberal government announced that it would cease funding 150 remote Aboriginal communities to force their closure and relocate the residents to towns and cities elsewhere, furthering the two-centuries-old agenda of Aboriginal dispossession.

If Australian governments continue to oppress the Indigenous population, there have been developments that seem to point in the other direction. In 2008, newly elected Prime Minister Kevin Rudd issued to great acclaim an Apology to the Stolen Generations, those Indigenous children removed from their families as a matter of state policy to "breed out the black". And today, the boards of Australia's biggest resources companies, which, thanks to the inadequacies of native title legislation, have won the right to exploit vast tracts of land, now seek to give themselves a progressive veneer, decking their corporate head offices with Aboriginal artworks, employing Indigenous workers on their mine sites and granting multi-million-dollar contracts to Black-owned businesses to provide services. In the name of representation and diversity, thousands more Indigenous university graduates have been appointed to well-paid jobs in government, community and NGO-run cultural, legal, educational and health institutions. Even the Abbott government embraced "constitutional recognition" of Indigenous peoples in 2015. Welcomes to Country or Acknowledgements of Country have now become almost universal in the world of big business, universities, parliamentary chambers and the big sporting codes. Aboriginal and Torres Strait Islander flags fly outside every major public institution. As tens of thousands turn out at annual Invasion Day rallies to protest the crimes of colonialism and ongoing oppression, many local councils have cancelled Australia Day events or tried to incorporate some recognition of Aboriginal history into them. Organisers of Anzac Day events now take care to incorporate the stories of Indigenous servicemen and women.

Much of this shift in official discourse has been superficial. The Apology to the Stolen Generations provided no compensation to those whose lives had been ruined and did nothing to disguise the continued removal of Indigenous children from their families in staggeringly high numbers. Resource companies may proclaim their support for Indigenous progress but continue to destroy sacred sites. The Abbott government's proposed constitutional recognition was so anaemic and so compromised by his government's day-to-day policies that Indigenous groups disowned it. The Queensland Labor government may acknowledge Country and fly Indigenous flags but suspended its own Human Rights Act twice in 2023 to rush through draconian laws to incarcerate Indigenous children. The military establishment may nod to the contribution of Indigenous personnel in far-flung wars but will not acknowledge those who fought the only invasion Australia has experienced. Black "empowerment" programs have created opportunities to enrich a few capitalists. Given the long history of racial discrimination and outright exclusion, the left cannot oppose diversity programs, but these have advanced only a narrow layer of Black professionals, while conditions of life for most Indigenous people are still wretched.

The Voice to Parliament was in this vein of tokenism. Starting with the Statement from the Heart drafted at a 2017 conference of prominent Indigenous figures in Uluru, the Voice to Parliament was to constitute an Aboriginal advisory body to parliament, eventually paving the way for a Treaty. From the outset of the referendum campaign in 2023, what was a weak proposal was diluted even further in the face of a growing right-wing backlash led by the Liberal Party. The referendum result, in which the Yes campaign won not a single state, was a devastating defeat and demonstrated how shallow had been much of the anti-racist discourse of the previous couple of decades.

The outcome of this horrible history is that Australia's Indigenous people remain among the most oppressed in the world as measured by ill health, mortality rates, life expectancy, housing and education, joblessness, access to government services, imprisonment and deaths in custody. Well over 500 Indigenous people have died in custody since the Royal Commission into Black Deaths in Custody handed down its report in 1991. Not a single police officer or prison officer has been convicted on charges relating to their deaths.

Racism in Australia extends well beyond the Indigenous population. Working-class immigrants also experience structural oppression. Bosses, politicians and landlords use laws, policies and practices that at times explicitly target, at others disproportionately affect, the racially oppressed. The immigration department both consciously and instinctively upholds racist inequality. Many immigrant communities are concentrated in the poorest areas in major cities, with lower average incomes, poorly funded schools, worse public amenities like transport and hospitals and a greater police presence than well-off neighbourhoods.

Governments have, in recent decades, skewed the immigration system to favour the wealthy. There is an open door for those with money and professional qualifications, such as accountants, doctors, engineers, IT professionals and lawyers. A wealth management company noted in 2023 with great satisfaction that "Australia consistently attracts sizeable numbers of millionaires every year, mainly from Asia and Africa, but more recently also from high-income countries such as the UK". Between 2002 and 2022, an estimated 82,000 people with investable wealth of more than US$1 million migrated to Australia.[5]

If the millionaires get red carpet treatment, others find the path strewn with boulders. There are nearly two million people without permanent residency or citizenship, many of whom labour in highly oppressive conditions. For non-citizen or temporary visa workers and refugees, including many international students and graduates and those on working holiday and bridging visas, hyper-exploitation in the workplace and the threat of deportation degrade their lives.

Capitalists always seek to minimise their costs and maximise their earnings, and politicians are happy to help them. Farm work is perhaps the most egregious example. The Pacific Australia Labour Mobility (PALM) scheme allows farmers and contractors to access a cut-price workforce sourced from Australia's impoverished Pacific Island neighbours. The scheme is open not only to farmers but also to meat processing, fisheries, hospitality and aged care bosses. A 2022 parliamentary inquiry into the scheme found such workers were horribly abused, earning perhaps $100 a week for 64-hour working weeks and housed in substandard accommodation where they were charged exorbitant rents.[6] The Albanese government states that it intends to crack down on the abuse of these workers, increasing fines and even threatening jail terms for employers who flout regulations, but abuse is baked into the system: its very purpose is to supply a workforce employed on substandard conditions living in fear of deportation should they speak up for their rights. Such treatment underpins racist ideas and attitudes as well as the experience of racism – real social inequality. The media ratchet up racist divisions wherever they can.

It is not only those directly subjected to racial oppression who are harmed by it. Inequality in the workplace can undermine unity between workers and thus harm the conditions of all. The ruling class has encouraged racism to undermine solidarity. Starting in the 1950s, a period of labour shortages, Australian bosses worked with the immigration department to organise mass immigration of working-age southern Europeans to fill semi-skilled blue-collar jobs. By the late 1970s, 50 percent of southern European men in Melbourne were employed in merely 15 percent of jobs, mostly production and labouring, and mostly low-paid. In the big Ford Broadmeadows factory, the company then divided them up by language group and from British immigrants, predominantly in trades jobs, to create divisions and suspicion, weakening trade unionism. When workers stood up to demand their rights, one of the first things they had to do was to break down these racial and ethnic barriers.

Racism is divisive even when employers are not consciously encouraging it. The experience of racism can make racially oppressed workers feel alone and defensive about raising grievances. They can feel support is forthcoming only in their ethnic community rather than from the workers' movement. And it can make non-oppressed groups hostile to those who should be their allies. Their allegiance to the nation means identification with the economic and political interests of their rulers, frequently against co-workers. Racial and national identities are so coveted by bosses, politicians and right-wing ideologues precisely because of this potential to obscure or eclipse class identification. Just think of the various racialised moral panics about terrorism or crime, which both divert attention away from politicians' failures in other areas, whether health or other social services, and create a scapegoat for the stress caused by those failures.

The undermining of collective consciousness creates barriers to advancing workers as a class, both in the workplace and in society.

Imperialism and racism

If stealing Indigenous land and undercutting workers' wages have been two drivers of racism, Australia's bloody imperialist history has probably been the most significant factor. Identifying an enemy has been important for prosecuting imperialist wars, both in sowing divisions at home and winning working-class support for war. Both have featured in ruling-class racist campaigns over the past two centuries. As the enemies of the Australian ruling class have changed, so have the targets of racism, emphasising that racism is not driven by popular ignorance but is a deliberate ruling class project.

The Irish were the first target. Irish resistance to British rule meant that the Irish in Australia were always regarded as disloyal and a threat, and racism served a useful purpose in oppressing what soon became a important component of the Australian working class. The newspapers in the colonies portrayed Irish people as repulsive in appearance, stupid, dishonest, always ready to fight, and sulky. This racism was part of a wider campaign to discipline an unruly working population by associating ignorance, dishonesty, immorality and laziness with Irishness.

Australia was established as a white colonial outpost of the British Empire in an area dominated by Asians and Pacific Islanders. It therefore faced challenges, real or imagined, from the hundreds of millions of non-white peoples of the region. Anti-Asian racism has, therefore, been a core feature of Australia's history.

For decades leading up to Federation, increasingly restrictive legislation was imposed on Asian immigrants, particularly the Chinese. In 1901, the new Commonwealth formally instituted the White Australia policy. For the following seven decades, this policy virtually defined what it meant to be Australian. Australian nationhood and whiteness were inextricably linked.

In World War I, when the British Empire went to war with Germany, Germans in Australia also became targets. They were rounded up and detained or deported, and thousands lost their jobs. In the 1920s, the focus shifted to southern Europeans, who by now had arrived in significant numbers. In the mining town of Kalgoorlie (WA), anti-migrant agitation, funded by the big mining companies, led to riots. The bosses aimed to divide the multicultural workforce and undermine the effectiveness of trade unions so that labour could be kept as cheap as possible.

During World War II, Germans were again interned, as were Italians and Japanese. In the postwar decades, facing labour shortages, conservative governments steadily diversified the sources of immigration but still sought to prop up White Australia. They demanded that non-Anglophone migrants assimilate into Australian society and leave their previous customs, languages and cultures behind. This sent a message that such migrants were not really

Australian. This policy also encouraged a sense of superiority among those who identified as British Australians, which (temporarily) strengthened the grip of the Liberal Party over postwar Australia.

The subsequent policy of multiculturalism may have tempered some of the worst excesses of the White Australia policy, but only to incorporate a layer of middle-class and capitalist ethnic community leaders into what is still a racist national project. As an imperialist country in a region populated overwhelmingly by people of colour who form the primary target for external oppression and exploitation, if not invasion, Australia cannot be anything other than racist so long as it is capitalist and, therefore, imperialist.

Following the 9/11 attacks on the World Trade Center, Muslims were at the centre of a sustained racist offensive. As occurred with Germans during World War I, Muslims were vilified to justify Australian involvement in wars and occupations in Afghanistan and Iraq. Muslims were subjected to waves of repressive "anti-terrorism" legislation and abuse by senior politicians and the media. The result of this Islamophobic offensive was a surge in racist attacks on Muslims on the streets, in shopping centres, on public transport, in schools and other public places, including most notoriously, the 2005 Cronulla riot, a media-fuelled lynch mob attack on anyone of "Middle Eastern appearance" in the Sydney beach suburb.

Africans, in particular young African men, are also targets of systematic racism. This includes harassment by the police. Young African men are stopped, questioned, demeaned and have their photos taken purely because of their skin colour, with Black men gathering in groups labelled by police and media alike as "gangs". But when Africans are themselves the subject of violent attacks, the police look the other way – a Black person's life is not worth much to them.

Refugees arriving by boat seeking asylum have been subjected to ever more cruel punishment by successive governments since mandatory detention was first introduced in 1992. Whether it has been the turning back of refugees from the Australian mainland, allowing unseaworthy boats to take to sea only to watch them sink, taking the lives of hundreds of refugees, or the sadistic treatment of refugees in places like Christmas Island, or the forced transfer of asylum seekers to hell-holes in Nauru or Manus Island, or the cruel system of temporary protection visas that kept refugees in limbo for years on end, or the forcible return of refugees to the countries from which they were fleeing – nothing has been beyond the imagination of Australian governments. The cost in terms of lives ruined is immeasurable.

The point of these vicious measures against refugees was to deter others from exercising their right to seek asylum in Australia, but they also had other benefits for the ruling class. The ruling class wants to crush any sense of social solidarity with the vulnerable and marginalised and to justify the strengthening of the repressive apparatus of the Australian state that jeopardises everyone's rights and civil liberties. Like the persecution of Muslims, attacks on refugees have been a means to crush any sense of social solidarity with the vulnerable and marginalised and to distract workers from the broader government agenda – the redistribution of wealth from the working class to the capitalists.

As Australia joins the US in preparing for war with China, it is likely that Chinese Australians will bear the brunt of a fresh round of racism. Already, some politicians refer to them as a "fifth column", the enemy within. If a shooting war breaks out, racism against Chinese Australians will only get much worse.

The interlocked twists and turns of racism and imperialism demonstrate the artificial and constructed nature of race. We cannot smash racism without attacking Australia's imperialist aggression.

Fighting back against oppression

The targets of racism in Australia have not accepted their lot passively. While racism can beat down minority groups, it can also spur them to fight back.

For many decades, Australian schoolchildren were told that Australia was settled peacefully, and that Aboriginal people accepted their dispossession, if not willingly, at least with no serious resistance. Their supposedly passive response was contrasted with that of the Māori in New Zealand, whose armed conflict and subsequent treaty with the British could not so easily be ignored.

This textbook version is a lie. Aboriginal people fought British invasion right across the country, sometimes for decades. The Dharug, living near the

Hawkesbury River in NSW, waged a war against the invaders from 1795 to 1816, led in the early years by guerrilla leader Pemulwuy. When pastoralism took off west of the Blue Mountains and along the Hunter River in the 1820s, the pastoralists faced determined resistance by the Wiradjuri people, and by the end of the 1830s, a war frontier stretched from northern New South Wales to western Victoria. In Western Australia, Yagan and his followers mounted resistance in the Swan River Colony in the early 1830s, while in Queensland, Dundalli left whites north of Brisbane living in fear as he led a guerrilla campaign for 14 years until his capture and execution in 1855. Decades later, the invasion still faced resistance. For 10 years, the Kalkadoon around Mount Isa harried the occupiers until they were crushed in 1884 at Battle Mountain. Thirteen years later, a three-year guerrilla resistance by the Bunuba people in the Kimberley in WA, led by Jandamarra, was put down, but not before the Bunubas had created panic in the ranks of the region's pastoralists.

Despite their immense bravery, Indigenous peoples were too fragmented and lacked the technology to win the war, particularly as their numbers began to decline and ever greater numbers of whites arrived on the continent. What bullets and poisoned food, water wells and blankets could not achieve, starvation, smallpox and other introduced diseases completed.

Military resistance gave way to other forms of fighting back. Indigenous people were active in the labour movement from at least the 1880s when they fought alongside white shearers, including in the great shearers' strikes of the 1890s.[7] A few became early activists with the ALP, the Industrial Workers of the World or the Communist Party. In 1937, William Ferguson, an Aboriginal union activist and ALP member, launched the Aborigines' Progressive Association, which demanded the abolition of the Aboriginal Protection Board and full citizenship rights for Indigenous people.

The 1946 strike on the sheep stations of the Pilbara in WA was the first big industrial strike by Indigenous people and a breakthrough in the struggle for Black rights. The pastoral workers demanded higher wages and better conditions when many of them were not paid cash wages at all. The strike received widespread support from other unions which was essential to keep the struggle going in the face of obdurate resistance by the pastoralists. Union power finally broke the deadlock in 1949 when the Seamen's Union banned the transport of wool from stations affected by the strike, forcing immediate concessions from the bosses.

In 1951, Aboriginal cooks, gardeners and labourers in Darwin struck for improved conditions on their reserve, award wages and equal citizenship. Again, they received support from trade unionists as far afield as Melbourne. The result was considerable gains for domestic workers in government service in the Northern Territory.

In 1966, two decades after the Pilbara walk-off, Indigenous pastoral workers at Newcastle Waters in the Northern Territory went on strike and were soon followed by stockmen at Wave Hill and other stations controlled by the giant Vestey company. In March 1967, after they had won concessions from some of the station owners, they decided to demand the land itself. Land rights came to the forefront of the Aboriginal struggle. The Gurindji moved to Wattie Creek (Dagu Ragu) and sent a petition to the Governor General asking for the return of 500 square miles of their traditional land. Eventually, in 1975, after many years of hard struggle, the Gurindji won their land.

Two other milestones in the 1960s were the 1965 Freedom Rides and the 1967 constitutional referendum. Following in the footsteps of a campaign by Indigenous and union activists on the NSW South Coast in the early 1960s, which broke the colour bar in pubs and cafes in Port Kembla, Wollongong and Nowra, a busload of white Sydney University students and two Aboriginal activists protested in 1965 against the colour bar in Walgett and Moree, forcing its partial repeal. The 1967 constitutional referendum was the culmination of a long-running campaign involving hundreds of activists, white and Black. Although the referendum started a long way back from the prospect of success, tireless campaigning across the country involving the ALP, CPA and churches saw a 90 percent yes vote.

A militant working-class upsurge in the late 1960s and early 1970s, combined with the strength of movements like that against the Vietnam War, inspired a new generation of Black activists who turned their back on the polite lobbying tactics that had characterised most Aboriginal campaigning in the 1950s. The Aboriginal Tent Embassy was set up on the lawns of Parliament House, Canberra, on 26 January 1972, after Prime Minister William McMahon announced Aboriginal people would not be granted ownership of their tribal lands. Police tore the tent down, but the protesters put it up again in a gesture of defiance. Again, the police pulled it down. On 30 July, about 400 Indigenous people and over 1,000 non-Indigenous supporters broke the law again, putting up the tent in front of 250 police. The Embassy symbolised a new Black assertiveness uniting urban and rural people. It attracted significant support from militant unions, like the NSW Builders Labourers Federation. The Communist Party was important in bringing Aboriginal activists, student radicals and left-wing trade unionists together in this period.

The 1980s was a time of working-class retreat, and this affected the Indigenous struggle as well. There were still important large Aboriginal mobilisations during the 1982 Brisbane Commonwealth Games and the 1988 Sydney bicentenary celebrations, but these were exceptions. The late 1990s saw a brief revival of Indigenous struggle around land rights when the Mirrar people fought for three years to prevent the development of the Jabiluka uranium mine on their land in Kakadu National Park in the Northern Territory, including a blockade of the mine site. Faced with this opposition, the company, North Ltd., pulled out, and the campaign won a decisive victory.

Indigenous struggles continue. The toll of deaths in custody continues to grow, but Aboriginal people have repeatedly taken to the streets in protest. Indigenous people have also put pressure on the police, governments and courts to fight for justice for those murdered by whites. In Redfern in Sydney and Palm Island in Queensland, Aboriginal people have rioted and, in Palm, burned down the police station. Socialists unequivocally support such actions. They are an entirely justified response to oppression and have the potential to spark more widespread protest and resistance.

Other victims of racism, too, have resisted their oppression. Irish nationalists transported to Australia were involved, along with many other nationalities, in the Eureka Stockade in 1854. Irish migrants were also central to the fight to establish trade unionism in the last quarter of the nineteenth century and against conscription in World War I.

Starting in the 1960s, workers from southern Europe often started and led some of the most militant strikes against ruthless employers: at General Motors-Holden in Fisherman's Bend in Melbourne in 1964, Ford Broadmeadows in 1973 and the Redfern Mail Exchange in Sydney in 1985.

European migrants brought left-wing and radical traditions from their home countries that enriched the Australian working class.

Asian workers have become an increasingly important component of the Australian working class. In 1980, Vietnamese workers played a major role in a long strike at the Toyota factory in Melbourne and were the most active picketers during the 1985 strike at the Redfern Mail Exchange in Sydney. In the 2010s and 2020s, migrant workers from Southeast Asia and Africa have been at the forefront of strikes in agriculture and food-processing, where they are subjected to rotten conditions and poor pay.[8]

Even in the most desperate of circumstances, the oppressed can resist. Asylum seekers in detention have sewn their lips together, gone on hunger strikes, broken out of the detention centres and staged rooftop protests to draw attention to their conditions and demand the right to asylum. In 2011, 250 asylum seekers rioted and tried to break out of the detention centre on Christmas Island, and in the following month, 100 asylum seekers torched nine buildings at Villawood detention centre in Sydney. Two years later, 130 or more burned down the detention centre in Nauru and in 2015, hundreds went on hunger strike and barricaded themselves in their compounds on remote Manus Island in PNG. As with Aboriginal riots, socialists defend the right of asylum seekers to fight back in this way.

Can workers unite against racism?

It is not only those who are racially oppressed who can fight racism. The entire working class can and must join this struggle. This may seem counterintuitive. Aren't white Australian workers racist? How could they be partners in such a struggle? In recent decades, a series of closely related arguments have become popular in university circles that challenge a class-based explanation of racism and, with it, the potential for workers of all backgrounds to join hands to fight it.

Privilege theory states that all white people, by virtue of their collective identity as whites and regardless of their class, are privileged and benefit from racism.[9] According to the "Racism: It Stops with Me" campaign run by the Australian Human Rights Commission, whites are privileged because they are the "one group or group of communities that benefits the most from racially inequitable laws, policies and practices".[10] These "privileges" include being treated fairly in the justice system and seeing yourself represented in the media, business and politics.

It is not just that whites are privileged in these ways, according to such theorists, but they are complicit in, if not responsible for, the system of racial oppression. Those who wish to overcome their complicity in racism, referred to as "allies", which can range from individual workers and students to football teams, mining corporations, universities and the armed forces, must "understand your own privileges and biases, the ways in which you might be complicit and take action to address these". This involves self-education, "thinking about your privilege" and "actively leveraging it to promote change", listening to those affected by racism, talking to friends and family, and respecting First Nations sovereignty.[11] This is the bread and butter of the many companies offering racism awareness workshops to corporations and government departments in which staff are expected to interrogate their culpability in racism. Evidently, such an approach completely buries the responsibility of the capitalists and state apparatus for racism. Privilege theorists never argue to eliminate the privileges of the capitalist class by dispossessing them and distributing the proceeds among the working class, those who lack any privilege, whether Black or white. And, by ranking the relative invisibility of people of colour (POC) from television shows alongside the experience of being framed, incarcerated or killed by the police and courts, this approach also trivialises racism and highlights its middle-class bias. Little wonder that the "Racism: It Stops with Me" campaign is funded by Australia's leading insurance companies; it gives them a progressive gloss while requiring them to do nothing substantive to combat oppression.

Privilege theory has at its heart the proposition that the experience of oppression confers an incontrovertible authority that alone qualifies a person to speak, analyse and present strategies to challenge or eliminate oppression. Those who do not share this experience can only play a passive role as allies, supporting those who do or else become complicit in the problem. This ties the validity of any argument to the identity of the person making it. What is being said becomes a secondary consideration to who is saying it.

The experience of being oppressed can and has stirred POC into fighting racism, and any mass anti-racist campaign will be led by POC. Identity politics, however, is a middle-class phenomenon that benefits only this narrow social layer. Its most enthusiastic proponents tend to be aspirational POC businesspeople and well-heeled POC academics and politicians, because it allows them to use their identity to dominate discussions and silence criticism of what are commonly conservative political projects. We see the same in the world of student unions and campaign groups when conservative and often self-appointed supposed representatives of particular ethnic or racial groups assume the authority to preside over all political activity that relates to their identity category. To defend their patch against challenges by socialists, such people try to discredit their opponents by writing them off as white (regardless of their race) or a lackey of "white socialist groups" and whose arguments are therefore suspect if not downright racist.

Identity politics is closely related to privilege theory in that it understands society as comprising a multitude of identities, some oppressors, others oppressed. One variant of identity politics argues for greater representation of POC in senior positions in the worlds of politics, business, academia and culture. Media coverage of POC who advance into such positions, most obviously figures such as former US President Barack Obama and British Prime Minister Rishi Sunak, inevitably foregrounds their ethnic background and hails their ascent as a step forward for all POC from such backgrounds and a blow against racism. The proposal for an Indigenous Voice to Parliament was also motivated by the idea that greater Indigenous representation in national politics would be a step towards racial equality.

There are more radical variants of identity politics that scorn the liberal idea that simply appointing a few "Black faces in high places" will do anything to tackle entrenched racism. It's clear that figures like Jacinta Price, Warren Mundine or Penny Wong will never fight racism. But in kicking identity politics out of the front door, it comes in through the back. The world is still seen as a clash of identities, it is just that the Prices and Mundines are deemed dupes or sell-outs to the white power structure, who have abandoned their Indigenous brothers and sisters for the sake of career advancement. What is needed, the radical identity theorists argue, is a radical Black nationalist movement to take on "whiteness" and "colonial power structures" and demand reparations of white people, including "paying the rent".[12] But simply removing class as the focus of analysis does not mean it vanishes; it just means that forces other than the working class dominate. Witness the record of Black nationalism invariably elevating a section of the Black middle classes into influential positions while leaving untouched the oppression of the Black working class.

The refusal to centre class also writes off the prospect of working-class unity to fight racism. Solidarity is based on the mutual understanding that the liberation of each depends on the liberation of all, and that racism must be smashed if the entire class is to advance. White workers must confront racism in their own ranks if they are to achieve the unity needed to fight the capitalists. Allyship, by contrast, suggests that capitalist society only needs a modest makeover and that the responsibility for this rests on the shoulders of an enlightened minority, capitalist and worker alike. With capitalists, it amounts to no more than corporate PR; with workers and students, it trades on guilt.

Settler colonial theory comes to the same conclusion as privilege theory. It suggests that the relationship between Indigenous people and "settler society", all those who have migrated to Australia since the initial invasion, is an exploitative relationship in which "settler society", including working-class "settlers", gains material privileges from the dispossession of the Indigenous population. One of the main exponents of settler-colonialism, Sai Englert, argues that:

> If settler workers are exploited as workers within the settler colony, they remain settlers. As such, they participate in the processes of accumulation by dispossession through the occupation of lands, the elimination or exploitation of Indigenous peoples, and the extraction of expropriated resources. Settler workers are both exploited by settler bosses and their co-conspirators in the dispossession of indigenous peoples. As such, class struggle within a settler society has a dual character: it is waged over the distribution of wealth extracted from their labour as well as over the colonial booty.[13]

Because the "settler" working class shares in colonial booty, a united working-class fight against racism is unlikely, if not impossible. Those who are settlers are told that to be a good ally means deferring to supposed representatives of the Indigenous community. Thus, the absurd situation in 2020 of Indigenous activists and their many white supporters on social media scolding as "settlers" young African immigrants who had called demonstrations in solidarity with Black Lives Matter protests. These Africans, themselves the target of regular police harassment, were slammed for not "centring" Aboriginal people and failing to recognise that only Indigenous people had the right to call Black Lives Matter protests. The Africans promptly took down their Facebook event and explained that they never intended to monopolise the rally. The outcome was a setback for a united fight against racism.

Privilege theory, identity politics and settler colonial theory are not only a set of misguided assumptions but a form of politics that systematically points away from the system responsible for oppression and away from the forces that have an interest in fighting it. They are an impediment to solidarity and struggle, focusing as they do on individuals and the most superficial of cultural phenomena, and provide cover for petty-mindedness and self-promotion. What they all have in common is that they deny the primacy of class and class interests in shaping political outlooks and practice. Class is foundational in a way that race is not. How, then, can we understand the relationship between class and race?

Working-class people can be racist, agree with racist government actions, or even take part in racist political movements, although it should be borne in mind that the middle classes – small business owners and the like – are the most significant vehicles for racism, contrary to the stereotype of the middle class's supposedly enlightened outlook. Racism can be pervasive across all classes because, as Marx argued in *The German Ideology*, "[t]he ideas of the ruling class are in every epoch the ruling ideas". Racism in Australia may become less intense in some periods, and yesterday's targets can be passed over today, but racism remains a running sore. Privilege theory, though, cannot explain why racism is malleable nor how it can be challenged.

Race is a social phenomenon. Racial identity is made meaningful by society and the differential position of particular groups within it. In each country, the ruling class – whether black-, white- or brown-skinned – creates and enforces racial division and oppression for its own purposes. Race is not a natural phenomenon stemming from biological factors such as skin or hair colour. This is obvious when we consider the category of "whiteness". Who is white is an extremely fluid concept. Many groups that today in Australia would be considered white, such as the Irish, Greeks, Jews, Germans, Italians and Eastern Europeans, have themselves at times experienced racism in Australia. That they are not oppressed today results from the changing priorities of the ruling class, in particular, which groups are identified with an imperialist enemy.

Racism is not a simple matter of white supremacy. Nor is "whiteness" or "Western culture" to blame for racism or singularly identified with capitalist values. Capitalism straddles the world and so, therefore, does racism. Divisions exist in Australia not only between native-born white Australians and non-white migrants but also between and within multicultural communities, such as Lebanese Maronite Christians and Muslims or between Kurds and Turks. In many countries, those subjected to racial terror are the victims of other people of colour, such as Muslims in India who face lynchings and pogroms by Hindu nationalists, Tamils facing genocide at the hands of the Sinhalese-chauvinist state in Sri Lanka, or Zimbabwean migrants attacked by Black South Africans.[14] Some of the most horrendous acts of racism in history have occurred between and among people who look similar to each other, such as the persecution of Jews in the Holocaust or Bosnians murdered by the Serbian government in the 1995 Srebrenica massacre.

Nor are whites as a racial category responsible for the structures and policies that allow racism to exist. White workers do not determine visa conditions, wages or the cost of rent. Nor do white workers command armed forces to imprison refugees attempting to reach Australia by boat or choose to lock up Indigenous kids for petty crime. These decisions are made or shaped by those with actual power – politicians, corporate bosses, magistrates, media moguls – whose overriding concern is generating profit and protecting the rule of the wealthy. Sustained employer, media and government attacks on Indigenous people, migrants and Muslims, combined with the competition that is injected into the ranks of the working class by the operation of capitalist markets which keep well-paid jobs and affordable housing scarce, are what is responsible for racism, not white workers simply struggling to survive.

Just as whites are divided by class, so too are the racially oppressed. In the US and Britain, Black presidents, prime ministers, home secretaries, defence ministers, ambassadors, police chiefs and judges have all taken power or been appointed in the past couple of decades. They have all been as enthusiastic as their white colleagues to wage wars in the Middle East, kill or incarcerate Black people, deport Central American and African migrants and destroy affirmative action programs. The same is true in Australia when we look at the record of politicians such as Foreign Minister Penny Wong and the Liberal Party's Warren Mundine. This is not because of a desire to "prove themselves" to their white colleagues or because they somehow suffer "false consciousness" and fail to recognise their kinship with other POC, as some advocates of identity politics suggest, but because of their own class interests. Senior state functionaries and capitalists who are POC benefit from the system that perpetuates oppression.

Counter to identity politics, simply experiencing racism is an inadequate foundation from which to develop an analysis of oppression or to devise political strategies to end it. It can be a trigger to fight racism, but it is inadequate to go much further. In part, this is because the experience of oppression is not uniform, and the oppressed are not a homogeneous bloc. There are as many experiences as there are individuals who suffer from oppression. The racism experienced by someone like US Vice President Kamala Harris, for example, is dramatically different from that experienced by a migrant worker on the minimum wage. The experience of conservative Indigenous figures such as Jacinta Price is a world away from that of an Indigenous bus driver or childcare worker.

Expecting to derive any meaningful understanding of oppression by passively listening to the experiences of the oppressed is doomed to chronic confusion and ultimate failure. So, too, is elevating to a principle the belief that experience alone gives an individual exclusive insight into what is needed to remedy oppression and understand its causes. Anyone who emphasises that anti-racists must take their lead from what "the Indigenous community" want would be politically paralysed. After all, which Indigenous leader should they listen to: Jacinta Price, Lidia Thorpe or Marcia Langton? "Listening to Aboriginal voices" gets you nowhere precisely because there are many Aboriginal voices, with varying political positions.

A theory of oppression and struggle for liberation is strongest when it is built on a theory of society that can account for all forms of oppression and inequality, accurately identify their causes, and provide a strategy for liberation. The strength of any such theory can only be tested by history and in ongoing struggle. Experience alone is an inadequate starting point from which to develop such a theory. All those committed to liberation and social equality have an obligation to engage actively with, question and test different theories of society and oppression, as well as learn from the lessons of struggle. This cannot be done without moving beyond the narrow politics of identity and experience.

United we stand, divided we fall

The best refutation of privilege theory, settler colonial theory and identity politics is the history of workers repeatedly taking common action across artificially constructed barriers of race and citizenship. There is a simple explanation for this, expressed in the slogan universal to the workers' movement the world over: "United we stand, divided we fall". Capitalists do their best to create and widen divisions in the ranks of the working class. The employers lobbying for cut-price migrant workers oppose the union movement as a whole. The politicians who blame immigration for high rents and crowded public amenities are also cutting funding for public housing, schools and hospitals. Racism is among the myriad tools capitalism relies on to keep workers ground down, distracted and failing to see the class reality at the core of the system. The more that workers accept such divisions, the weaker they are, the more that the bosses can exploit them and drive down the conditions for all. The nineteenth-century US abolitionist Frederick Douglass put it well:

> The hostility between the whites and blacks of the South is easily explained. It has its root and sap in the relation of slavery and was incited on both sides by the cunning of the slave masters. Those masters secured their ascendency

over both the poor whites and the blacks by putting enmity between them. They divided both to conquer each.[15]

Slavery may have gone, but the same method of divide and rule is applied today. Not for nothing are wages and union organisation in the US lowest in the South, where racism is most entrenched. With migrant workers in aged care or meat processing, Australian bosses use the fear of deportation to keep them from fighting back, weakening unionism and pushing wages down, hurting *all* workers.

The fight against racism, therefore, cannot be separated from the class struggle. The special oppression faced by one part of the working class – Indigenous people, migrants, refugees, Muslims – drags down the rest. Conversely, the liberation of the oppressed is the condition for lifting all.

Three things are necessary to fight racism within the working class. First, a broader class fightback that unites workers across racial lines; second, a campaign against the conditions (bad jobs, housing, education, etc) that create the opening for racists to stir divisions within the working class; and third, the conscious intervention of anti-racists to oppose racism in all its manifestations and to win support for interracial class solidarity.

We see some or all of these in many episodes in Australian history. The big Indigenous strikes of the 1940s, '50s and '60s saw white trade unionists throw their support behind the fight for justice. It was no accident that the unions involved had strong left-wing traditions. Socialists in these unions understood that the oppression of Indigenous peoples held back the conditions for white workers as well. This was obvious on the sheep and cattle stations of the Northern Territory, where the pastoralists played workers off against each other. Aboriginal workers suffered the most, of course, but the white stockmen worked long hours without proper overtime pay and received the lowest wages of any white workers in Australia. Socialists who conducted agitation for solidarity with the Indigenous struggle could argue that it was in white workers' interests to do so, as a united working class could lift the wages and conditions of all workers, Black and white.

Decades later, in 1993, the leaders of the mineworkers' union made the same point when campaigning against the mining companies who were running a scare campaign that the granting of Indigenous land rights would throw mineworkers out of their jobs. The mineworkers understood that the bosses fighting against land rights were also out to get them. Union secretary John Maitland told members in the union newspaper:

> What is driving CRA, BHP, MIM and the rest in their campaign of vague and dreadful threats about withdrawing investment is exactly the same pressure that drives them to lecture the United Mineworkers Union about "unreasonable wage claims" and "restrictive work practices" – the lust for profit. The blackmail is the same, only the targets differ.[16]

Again and again, it has been workers who have been involved in a struggle for their own rights who have been the most receptive to the anti-racist message. Wharfies, seafarers, metal workers and builders' labourers, unions with a consistent anti-racist tradition, learned of the need for unity in their own ranks through their own strikes and campaigns. This applies not only to certain groups of workers but also in certain periods: solidarity with Indigenous struggle was at its height after World War II and in the late 1960s and early 1970s when the working class was on the offensive. The struggles of both strengthened each other: seeing white workers fight for their rights could inspire oppressed groups to enter battle themselves, while Aboriginal struggles could give white workers the confidence to fight for more. With most of the Indigenous population now living in big towns and cities, the prospects for this kind of united struggle are greater than ever before.

White workers in Australia have taken a stand alongside other oppressed groups as well. Australians today take equality between Catholics and Protestants for granted, but there was no such equality a century ago; it had to be fought for, and struggle in the early trade unions and Labor Party was crucial. In both Kalgoorlie and Broken Hill in the interwar years, radicals within the union movement fought for class unity across the ethnic divide.

Competition within the working class constantly throws up the potential for racism to strengthen its grip. However, the common experience of living and working alongside each other and facing oppression, even if some are more oppressed than others, also generates the potential for solidarity. The late 1960s and 1970s saw an upsurge in anti-racist working-class activism and solidarity. Alongside working-class migrant militancy, there were massive political campaigns against the Vietnam War and against apartheid in South Africa. These had to tackle the racism used by governments to justify oppression and war.

The retreat of working-class militancy since the 1980s has also seen a retreat in conscious anti-racist activism, but it has not disappeared. Years of anti-refugee propaganda has seen support for the rights of asylum seekers stuck at only 30 percent, but a series of unions have passed motions denouncing the inhumane treatment of refugees. Trade unions have been some of the most prominent organisations backing Indigenous rights in recent decades, and trade union members were among the few groups to back the Voice to Parliament in the 2023 referendum.

Even if workers do not consciously challenge racist offensives by governments, their class hostility to right-wing governments can nullify their effect. In 2014, opposition to the Abbott government's budget cuts was so great that its anti-Muslim offensive of that year did nothing to boost its popular support.

If struggle forges closer links between workers from different backgrounds, it also exposes the class differences among racial and national minorities. In tens of thousands of businesses across Australia, from convenience stores and restaurants to construction businesses, farm labour contractors and commercial cleaning companies, employers from migrant backgrounds employ workers from their "community" and rely, just like native-born bosses do, on migrant workers' fear of deportation and their lack of knowledge of employment rights to exploit them. The migrant landlord with a couple of dozen investment properties does the same with their migrant tenants. The Coalition or Labor politician from a migrant background is as committed to racist immigration policies as their native-born colleagues, while the managers of Indigenous-run housing corporations have no compunction in leasing land to offices and expensive student housing. The racist campaign to defeat the Voice to Parliament in 2023 was spearheaded by Jacinta Price and Warren Mundine, who blame Indigenous people for their own oppression and even deny the reality of the genocide that followed colonisation.

The interests of capitalists and workers are totally counterposed, no matter the colour of their skin. Migrant bosses may be subjected to racist abuse by the Australian state, but they will call on that same state, including its virtually entirely white police force and Border Force, to break picket lines, evict tenants and deport migrant workers. The growing class division within the Indigenous population is spurring the same dynamic, with Indigenous bosses and professional middle classes looking to one arm or the other of the state for protection. Any strategy to fight by workers and the oppressed that rests on some supposed common interest of all migrants or all Indigenous people is doomed to fail.

Workers can improve their own lives only by casting off the divisions spurred by racism and all such oppression. Racism, however, will never be eliminated so long as capitalism is in place. It is too useful for the ruling class for it to abandon it. That is why the fight against racism, if it is to be successful, cannot be restricted to a liberal campaign for human rights, still less the obnoxious idea of "tolerance", but has to incorporate an anti-capitalist perspective and be led by the working class, Black and white, migrant and native-born. Racism can be ended only when the economic structures that uphold it, along with all other forms of oppression, are destroyed and replaced by a system geared around meeting people's needs, not generating profit.

Socialists must champion all struggles against racism – in their workplaces, on university campuses and in the streets. We must rebuild anti-racist politics in the workers' movement and campaign against racist ideas that divide and weaken the working class. This is a longstanding position of Marxists and revolutionary socialists – we argue that the workers' movement must consciously fight against racial oppression. First, because only the working class has a genuine interest in destroying racism and the power to win liberation. Second, because workers cannot overthrow the capitalist system unless their fight takes up the causes of all the oppressed.

In summary

Oppression is a structural phenomenon, not a matter of bad attitudes or intolerance. It is embedded in all the major structures of capitalist society, from the schools to the prisons and from business to sports and takes the form of systematic disadvantage for those on the receiving end.

The working class is the largest oppressed group in society. Oppression contributes to further exploitation, and exploitation is itself a form of oppression. Other layers of society are also oppressed based on gender, sexuality, race, physical traits and age. The ruling class fosters oppression because it weakens the working class and assists the capitalists in exploiting the working class by keeping it divided. Capitalism needs oppression but did not invent it. It has appropriated older forms and has moulded them to its own needs.

Racism was developed over the years in response to a need for the capitalists to justify the human degradation of slavery and colonialism and, since then, has been a cornerstone of the smooth functioning of economic exploitation across the planet. It does not remain the same, however. As capitalism changes, so too does racism. Racism can be mobilised by the ruling classes across the world at times of crisis, change and challenge because it is such a malleable ideology and set of practices. Racism has been used against many targets and is cloaked in many designs. However, its basic premise remains the same – to "divide both to conquer each". Despite its surface modifications, racism is always used to pit workers against each other and to entrench the rule of the capitalist class.

Working-class people can be and often are racist, but they have no material interest in racism. So, the ruling class's attempts at fostering racist hostility are not always entirely stable. This means racism can be challenged and overcome. The brutality and unfairness of capitalism can reveal to workers, both Black and white, who their real enemies are. The everyday grind of capitalism, marked by regular economic crises and wars, can lead to a questioning of society and a challenge to racism.

Because racism is part and parcel of the capitalist system, the fight against racism requires a challenge to capitalism if it is to win. Previous struggles against racism, from the civil rights campaigns in the US to the immigrant and Indigenous struggles in Australia, while inspiring, have not struck at the heart of this system. While some Indigenous people and oppressed migrant groups have escaped the worst aspects of racial oppression and, in some cases, have joined the oppressors themselves, for the vast majority of those oppressed by racism, life continues to be wracked by hardship. Their hopes for social and economic equality have been dashed. Ending the structural racism that blights the lives of so many people means eliminating the capitalist system that constantly reproduces it.

Notes

1. This chapter incorporates extracts from: Priya De, "What's the point of racism?", *Red Flag*, 18 February 2022; Jordan Humphreys, *Indigenous Liberation and Socialism*, Red Flag Books, 2023; Louise O'Shea, "The problem of identity politics", *Red Flag*, 6 July 2017; Diane Fieldes, *Land Rights Now*, Socialist Alternative, 1997; Mick Armstrong: "Aborigines: problems of race and class" in Rick Kuhn (ed.), *Class and Struggle in Australia*, Pearson Longman, 2005; Tom O'Lincoln, "From invasion to resistance", *Red Flag*, 25 January 2014; Phil Griffiths, "Racism: whitewashing the class divide" in Kuhn, *Class and Struggle in Australia*.

2. Karl Marx, *Capital*, Vol. I, chapter 31.

3. Stella Young, "Why fund NDIS? Because one day you might need it", *The Drum*, 1 May 2013.

4. Bridget Brennan and Kirstie Wellauer, "More evidence of 'genocidal killings' of Aboriginal people in frontier times, University of Newcastle research reveals", ABC News, 16 March 2022.

5. Andrew Amoils, "Where and why millionaires are migrating in 2023", https://www.henleyglobal.com/publications/henley-private-wealth-migration-report-2023/global-insights.

6. Rayan Tamer, "Pacific Islander farm workers demand justice after claims of 'modern slavery'", SBS News, 6 February 2022.

7. For more of the history of Aboriginal resistance from this period onwards and its links with the working-class movement and the Communist Party, see Humphreys, *Indigenous Liberation and Socialism*.

8. Ben Schneiders, *Hard Labour: Wage Theft in the Age of Inequality*, Scribe Press, 2022.

9. Privilege theory extends far beyond racism and is often used to explain every form of oppression, which creates ever-more complex hierarchies of privilege and oppression that end up in a tangle of indeterminacy. In this chapter, I focus on racism. For extended critiques of privilege theory, identity politics and settler colonialism theories, see Sarah Garnham, "The failure of identity politics: A Marxist analysis", *Marxist Left Review*, 22, Winter 2021, and Jordan Humphreys, "Capitalism, colonialism and class: A Marxist explanation of Indigenous oppression today", *Marxist Left Review*, 21, Summer 2021.

10. Australian Human Rights Commission, "Racism. It Stops with Me", https://itstopswithme.humanrights.gov.au.

11. Australian Human Rights Commission, "Racism. It Stops with Me".

12. Warriors of the Aboriginal Resistance, "Manifesto", 2014; https://paytherent.net.au/about-us/; Clare Land, *Decolonising Solidarity: Dilemmas and directions for supporters of Indigenous struggles*, Bloomsbury, 2022 [2015].

13. Cited in Humphreys, "Capitalism, colonialism and class", p.77.

14.   Rana Ayyub, "The world continues to ignore the radicalisation of India", *Washington Post*, 17 October 2022; Ayanda Charlie & Tamasin Ford, "Inside South Africa's Operation Dudula: 'Why we hate foreigners'", BBC News, 18 September 2023.

15.   Frederick Douglass, *My Bondage and My Freedom*, ed. William L. Andrews, University of Illinois Press, 1987, p.188.

16.   John Maitland, "A look at Mabo mining myths", *Common Cause*, 58 (7), August 1993, p.7.

Chapter eight

Women's and LGBTI oppression[1]

According to the materialist conception, the determining factor in history is, in the final instance, the production and reproduction of immediate life. This, again, is of a twofold character: on the one side, the production of the means of existence, of food, clothing and shelter and the tools necessary for that production; on the other side, the production of human beings themselves, the propagation of the species.

—Engels, *The Origins of the Family,*
Private Property and the State, 1884

S EXISM IS OBSERVABLE VIRTUALLY EVERYWHERE TODAY. The almost universal question asked upon the arrival of a new baby – "Is it a boy or a girl?" – points to the primacy of gender as a social category. It informs how people relate to each other; if it's a boy, he'll have toy trains and tractors and be treated as a self-confident child who enjoys rough play. A girl will be smothered with coos, dolls and dulcet tones of speech. This life-determining identity plays a large part in setting up the opportunities open to individuals and how governments, employers and family treat us. From our first days of school, we are subjected to sexist conditioning. There are different uniforms, bathrooms and sporting teams, even entire schools, for boys and girls. Girls are expected to do well in humanities and arts and crafts but less so in maths and science.

Sexism is also central to shaping our sense of self-worth and identity. Advertising featuring degrading or patronising images of women is used to sell everything from washing-up liquid to bank loans. Pop culture is saturated with demeaning, hyper-sexualised or otherwise stereotyped portrayals of women. Consumer goods, from cars to toys and even pens, are designed and marketed in a highly gendered way that borders on the ludicrous. Childcare is expensive and hard to access, and women continue to carry the major burden of domestic work in the home, especially when there are children. And, as the Everyday Sexism Project and #MeToo movement have confirmed, women experience sexual harassment, family violence and rape at disturbing levels.[2]

Gender roles, the socially created expectations of what constitutes a man and a woman, are widely thought to be the natural result of biology: women are "empathetic" while men are "analytical". This kind of argument has been used for centuries, in various forms, to explain the allegedly innate inferiority of women. Although neuroscientists have shown no fundamental distinction between the brains of men and women, the idea that men and women operate in separate mental worlds is used to reinforce in the minds of the oppressed that they are trapped within the limits society has set for them. Yet, when it comes to medicine, until recently, experiments and medical models were all based on the male body. So, conditions specific to the female anatomy still go undiagnosed or are treated inappropriately. Marxists reject the false binary of men and women and the prejudices and stereotypes that go with it.

Women remain oppressed despite the significant gains made since the 1960s. Women today, at least in most of the developed world, are free to take out bank loans, stay at work after marriage and enjoy at least a modicum of legal protection from rape by their husbands, rights that did not exist several decades ago. Nor are girls raised today to think their highest mission in life is to get married and have babies, as their grandmothers were. But sexist discrimination, stereotypes and attitudes still shape women's expectations and achievements in life. The achievement of formal legal equality and the entry of a minority of women into the ranks of the ruling class has not created a situation where most women are on an equal footing with men.

This is because, for all the changes in women's lives, the basis of sexist oppression has not been eliminated. The fundamentals of capitalism upon which oppression rests have survived the challenges of the 1960s and '70s and remain intact. Bosses continue to rely on the exploitation of the majority to keep their profits rolling in, and they benefit from the additional exploitation and oppression of women that occurs as part of that process. And women continue to be subject to the pressures and demands of the family unit, with the myriad responsibilities this entails. These are the two related pillars on which women's oppression today rests.

Women in the workforce

Women now form one-half of the Australian workforce, and the vast majority will spend most of their lives working for a wage. But while at work, they are systematically disadvantaged. Women are much more likely to work part-time, which is a crucial contributor to their lower pay and status at work. Women also tend to be concentrated in female-dominated occupations and these are low-paid jobs, such as sales assistants, nurses, clerks, carers, primary school teachers, teachers' aides, hospitality, cleaners and receptionists.[3] But in every industry and occupation, women earn less than men, nearly 30 percent less in construction, finance and insurance, and professional, scientific and technical services. Getting promoted or attaining higher qualifications is no protection against lower pay: male managers, professionals and tradespersons are paid substantially more than women. The outcome is that women earn, on average, 23 percent less than men.[4] Lower pay and career breaks mean that women also have significantly lower superannuation balances, setting them up for hardship in old age.

Women workers face a series of other barriers that disadvantage them, both economically and socially.[5] The cost and limited availability of childcare often make it impractical for both parents with preschool children to work. Because women typically earn less than men, women in heterosexual relationships are much more likely to drop out of the workforce to care for young children than men. Economic necessity dictates, for all but the wealthy, that the higher-earning parent continues working while the other takes a break, regardless of the wishes of those involved. This reduces women's earning capacity and associated financial independence in the immediate and long term and reinforces the idea that women's key responsibility and natural inclination involve caring for others, with paid work having to fit in around these demands. If men take up sexist ideas of women's supposed inferiority and sexism, this undermines women's confidence at work, undermining the capacity for collective struggle, directly helping the bosses.

Economic inequality does not affect all women in the same way. For Indigenous women in remote communities, the issues they face – including unemployment, lack of services, the threat of incarceration or having their children stolen – differ from those affecting women in low-paid industries in the big cities. So, too, do those facing refugee women or women with disabilities. But a common theme running through the experience of oppression among different groups of women is inadequate income, discrimination at work and lack of access to services and disadvantage relative to the men in their lives. Across the board, the workplace is a crucial area where women's oppression is keenly felt, whether due to low pay, poor conditions, lack of adequate support or outright exclusion leading to poverty. This experience shapes and affects the self-confidence, economic independence, personal choices and standard of living of most women.

Women who belong to the upper middle class sometimes experience discrimination, but their privileged position protects them from its roughest edges and makes them beneficiaries of the system that oppresses their sex. Take Kathryn Campbell, the head of the Department of Human Services between 2011 and 2017, who oversaw the Robodebt scheme that manufactured fake Centrelink debts and sent threatening letters to hundreds of thousands of the country's poorest people, many of them women, to compel them to repay their imaginary debts. Campbell was eventually forced to resign in disgrace from the public service in 2023, but not before she had destroyed the lives of many working-class women and men.

Or take Margaret Gardner, Governor of Victoria. Gardner was appointed to the position in 2023 after nearly two decades as a vice-chancellor at RMIT and Monash University, where she was paid a salary of $1.2 million. Gardner set herself up as an advocate for women but turned a blind eye to years of underpayment of thousands of casual staff, low-paid tutors and research assistants, the majority, likely again, to be women, robbing them of at least $8.6 million.[6] Or businesswoman Sarina Russo, whose job agency has earned hundreds of millions of dollars from government contracts to harass the unemployed through "mutual obligation" schemes. Russo herself is "worth" $260 million.

Women make up one in eight of the world's billionaires. The richest woman is L'Oréal cosmetics heir Françoise Bettencourt Meyers, "worth" $100 billion in 2023, money made from an industry that explicitly relies on gender stereotypes that lead women to use cosmetics to boost their confidence in their appearance. Her investment fund backs enterprises such as private hospitals, which rely on thousands of low-paid women to keep boosting her wealth.[7]

Ruling-class women who have children and full-time careers also rely on low-paid women for childcare and domestic services.

Far from sharing common interests with working-class women, female heads of government departments and corporations and the super-rich directly benefit from and perpetuate the oppression of other women. There can never be meaningful solidarity between these women and those they oppress.

Women and the family

Historically, women's oppression has been rooted in the institution of the family. The family is not unique to capitalism but has existed in various forms for thousands of years. The idealised model of the nuclear family that dominates under capitalism has been adapted from preceding forms of class society. In chapter four, we saw that egalitarian relations between men and women predominated for most of human history. This changed with the emergence of class differentiation, a process that was complex and uneven. It took place over thousands of years (and not until colonial invasion in the eighteenth or nineteenth centuries in some areas of the globe, including Australia).

To explain how women's oppression became integral to class societies, we need to uncover the relationship between objective developments in production and changes this brought about in social relations, including how reproduction was restructured. Early anthropologists, mostly male, assumed a strict division of labour between women and men in pre-class societies. The "Man the Hunter" view assumed that this role meant they dominated, and women's oppression was universal. Gradually, the radicalism of the 1960s had a big impact on thinking, and researchers began to accept that oppression of women or any other group did not exist in such societies as there was no material basis for such a thing. A considerable body of anthropology shows that in societies such as the !Kung of the Kalahari Desert and the Mbuti of what is now the Democratic Republic of the Congo, women, until recently, took part in decision-making as equals with men, controlled their own sexuality and contributed as equals to productive activity.[8] By the late 1980s, Richard Lee, a renowned anthropologist, accepted, with little controversy, that:

> Before the rise of the state and the entrenchment of social inequality, people lived for millennia in small-scale kin-based social groups, in which the core institutions of economic life included collective or common ownership of land and resources, generalised reciprocity in the distribution of food, and relatively egalitarian political relations.[9]

This is the consensus that unites the research brought together in the 2014 *Oxford Handbook of the Archaeology and Anthropology of Hunter-Gatherers*.[10] While there are many gaps in what is known with certainty, we can confidently state that humans lived free of oppression for most of our history.[11]

With the division of society into classes, women's oppression became entrenched in the new structures that enforced inequality and exploitation. Around 20,000 years ago, as the last Ice Age began to come to an end, gatherer-hunters settled at least seasonally where rivers and coastlines swollen by melting ice sheets created new areas of abundance. Over time, by management of fish stocks and some rudimentary horticulture, they could produce something of a surplus above the everyday needs of the community. At first, this did not change the egalitarian, collectivist nature of society. But gradually, this surplus required some management. Archaeologists and anthropologists think that responsibility for this would have been allocated to trusted individuals, groups, or perhaps religious figures – any of whom could have been women, given their equal status with men. This point is important because social theorists have often assumed that the inequalities of our society are universal, and so they assume only men controlled the surplus. These individuals or groups played a necessary social role involving reciprocal responsibilities, coordinating increasingly complex production methods, and storing and distributing resources as needed. For thousands of years, this did not give them undue power over society, even though they may have a high status and access to extra wealth.

But over time, this led to a cleavage in society where those with control over the surplus emerged as a ruling group backed up by coercive power to enforce their decisions, whether or not others agreed. For this group to develop the mentality of ruling exploiters, they would have had to come to identify the interests of society with their control of production. They did not necessarily think of themselves as introducing oppressive relationships. The long-term evolution of class and state structures was not a seamless process. And it occurred in different ways in different parts of the world. There is evidence that emerging ruling groups could well have met with resistance from both women and men. So, to maintain their authority to manage the surplus, they would most likely have begun to codify the obligations and rights of community members. And as they became more controlling, their position was increasingly entrenched by rules and laws, so society's expectations changed. Gradually, any challenge to them would have become a crime against not only them but against society.

As ruling groups made efforts to stamp their authority and control over society, they began to control women's sexuality, abolishing their former sexual freedom and equality with men. This was critical if they were to consolidate their position, with the wealth they controlled passing from one generation to the next. Thus, an increasingly repressive cycle ends with the woman as "a mere instrument for the production of children", as Engels put it. He identified this as "the world historical defeat of the female sex", which had taken centuries to arrive at this point.[12]

As Marx and Engels argued, the ideas of society are necessarily the ideas of those who rule. So once ruling circles accepted new attitudes toward women, they would naturally impose those ideas on the exploited. That exploited men could well be producing an increasing percentage of the surplus while women were being encouraged to bear more children as future labourers to be exploited would have underpinned this process.

The capitalist family

If women have been oppressed since the division of society into classes, the family as we know it today was established as the result of the specific development of capitalism. The historical path this transition took was not smooth. The Industrial Revolution in England had a severe effect on the newly emerging working class by undermining old family ties. Everyone – men, women and children – was forced into long hours of back-breaking labour. The result was a collapse in life expectancy and a soaring rate of infant mortality. While new labour was available from displaced peasants and rural workers coming to the new industrial towns in search of work, this was a situation the capitalists were happy with. But at a certain point, that source of labour began to dry up, and the more far-sighted bosses began to realise they needed to ensure the reproduction of a working class at least healthy and alert enough not to fall asleep at the machines. And more and more, they needed an educated, skilled workforce.

The solution they came up with was the nuclear family. This is hardly surprising when we consider that the bourgeoisie themselves lived in the family. Workers fresh from the countryside were used to working and living in peasant families. It was accepted without question that women should be responsible for childcare and most domestic duties. The second half of the nineteenth century saw a massive ideological campaign by the middle and upper classes in Britain to reverse the trend away from the working-class family and to force women more decisively into the roles of wife and mother. This was backed up by attempts to address at least the worst aspects of working-class life, especially those that endangered women and their ability to produce healthy children.

The same process was repeated here in Australia. The family was even more severely disrupted because of the transportation of convicts and the general lawlessness of the frontier society in the first years of the nineteenth century. Shortages of labour were acute in the early years of the colony because of the distance from the home country and the lack of free settlers. This pushed the colonial ruling class to find a solution even earlier than in Britain. Connell and Irving comment on the earliest signs of changing attitudes among the colony's ruling class:

> In the 1820s, a tightening began. The movement in England by evangelicals against the sexual laxity of the aristocracy soon acquired colonial agents. The Protestant clergy were prominent... Particular venom was directed against the homosexual relationships formed by many convicts and pastoral workers, though unmarried women got a fair pasting as sluts and whores. The 1812 Parliamentary inquiry into transportation had hardly raised a question about sex; the 1837 inquiry and report positively smouldered with innuendo, scandal and moralising.[13]

Connell and Irving situate the attempts to confine women to the home, to establish the "feminine" stereotype, firmly in the ruling class's drive to stamp their authority on the new colony. They argue that women "disappeared into domesticity in the age of the bourgeois ascendancy". From then on, we no longer see women entrepreneurs like Mary Reibey or Rosetta Terry, who had run successful businesses and been prominent in other public ventures in the earlier years of the settlement.[14]

Caroline Chisholm, a noted philanthropist, led the way in the campaign to establish the working-class family in 1847. She advised the British government that if they wanted to establish a "good and great people", they must appreciate that:

> For all the clergy you can despatch, all the schoolmasters you can appoint, all the churches you can build, and all the books you can export, will never do much good without what a gentleman in that Colony very appropriately called "God's police" – wives and little children – good and virtuous women.[15]

Connell and Irving argue that "by the 1860s, the lack of parental guidance and education among working-class children was recognised as a major problem of social control".[16] After the 1870s, living standards declined as the cities grew rapidly. In the 1880s, infant mortality rates were higher in Sydney than in London. The campaign for the family was even more strident here than in

Britain, and it was led by the ruling class, male and female, and its middle-class supporters, both male and female.

This argument is not meant to idealise workers. Sexist ideas about women are as old as class society. It is not surprising that male workers were sexist and accepted the standard stereotyped view of women. But this does not mean they strove to establish the stifling, restrictive existence of the nuclear family. It simply means they were the product of given social relations not of their own making.

It was the ruling class, via magazines produced for workers, who argued for women to become homemakers, wives and mothers above all else. That is why every mass-circulation magazine and every middle-class voice proclaimed the virtues of womanhood – a certain kind of womanhood, that is (as they still do today). And the overwhelming arguments for women to be primarily housewives came from women.[17] There was nothing unusual in that. Women in ruling groups throughout history have benefited from and enforced the exploitation and oppression of women. Such women promote the stereotypes that justify systematic discrimination, even against themselves within their circles, to maintain their class's power and prestige. While ruling-class women experience oppression, they also have access to power and wealth by virtue of their class position, which depends on maintaining both the class and gender oppression of those their class exploits.

The family and women's oppression today

The stereotypical nuclear family of a working father, housewife and several children was dominant only for a relatively brief period, from the late nineteenth century to the 1940s. Since that time, gender roles and families have changed substantially.[18] People marry later, and many more never marry. In 1971, just under two-thirds of adults aged over 15 were in a registered marriage; today, less than one-half. De facto relationships, what used to be called "living in sin", were not even recorded in the 1971 Census; today, 12 percent of the population over 15 are in such relationships. Twelve percent of adults are divorced or separated, three times as many as in 1971. There are more than one million one-parent families today, about one in six of all families. Women are putting off having children – nearly two-thirds of babies are now born to women aged 30 and over, compared to one in five in 1975 – and having fewer of them.

Domestic life is much less the centre of women's existence today. In 1971, the Census found that "home duties" was the "major activity" for two-thirds of women (the figure for men was not even recorded). Only one-third said that "working in a job" was their major activity (with 98 percent of men falling into this category).[19] Today, most women work in jobs for most of their lives after completing their education, taking only a few years off at the birth of a child or children.

LGBTI families are much more common today. Even though homophobia still leads to substantial under-reporting of same-sex relationships, the 2021 Census still found 80,000 same-sex couple households, up from a reported 10,000 in 1996.[20]

The family has not, however, disappeared. In 2021, nearly 17 million people lived in a couple family, with or without children, and another 2.8 million people lived in a one-parent family, accounting in total for 80 percent of the population.[21] Fourteen million people lived in households with children. The family continues to play a key economic and social role in capitalism today. It is the key mechanism through which the vital work of caring for, nourishing and socialising children is done. This is an essential service from the bosses' point of view, as without human beings being prepared and healthy enough to work and to accept as compensation only a fraction of the value they produce, and without a new generation to work in the future, there would be no profits, no capital accumulation and no attending power and privilege for the capitalist class.

Most times, workers themselves understandably desire to replicate the institution of the family, readily carry out its functions with no expectation of compensation and accept family duties as their personal responsibility. This makes the family an extremely efficient and cost-effective mechanism for carrying out these tasks, which explains the robust and enduring nature of the family structure under capitalism.

Women occupy a subordinate position within this structure. Their roles as wives, partners and/or mothers are loaded with expectations and responsibilities that do not apply to men. So, although women and men in Australia spend almost an equivalent number of hours working every week (when the total of waged and unwaged work is considered), women still perform a greater share of the unpaid work around the home, particularly when they are caring for young children.[22] And the sense of responsibility for the home and children continues to be felt more keenly by women.

The family is also the basis for the gender roles that play such a pernicious part in undermining the confidence, aspirations and participation of women in public life. Whether it's the degrading and objectifying image of women as sexually attractive partners – now covering almost every stage of women's and girls' lives, not only young adulthood – potential child-bearers, unfulfilled and childless career women or the demeaning and patronising presentation of women as sink-bound figures in perpetual maternal service (or a combination of the above), the various stereotypes of women rest ultimately on the roles they are expected to assume within the family structure.

The unpaid and unappreciated nature of women's work both in and outside of the home underpins the economic disparity within male-female relationships and contributes to a situation where many women, to a greater or lesser extent, depend on male earnings. The rising cost of housing means that even where women earn a reasonable full-time wage, they are often not in a position to leave unsatisfactory relationships because they cannot afford to start out again.

Combined with the lack of adequate childcare and maternity leave, this creates a situation where women are more likely to be marginalised and disadvantaged in the workplace and economically dependent at home. Frequently, public policy and service provision acts to promote and further entrench this reality.

All in all, work and family have a reciprocal relationship that entrenches women's subordination. Expectations in the family funnel women into part-time work in low-paying industries. Insufficient parental leave and the unwillingness of bosses to give fathers time off for childcare reinforce gendered roles in the family.

The whole set-up continues the gendered socialisation of men which begins at birth, thereby fostering sexist assumptions among men, creating a further barrier to working-class unity. So, sexism underpins the nuclear family and the underpayment of women but also because by encouraging demeaning and hostile attitudes to women on the part of men and discouraging women from fighting their oppression, it makes it harder for workers as a class to fight for a world based on social solidarity. It is, therefore, incumbent on socialist men to reflect on their own behaviour in their personal lives and to stand up against sexism wherever we witness or experience it, at work, on social occasions, in our families and in our personal lives.

LGBTI oppression

The idealised nuclear family contributes not only to the oppression of women. It is also the basis for the oppression of those whose gender identity or sexuality does not conform to the heterosexist norm consistent with the family structure. The liberation of women is therefore inseparable from that of lesbians, gay, bisexual, transgender, non-binary and intersex (LGBTI) people.

The level of acceptance in society of LGBTI people in Australia and many other countries has increased over the past few decades. There are more positive portrayals of LGBTI characters in film and television, and marriage equality is now a reality in many countries, usually won through popular struggles or votes. In several countries, including Australia, there have been some limited legal improvements for trans people, especially in granting access to gender-affirming healthcare. Overall, attitudes towards trans people have been improving. Research from 2021 found that 78 percent of Australians agree that trans people deserve the same rights and protections as other Australians.[23]

LGBTI people still face discrimination on a range of fronts. Before children understand or experience their own sexual desires, they know which ones are punishable. For gay and lesbian kids, heterosexual-focused sex education compounds the feeling of being sick or a freak. For transgender people, the struggle for free expression and recognition feels almost insurmountable. For trans and non-binary people, navigating a world so fixated with (biologically determined) gender is a minefield of prejudice, discrimination, anguish and pain.

The persecution and oppression of trans people is worth particular consideration because it has become a key focus for conservatives and the far right in recent years. In part, this is because of the increasing visibility of trans people and increasing support for trans rights. At the same time, the far right have been on the offensive and, in several places, have been successful in pushing back trans rights. The US is one of the best-known examples of this. Beginning with President Trump's "bathroom bills", there has been a concerted campaign from Christian groups and Republicans to prevent trans people from accessing healthcare and legal rights, and an aggressive ideological campaign against the so-called "trans lobby" and its "corruption" of children.

Conservatives ferociously oppose trans rights because they believe in the strict social order of the traditional nuclear family. Biologically determined gender roles are key to upholding this institution, and the very existence of trans people is seen as a challenge to it. "Trans critical" feminists are another group that actively promotes transphobia. They use the issue of women's oppression to attack trans rights, and their focus is on trans women, who they argue are men dressed as women. In the UK, groups such as "Standing for Women", founded by right-wing transphobic activist Kellie-Jay Keen, have campaigned for years to prevent trans people from being legally recognised as their gender. In most places, including Australia, trans-critical feminists, though despicable bigots, are a minority that makes little impact, but beyond the campaigns of these groups, trans oppression and transphobia exists more broadly in society.

The result of social disapproval and institutionalised proscriptions is that self-loathing and mental anguish are part and parcel of growing up LGBTI. Bullying, familial rejection, street attacks and discrimination in housing and jobs are common. LGBTI people experience higher rates of food and housing insecurity and often lack even a small cash buffer to meet unexpected expenses. Little wonder that 41 percent of young LGBTI respondents to a 2013 University of Western Sydney (UWS) survey had thought of self-harm or suicide, 33 percent had harmed themselves and 16 percent had attempted suicide.[24]

Oppression of LGBTI people has to be understood historically because the ongoing and insistent homophobia and transphobia they face today are not found in all societies throughout history. Attitudes and practices regarding sex, sexual behaviour and gender identity have differed significantly over time. As historian David Greenberg has noted, "some societies are comparatively hostile to homosexuality, while others tolerate or even fully accept and institutionalise it" – perhaps most famously the ancient Greeks.[25]

There are many other examples of same-sex relations in different cultures. In the Gold Coast in West Africa (now Ghana), lesbian affairs were virtually universal among unmarried Akan women. In Southern Africa, Khoikhoi men who entered a compact of mutual assistance often become lovers. Censure or approval of particular sexual acts or gender identities is closely related to dominant family types, which are, in turn, related to the needs of production or the class that dominates production. In pre-class societies, men and women enjoyed a high level of sexual autonomy in which sexual relationships were not tied to immediate family responsibilities or moral obligations. The absence of any systematic classification of people based on their gender or restrictive moral codes regarding sexual relationships explains the acceptance among Native Americans of "two-spirit people", a cross-gender transfer in which men or women who preferred the activities of the opposite sex could be initiated into that gender and would carry out economic and social duties according to their acquired gender, including sexual relations and marriage with members of the same sex. Such "two-spirit people" could be found across a wide range of pre-colonial civilisations of Central America, including the Aztecs and Mayans, and have also been part of Ashanti culture in West Africa and in other African civilisations.

The relative fluidity of acceptable sexual roles and identities began to change in Western Europe from the 1300s onwards, during the development of the world market prior to the rise of industrial capitalism. From this point on, sexual behaviour came to be acceptable only when it was linked to procreation in families. Sexual relations that happened outside that relationship, which were considered "crimes against nature", were punished. Homosexual acts came to be considered unnatural, but so did heterosexual anal and oral sex and even masturbation – all of which fell under the more broadly defined category of "sodomy". In this period, same-sex acts were sometimes proscribed and sometimes punished, but there was no conception of homosexuality as an attribute of a particular type of person.

It was not until the 1870s that there developed, in Europe and the United States, the concept of "the homosexual" as a distinct identity. The medical profession pioneered the idea of the homosexual as a person or people who, by their very nature, deviated from societal and biological norms of sexuality. LGBTI people were defined in this pseudo-scientific ideology as sick, degenerate or mentally defective. The European labelling of LGBTI people in this way was then carried over to their colonial possessions, and it is here that the anti-gay laws for which countries like Uganda are now notorious were established.

Homophobia and transphobia are thus intimately linked to the broader structure and organisation of society. Capitalism promotes the family and denigrates non-conformist sexualities and gender identities in part to corral men and women into roles suitable for raising and socialising the next generation of workers. But it also has a useful effect in helping to discipline the working class. Homophobia and transphobia have an effect in pushing down gays and lesbians and trans people at work. Rather than face bullying and social exclusion, many LGBTI people hide their sexuality or gender identity at work. This brings its own problems: if LGBTI workers cannot be confident to tell their workmates what they did at the weekend or can't put a photo of their partner on their desk or must hide their gender identity, it can undermine their confidence in the workplace. By denying workers control over the very things that in our society are supposed to be the most personal and intimate, the ruling class is better able to exercise control over what seem to be the much bigger questions of public life, like industry, social services and the workplace.

Some trans people and trans advocates describe transgender identities as biologically determined, as an argument against the idea that certain genders naturally correlate with sex. Marxists, however, reject the idea that any gender is innate. Gender is a social construct that arose with sexism and has become deeply entrenched. Gender is socially assigned based on biological sex, but, because humans are various and our societies are complex, gender is also something that is based on human agency and self-identification. There is nothing more or less "real" about the gender identity of those who take on the gender they have been biologically and socially assigned and those who take on a different gender. Socialists should confidently argue that trans women are women and trans men are men. Fighting for the rights of both trans and non-binary people is important in its own right and as part of challenging LGBTI and women's oppression as a whole.

Sexual freedom and the sex industry

Women's changing role in the workforce and their greater economic and social independence, combined with readily available and reliable contraception, have broken women free from many of the most stultifying stereotypes and sexual codes that they were expected to conform to in the 1950s. It is now acceptable for women to engage in premarital sex, to cohabit with their partner and to divorce. While greater sexual freedom for women is welcome, there are contradictions inherent in it as well. Too often, it has been used to repackage sexism and has led to the creation of new and equally oppressive stereotypes, often more insidious because they use the language of "liberation" and "empowerment" to market the continuing subjugation of women.

What is called sexual freedom in capitalism is a culture that encourages both women and men to view women primarily as objects to provide sexual gratification to men rather than autonomous human beings with desires, thoughts and agency. This creates pressure on women to fulfil impossible and harmful stereotypes, leading to a situation where women, even as young as mid-teens, are increasingly anxious to undertake plastic surgery in the pursuit of the supposedly ideal body which is projected to them through this sort of imagery. This culture expects women to actively embrace their sexual objectification rather than question or challenge the relentlessly sexist and demeaning presentation of women. The only beneficiaries of this are advertising executives, the beauty industry and associated parasites.

This is not liberation, as some assert; it has nothing to do with increasing the ability of women to fulfil their sexual desires, exercise greater control over their sexual relationships, or enjoy more pleasurable sex. Rather, it fuels greater insecurity, anxiety and abuse and exacerbates the very real daily encounters with harassment, violence and discrimination that women endure.

Worse still is the idea that has emerged on the fringes of progressive circles that women selling their bodies on the market through the sex industry is empowering. Or, if not empowering, at least something that is a legitimate choice and defended against feminist criticism. So, for example, Melbourne University academic Lauren Rosewarne argues:

> If the sisterhood can support my decision to swallow contraceptive pills or terminate an unwanted pregnancy, then there is a duty for them to support my choice to have as much or as little sex as I like and, if I so choose, put a price tag on that sex.

> For me, it's a matter of consent, of bodily autonomy. If feminists aren't fighting for my right to use my body how I choose, then they've dramatically detoured from their mission.[26]

This perspective seeks to sanitise the industry and obscure its sexist nature and is a grotesque distortion of genuine sexual freedom.

The sex industry reflects sexism, as most people engaged across its various fields – prostitution, strip clubs, camming (performing sexual acts in front of a webcam for paying clients), pornography or chat lines – are women, and most buyers are men. It therefore entrenches the most repugnant social norms, in particular the idea that women's sexuality is an object for male consumption without concern for the desire, pleasure or needs of the women involved. Outside the sex industry – where money is not involved – such relationships would rightly be considered assault and rape, not empowered and consensual.

Rosewarne defends the sex industry on the basis that the women involved choose to do so. While the coercion women in the industry experience may vary, for the vast majority, especially in the sex tourism industry of Southeast Asia frequented by Australian men, it is based on options dictated by the reality of class society, poverty and sexism. The so-called choice of such women to work in the industry is the culmination of two things – material inequality, poverty and deprivation that affect the most oppressed people in society, and the sexist ideas and stereotypes which permeate every aspect of our society that portray women as sex objects.

Violence and involvement in the criminal underworld are features of the industry, but even if the industry were fully decriminalised, that would not make it any more acceptable. While decriminalising sex work, as has occurred in Victoria and NSW, may be supportable, providing women in the industry greater opportunities to find safety and seek legal redress for mistreatment, it does not nullify the sexism inherent to the industry. The problem is not that sex work is illegal in some jurisdictions; it is that the entire industry is founded on and perpetuates the abuse of women. Indeed, decriminalisation normalises the sex industry, allowing it to spread unchallenged into the entertainment industry and broader society. Decriminalisation also gives brothel owners and pimps, whose business model depends on women's oppression, the opportunity to promote themselves as legitimate businesspeople, even "community leaders", and to receive tax and other benefits that flow from that.

The prevalence of sex work and the sexism it helps perpetuate hold back the fight for a better world, which requires that the working class be organised as a revolutionary mass that brings together all the oppressed. That involves overcoming the divisions created by sexist ideas. Working-class men cannot be genuinely anti-sexist and fight for women's liberation if they regard women as mere sex objects to be bought for their own gratification. A socialist society would abolish the sex industry because such a society would not permit women's bodies to be treated as commodities for purchase and because building a society based on human need would end the inequality and oppression that forces many women into the industry.

Socialists and the fight against oppression

The oppression of women and LGBTI people, and indeed all oppressed groups, results from the needs of class society, specifically capitalist society, which profits from it both materially and ideologically. Challenging this oppression is the duty of socialists. Socialism is not only a theory of the liberation of the working class. It is a theory of the liberation of the working class as the foundation for the liberation of all of humanity – and not only from class exploitation but all forms of oppression.

Class and oppression cannot be separated but are part of an integrated whole. Oppression cannot be overcome unless capitalism is overthrown, and there will always be pro-capitalist reactionaries while the system continues. But no successful challenge to capitalism is possible unless it also involves a struggle against oppression in its many forms. This is true not only because without supporting these struggles, it is impossible to build the working-class unity that is required to challenge the system, but also because the struggles of the oppressed have a powerful role to play, as they always have, in the struggle for a different world. Revolutionary movements demand much more of workers than simply seizing control of production. Revolutions are, in Lenin's words, "festivals of the oppressed and exploited", in which all those in society who have been beaten down in various ways rise up and challenge everything that has held them down, crushed their lives and stultified their personalities.[27]

A moral identification with the oppressed and sympathy for capitalism's oppressed victims is a necessary component for building links between different movements and struggles of the oppressed, but it is not sufficient; there must also be a material and social basis, some common ground, that provides the basis for such solidarity. That ground is the common class interests that potentially unite workers of all races, ages, nationalities, ethnicities, languages, abilities, sexualities and gender identities.

We only have to look at the experience of fighting the oppression of women and LGBTI people in Australia to see the importance of left-wing politics and working-class struggle. Class politics was an important feature of the fight for equal pay, for example. Although unions had been prominent in the campaign since the late nineteenth century, it was the left-wing metal industry and meat industry unions, both of which were male-dominated, that were crucial to winning the demand in the 1960s.[28] The Communist Party of Australia (CPA), whose members occupied leading positions in these unions, played an important role in this struggle and had done so since the 1920s. When Zelda D'Aprano, a CPA member employed by the meat workers' union, chained herself to the doors of the Arbitration Commission in 1969 to support equal pay for women, her action symbolised a campaign that had been going for decades. In 1969, the Arbitration Commission made its first ruling for equal pay, and under pressure from the unions, a second in 1972, which importantly established the right to equal pay for equivalent work.

The timing of this victory was no accident. This was a period when the working class was strong, confident, well-organised, and prepared to take on the bosses and government. The strike rate was rising, workers had won victories, and unionism was growing on many fronts. This politicisation, combined with industrial confidence, meant the workers' movement readily took up issues of broader social justice as well as the immediate workplace conditions.

For this reason, it was unions with the greatest commitment to and experience of fighting the bosses and government, not the most female-dominated ones, which were at the forefront of the campaign for equal pay. These unions, despite being largely male-dominated, recognised the importance of unions taking up broader issues of social equality as a means by which to both weaken the bosses and strengthen the bonds of solidarity between workers that are necessary for victory. So it was the meat and metal workers' unions that pushed for equal pay, the militant Builders Labourers Federation which campaigned for women's right to work on building sites and struck in defence of gay students in the 1970s, and the Communist-aligned waterside workers and seamen who took up issues of Aboriginal rights.

The late 1960s was a period of advancement not only for working-class women but also for LGBTI people. The riot at the Stonewall bar in New York in June 1969 kicked off the gay liberation movement around the world. After years of police harassment, patrons at the Stonewall bar in Greenwich Village, an underground bar frequented by working-class lesbians, gays and transgender people, many of them Hispanic and Black, had had enough one night and fought back. A three-day riot ensued, and when word got around the city hundreds of other LGBTI New York residents turned up to join the fight. The mood was exhilarant:

> Graffiti calling for Gay Power had appeared along Christopher Street. Knots of youth – effeminate, according to most reports – gathered on the corners, angry and restless. Someone heaved a sack of wet garbage through the window of the patrol car. On nearby Waverly Place a concrete block landed on the hood of another police car that was quickly surrounded by dozens of men, pounding its doors and dancing on its hood… trash fires blazed, bottles and stones flew through the air, and cries of "Gay Power!" rang in the streets as police numbering 400 did battle with a crowd estimated at 2,000.[29]

The rioters had had enough of hiding and cowering, and within days a new organisation, the Gay Liberation Front (GLF), had been launched. Soon, gay liberation groups were being established in Canada, across Europe and in Australia and New Zealand. The connections between gay liberation and the wider revolutionary mood among many millions of young people is indicated by the very name Gay Liberation Front, which was taken directly from the National Liberation Front fighting in Vietnam against the US invasion. "Gay Power" borrowed from the well-established slogan "Black Power", and one of the first GLF actions was to issue a call for solidarity with imprisoned Black Panther leader Huey P. Newton. Most of the early activists in the movement around the world had been involved in the struggle against the Vietnam War and saw themselves as revolutionaries. They were not interested in piecemeal reform but wanted to overturn the whole oppressive system that bred not only homophobia but war, racism and exploitation. The founding statement of the GLF declared:

> We are a revolutionary group of men and women formed with the realisation that complete sexual liberation for all people cannot come about until existing social institutions are abolished. We reject society's attempt to impose sexual roles and definitions of our nature. We are stepping out of these roles and

simplistic myths. We are going to be who we are… Babylon has forced us to commit to one thing – revolution.[30]

When asked what they meant by "revolution", GLF responded:

> We identify ourselves with all the oppressed; the Vietnamese struggle, the third world, the blacks, the workers, all those oppressed by this rotten, dirty, vile, fucked up capitalist conspiracy.[31]

After the first Gay Pride demonstration in the following year, the GLF paper *Coming Out* reported: "These days mean something special for every lesbian and homosexual – they mark the first time that gays took to the streets, angry, proud, joyous – tearing down the prisons in which sexist society has chained us".[32]

In Australia, the more respectable homophile groups that campaigned merely for "acceptance" gave way in 1972 to a more radical gay liberation current under the impact of developments in the United States.[33] The movement surged for a couple of years, spurred on by left-wing groups and student radicals, and then retreated before advancing again from 1975 and culminating in the 1978 Mardi Gras march and police riot. At the 1978 Mardi Gras, 53 people were arrested when police attacked the 2,000-strong march demanding the repeal of homophobic laws and expressing solidarity with struggles elsewhere. One reveller recalls:

> The Stonewall riots may have been a watershed for the worldwide gay and lesbian rights movement but for Australia, the Mardi Gras of 1978 was our first very public act of resistance and a turning point in our struggle against oppression.[34]

As with the fight for women's oppression, the struggle for LGBTI rights found a hearing in the working class in Australia. In 1973, the NSW BLF took industrial action in defence of the rights of a gay student, Jeremy Fisher, who had been thrown out of his college at Macquarie University. Later that same year, again at Macquarie, teacher trainee Penny Short lost her scholarship after publishing an explicit lesbian poem. When the Education Department refused to reinstate the scholarship, the Teachers Federation pledged its support, and the Communist-dominated BLF threatened to stop work on the campus. By 1976, anti-discrimination policy had been adopted by all the peak union councils, including the ACTU, and by 1978, these councils had specific lesbian and gay anti-discrimination policies in place. These had an important effect in shifting policy within the ALP. Again, it was the left unions that took the lead. The Plumbers Union, with CPA members in leading positions, adopted a policy stating: "Homosexual discrimination is an industrial issue and has to be fought on that basis".[35]

Struggle in the workplaces, in the schools and in the streets has won important gains for women and LGBTI people. It has shown the potential that exists to unite all workers, both those subject to particular forms of oppression and those who are not, behind the demand for equality and liberation. This is not always an automatic process. In the 1960s and '70s, for instance, resistance among some workers to the fight for equal pay had to be challenged and overcome through political argument by socialists committed to the cause of women's liberation and who could convincingly demonstrate that a win for women was a win for the entire working class. There is the potential to unite the working class around these demands because, ultimately, the entire class will benefit from the improved position of their female and LGBTI workmates. The same cannot be said for female CEOs or LGBTI bosses.

Important as they are, partial struggles can never entirely eliminate the basis for continued sexism, homophobia or transphobia. For that, a revolution is needed to overthrow capitalism, transform the social and economic structures that give rise to inequality, and lay the basis for a society where people can relate to each other as equals, not as exploited and exploiters. The gains won for women and LGBTI people when the Russian Revolution of 1917 was at its height, including voluntary no-fault divorce, abortion on demand, an end to child illegitimacy, same-sex marriage and gender reassignment surgery, demonstrate the liberatory potential of the working class when it is able to exercise control over society.

In summary

The position of women has changed since the 1960s, but oppression continues. Women's oppression rests on two key pillars: women's direct exploitation in the workplace and their subordinate role in the family, the means by which the capitalists ensure the maintenance and reproduction of the working class. The unequal position of women at work helps the capitalist class by degrading pay and conditions for all workers by increasing competition among their ranks and weakening union organisation.

Women are divided by class, and their experience of oppression is mediated by their class position. Ruling-class women benefit from the oppression of working-class women because it boosts the profits from which they live.

The family is a source of oppression because it foists the burden of raising the next generation of workers squarely on the shoulders of women. The family is also the basis of gender roles, which impact women at every stage of their lives and afflict the lives of LGBTI people. It also plays a role in training working-class children in the discipline, subordination and respect for authority that are required in the capitalist workplace.

Attitudes toward LGBTI people have changed substantially since the 1970s, but, like women, they are still oppressed. Their oppression is not the result of religion or lack of education, but because of the regimented sexuality identified with the family. Homophobia, as in the oppression of people identified by their sexuality, only took shape in the latter half of the nineteenth century, at the same time as the nuclear family was consolidated.

Both homophobia and sexism play an important role in enhancing social control. The more oppressed women and LGBTI people are, the more the working class is weakened. Challenging oppression is therefore essential for socialists, not just because of moral repugnance at injustice, but because fighting sexism, homophobia and transphobia is necessary to break down divisions in the working class and to fight for unity.

Sex work is not liberation or empowering, but epitomises some of the most degrading elements of women's oppression.

The history of the struggle for women's liberation and LGBTI liberation shows that it advances most rapidly as part of the broader struggle for social liberation in which the working class plays a central role. This is not only because most women and LGBTI people are working-class but because the working class has an interest in fighting the capitalist system that oppresses both groups and also is best equipped to do so.

While women and LGBTI people can make progress under capitalism, real liberation requires the smashing of capitalism.

Only in a society in which human satisfaction comes before the profits of a tiny few can there be genuine liberation and freedom from the pressure to conform to gender roles. Such a society would not depend on the private nuclear family, which puts women in a hidden subordinate place and punishes those who defy the regulation of a gender forced upon them. It would banish all political content from the categories of "men", "women", "gay", "straight", "trans", "cis" and so on. This would lay the basis for a society in which gender and sexuality is either a purely personal matter or no matter at all.

Notes

1. Priya De and Sarah Garnham wrote the sections on sex work and transphobia in this chapter, respectively. It also includes extracts from: Louise O'Shea, "Marxism and women's liberation", *Marxist Left Review*, 7, Summer 2014; Sandra Bloodworth, "The origins of women's oppression – a defence of Engels and a new departure", *Marxist Left Review*, 16, Winter 2018; Sandra Bloodworth, "The poverty of patriarchy theory", *Socialist Review*, 2, 1990; Paul D'Amato, *The Meaning of Marxism*, Haymarket Books, 2014 and Hannah Dee, *The Red in the Rainbow: Sexuality, Socialism and LGBT Liberation*, Bookmarks, 2010. Thanks to Sandra Bloodworth for her extensive comments on this chapter.

2. www.everydaysexism.com.

3. Australian Bureau of Statistics, Census of Population and Housing: *Income and work data summary, 2021*.

4. Women's Gender Equality Agency, *Australia's Gender Equality Scorecard December 2022*, 2022.

5. Diane Fieldes, "The impact of women's changing role in the workforce", *Marxist Left Review*, 6, Winter 2013.

6. Ben Eltham, "The piece Monash Uni refused to publish on wage theft and Victoria's new governor", *Crikey*, 22 August 2023.

7. https://www.forbes.com.au/news/billionaires/the-top-10-richest-women-in-the-world-2023/.

8. Karen Sacks, *Sisters and Wives: The past and future of sexual equality*, Greenwood Press, 1979; P. Draper, "!Kung Women: Contrasts in Sexual Egalitarianism in Foraging and Sedentary Contexts", in R. Reiter (ed.), *Toward an Anthropology of Women*, Monthly Review Press, 1975.

9. Richard Lee, "Reflections on primitive communism", in T. Ingold, D. Riches and J. Woodburn (eds), *Hunters and Gatherers*, Vol. 1, Oxford University Press, 1988, cited in Chris Harman, *A People's History of the World*, Bookmarks, 1999, p.3.

10. Vicki Cummings, Peter Jordan and Marek Zvelebil (eds), *The Oxford Handbook of the Archaeology and Anthropology of Hunter-Gatherers*, Oxford University Press, 2014.

11. Bloodworth, "The origins of women's oppression".

12. Friedrich Engels, *The Origins of the Family, Private Property and the State*, 1884.

13. R.W. Connell and T.H. Irving, *Class Structure in Australian History*, Longman Cheshire, 1982, p.65.

14. Connell and Irving, *Class Structure*, p.65.

15. Anne Summers, *Damned Whores and God's Police*, Penguin, 1977, p.291

16. Connell and Irving, *Class Structure*, p.126.

17. Connell and Irving, *Class Structure*, p.53.

18. Data in this paragraph are drawn from Census of Population and Housing, 30 June 1971, Bulletin 1: Summary of Population, Part 9: Australia; Australian Bureau of Statistics, "Household and families: Census", 28 June 2022; Australian Bureau of Statistics. "Births, Australia.", 2022; Australian Bureau of Statistics, "Australian women having fewer children and later in life", Media Release, 18 October 2023.

19. Census of Population and Housing, 30 June 1971, Bulletin 1: Summary of Population, Part 9: Australia. The Census records an "other category" totalling 700,000 out of 8.7 million adults, presumably the unemployed, the retired, those living with disabilities or in institutional care or prisons. I have excluded them from this count.

20. The ABS did not collect data on same-sex couples before 1996.

21. Australian Bureau of Statistics, "Household and families: Census", 28 June 2022.

22. Australian Bureau of Statistics, "How Australians Use Their Time", 7 October 2022.

23. Equality Australia, "New research shows overwhelming support among Australians on trans equality", 18 January 2021.

24. LGBTIQ+ Health Australia, *Snapshot of mental health and suicide prevention statistics for LGBTIQ+ people*, October 2021; Ana Hernandez Kent and Sophia Scott, "LGBTQ+ adults report struggles with food, housing costs and mental well-being", Federal Reserve Bank of St Louis, 20 December 2022; Kerry Robinson, Peter Bansel, Nida Denson, Georgia Ovenden and Cristyn Davies, *Growing Up Queer: Issues Facing Young Australians Who are Gender Variant and Sexually Diverse*, Young and Well Cooperative Research Centre, Melbourne, 2014.

25. David Greenberg, *The Construction of Homosexuality*, University of Chicago Press, 1990, p.3.

26. Lauren Rosewarne, "Radical feminists' objection to sex work is profoundly un-feminist", *The Conversation*, 9 August 2017.

27. V.I. Lenin, *Two Tactics of Social Democracy in the Democratic Revolution*, 1905.

28. Liz Ross, "What do we want? Equal Pay! When do we want it? Now!", *On Line Opinion*, 22 June 2011.

29. John D'Emilio, *Sexual Politics, Sexual Identities*, University of Chicago Press, 1983, p.232.

30. Jeffrey Weeks, *Coming Out: Homosexual Politics in Britain from the Nineteenth Century to the Present*, Quartet Books, 1990, p.188.

31. Dee, *The Red in the Rainbow*, p.96.

32. Dee, *The Red in the Rainbow*, p.98.

33. The following account of the gay liberation movement in the 1970s relies heavily on Liz Ross, *Revolution is for Us: The Left and Gay Liberation in Australia*, Interventions, 2013.

34. Ross, *Revolution*, p.88.

35. Ross, *Revolution*, p.82.

Chapter nine

The Russian Revolution[1]

We have seen above, that the first step in the revolution by the working class is to raise the proletariat to the position of ruling class to win the battle of democracy.

—Marx and Engels, *The Communist Manifesto*

THE RUSSIAN REVOLUTION WAS THE MOST IMPORTANT EVENT in modern history. It was the first time that the working class anywhere in the world had taken power. The Russian Revolution demonstrates the capacity of workers, even in the most repressive circumstances, to rise up against capitalism, smash the state and institute workers' democracy. That Russian workers did this in wartime conditions and in the face of repression by a highly authoritarian government that had at its disposal a fearsome army, millions strong, of police and spies makes their feat even more impressive. The revolution inspired workers worldwide, and even today, it speaks to us vividly and with force.

The lessons of the revolution are essential to anyone in the twenty-first century who wants to fight the capitalist system. We learn from the Russian Revolution about the conditions that can give rise to revolution and how a seemingly impregnable political order can fall to pieces in a matter of days. We learn about the ability of even the most downtrodden groups to make a stand during a revolution, shaking off decades of oppression. We see how the act of winning victories emboldens the working class to demand more and, conversely, how setbacks demoralise the working class and allow reactionary forces to seize the initiative. We witness the existence of "dual power", an unstable situation in which neither the capitalist class nor the working class can definitively impose its will on the other, but which must give way ultimately to the defeat of one of them – either through counter-revolution or workers' power. We see how, during the revolution, workers come to an understanding of their own power and the nature of the forces arrayed against them. Finally, we learn about the role of a revolutionary party, the obstacles placed in the way of a revolution by liberals and reformist forces, and the need for revolutionaries to convince workers who may initially be under the influence of these obstructive forces.

It is for all these reasons that conservatives, liberals and reformists alike have attacked the revolution from the moment it took place. They say that it was a coup, the act of a tiny minority lacking popular support, or that Lenin and Bolsheviks tricked the working class into supporting them, or that it led inexorably to Stalin's gulags. They want to convince us that the revolution was a terrible thing and that the goal of workers' power is an impossibility, to persuade us that the current capitalist system, with all its horrors, is the best humanity can come up with. Understanding what took place is, therefore, not merely a history lesson but is critical in asserting the viability of a socialist solution to the ills of the world. In this chapter, we look at the revolution itself; in chapter ten, we turn to its defeat.

The February Revolution

On 23 February 1917, in the Russian capital, Petrograd (known before World War I and today as St Petersburg), many thousands of angry women textile workers celebrated International Working Women's Day by stopping work and holding protest meetings in their workplace. Before the morning was out, tens of thousands were on strike. They were fed up with low-paid, 12-hour working days in dirty, unhealthy conditions. Joined by housewives, angry at food shortages and war privation, these women then left the mills and moved in their hundreds from factory to factory, calling out other workers on strike and engaging in violent clashes with police and troops. They demanded solidarity and insisted on action from men, especially those working in skilled engineering and metal factories who were regarded as the most politically conscious and socially powerful of the city's workforce. Gordienko, a worker at the Nobel Machine-Construction Factory, recalled:

Masses of women workers filled the lane, and their mood was militant. Those who caught sight of us began to wave their arms, shouting: "Come out! Quit work!" Snowballs flew through the window. We decided to join the demonstration. A brief meeting took place outside the main office near the gates, and we poured out into the street.[2]

By the end of the day, over 100,000, one-third of the city's industrial workforce, were on strike. The days that followed, in which working-class women continued to play a leading role, were to result in the downfall of the repressive and hated tsar.

On the next day, 24 February, meetings, proclamations and marches continued as increasing numbers of workers joined the strike wave. By the end of the day, 200,000 had swelled the ranks of the angry strikers demanding bread to feed their starving families. Calls for an end to autocracy and the war soon followed. The soldiers wavered. A friendly wink from one of them told the workers that the troops would not fire on their demonstration. On the 25th, thousands of students joined the workers' demonstrations, and now 240,000 were on strike. Recalling the experience of the 1905 revolution in Russia, workers in Petrograd immediately set up a workers' council, or soviet, with elected representation from the big workplaces.

By the afternoon of the 27th hundreds of thousands of workers, soldiers, students, and housewives were in the streets of Petrograd. Many of them were armed. The regime was shaking, and on hearing that similar numbers of workers in Moscow had also taken to the streets, wrecked police stations, freed political prisoners, created a workers' committee and inspired soldiers to refuse to fire on them, the tsar abdicated, and government authority collapsed. A revolution begun by working women, some of the most oppressed and downtrodden in Russian society, had deposed one of the most authoritarian regimes in Europe in a few short days.

Background to the revolution

Before the revolution, Russia was a mass of contradictions. Superficially, the country was a backward relic of feudalism in a continent that, over the preceding two centuries, had been shaken by revolutions. The tsar, whose family, the Romanovs, had ruled Russia for three centuries, was an absolute monarch, one of the last in Europe. The political order was dominated by the landlords who owned enormous estates and who, until as recently as 1861, had also owned the peasants who laboured on their lands. They were backed by the generals, who ruled with an iron fist over the world's biggest army, made up mainly of poor peasants. The Russian Orthodox Church, a large landholder, cloaked the tsar, the landlords and the high command with religious authority.

Most of the population were peasants, many of whom had suffered from their "emancipation" in 1861, an act that had enriched a minority, plunged many others into debt and driven their sons and daughters to the big cities to find work. The peasants had periodically risen in revolt but were crushed brutally on every occasion.

The tsar also ruled over a vast population of oppressed nationalities stretching all the way from the border with Germany in the west to the Pacific Ocean in the east and from Finland in the north to the borders of Persia (now Iran) and Afghanistan in the south. Within this territory, Jews were cruelly persecuted at the hands of tsarist legal restrictions and lynch mobs. The Russian state's constant imperial expansion brought it up against other powers, particularly the British, the Turkish and, lately, the Japanese.

But Russia was also rapidly plunging into industrial capitalism. It was late to develop compared to Britain and Germany, but when capitalism arrived, it came with a bang. Moscow was the centre of the textile industry, but St Petersburg had the biggest factories, which were mostly foreign-owned or financed. International investors brought the latest industrial techniques with them, meaning that St Petersburg simply skipped the early stages of the Industrial Revolution and jumped straight into factories that were larger than the biggest in Western Europe.

With the factories came hundreds of thousands of workers, many wrenched straight from the smallest villages. Almost overnight, a Russian working class came into being, three million strong. Russia under the tsar was an autocracy. There was no parliamentary democracy, no free press and no free trade unions or labour parties. Political opposition in the cities was severely repressed, meaning that the main workers' parties, the revolutionary Bolsheviks and the more moderate Mensheviks, had to operate in secrecy, their leaders often in prison or in exile abroad. Denied any rights, the workers' struggles for economic and political justice had an explosive content.

The late-developing Russian capitalist class was divided. Many elements of this class benefited from and warmly supported the tsarist order. A minority, however, resented the autocratic rule of the tsar, arguing that the parasitic feudal order limited capitalist development. They looked to countries like the United States, a capitalist country but with a republican and parliamentary system that they believed fostered rapid economic growth. These capitalists, along with some landlords, demanded a Constituent Assembly to prepare a new constitution and the election of a democratic parliament, which would introduce measures to speed up capitalist development. But, being capitalists, they also feared the threat posed by the new working class upon whom their fortunes depended – by the turn of the century, these workers had shown that they were prepared to fight for their rights as strikes mushroomed. Also, dependent on European loans, the Russian capitalists were averse to doing anything to upset the country's relations with Britain and France, the homes of their major financiers. This section of the capitalist class sponsored a new party, the Constitutional Democrats, better known as the Cadets.

The result of all these factors was a country that appeared stable, but which was experiencing immense social strains. Unexpected defeat by Japan in a war in 1904 sparked off the first revolution of 1905. Defeat showed the empire's vulnerability, not only to Japan and other rival imperialists, but also to the population at home.

On 30 January 1905, a demonstration in St Petersburg of workers and peasants demanding that the tsar ease the lot of the poor was put down bloodily, with the loss of 1,000 lives.

Such massacres had occurred many times before. This time, however, it sparked off a year of revolutionary struggle. Peasants rose in their millions to take the land and drive out the landlords. Soldiers and sailors revolted against their officers. But it was the working class in the biggest cities that led the way with a series of massive strikes for improvements in their conditions, an end to punitive treatment by supervisors and bosses and an end to autocracy.

The workers' struggle culminated in a general strike in St Petersburg in October and a rising in Moscow in December. Amid these strikes, the St Petersburg workers set up a city-wide soviet, or workers' council, composed of deputies elected from the big factories. This was the first time in world history that workers had set up such an organisation, an example of how a relatively "backward" group of workers can, at times, leap ahead of their more experienced brothers and sisters.

Initially, the job of the Petersburg Soviet was simply to coordinate the struggle, but soon it started to perform the functions of a government, organising food supplies, housing, transport and so on. Leon Trotsky, who was not a member of the Bolsheviks at this stage, was elected as its chairperson. That a 26-year-old Jewish revolutionary could be elected chair of the main workers' body is some sign of the transformation that was taking place in workers' consciousness because of the struggle. Other cities followed with their own soviets.

Sections of the middle class and capitalists initially supported the demand for political reform, but the tsar's offer of a token parliament, the Duma, saw them surrender to the regime, their timid demand partially met, while repression and general exhaustion saw the working-class challenge recede.

The next six years were ones of tsarist repression, including the execution, imprisonment or exile of thousands of workers, peasants and revolutionaries. Leaders of the Bolsheviks such as Vladimir Lenin and independent Marxists like Trotsky fled to Western Europe or the United States.

Working-class struggle surged again from 1912 and lasted two years. But the outbreak of World War I struck a blow against the rising struggles. Because the Bolsheviks were intransigently opposed to the war, there was working-class resistance, but middle-class hysterical patriotism made it difficult to build a broad movement. The Bolsheviks' isolation was made all the harder to bear because of the betrayal by most of the social democratic (i.e. labour) parties around Europe, which, having just passed resolutions opposing imperialist war on the eve of August 1914, now called for their members and supporters to go off and kill the workers of the other belligerent countries.

The war brought poverty and misery to millions of workers and peasants as they eked out a living. In the trenches, the men suffered terribly. Of course, as in all wars, the rich in the cities and landlords in the country were not starving. Far from it. Anger grew.

Bread shortages in Petrograd were simply the issue that lit the fuse of simmering discontent in February 1917. One historian says: "Strikes and demonstrations became daily events, with student demonstrations at Petrograd's higher educational institutions and strikes in other cities adding to the growing turmoil".[3] On 22 February, the day before International Working Women's Day, management at the giant Putilov metal works, Russia's largest plant, had locked out 30,000 workers.

The impact of the February Revolution

The overthrow of the hated tsar filled workers and soldiers with elation and expectations. Decades of oppression and the hatred it bred drove workers to take their chance at a better life. One account by a leading participant describes the situation thus:

> The revolution had spread like wildfire over the whole face of Russia. From all parts, there came hundreds and thousands of reports about the upheaval that had taken place easily, instantaneously, and painlessly [and] sprinkled with living water the oppressed and stagnant masses of the people and called them to life.[4]

Workers created factory committees that challenged capitalist rule by demanding the eight-hour day, decent wages and equal wages for women workers with men. They did not just demand things from the bosses; they began to take charge, organising everything from the soap in the washrooms to fixing light bulbs, organising rosters, outlawing excessive overtime, disciplining unruly workers, controlling drunkenness, presenting cultural events and organising political discussions – and, of course, taking control of production. Workers in the factories now began to lift their heads and demanded respect from the bosses. They burned factory rulebooks and lists of fines and other punishments for breaking the humiliating rules of the old order. To make their point, workers, especially women, spent the first weeks after the revolution throwing out managers known for humiliating workers, with the worst treatment meted out to those with a reputation for sexual harassment. Servants started to answer their masters back, and the masters complained to each other in their clubs about how unruly they had become.

The upsurge in political activity threw open the doors of culture to the working class. The factory committees brought in students to teach workers to read and write. US socialist journalist John Reed tells the story of arriving in Riga in the Russian colony of Latvia:

> [G]aunt and bootless men sickened in the mud of desperate trenches; and when they saw us, they started up, with their pinched faces and the flesh showing blue through their torn clothing, demanding eagerly, "Did you bring anything to read?".[5]

It wasn't just reading. Lectures, meetings and debates issued forth in huge numbers in the factories, the barracks, in theatres or any other venue available. Every street corner was a tribune; tram carriages, railway stations, wherever people gathered became the scene of impromptu debates.

The factory committees had to defend their gains. They quickly organised workers' militias to defend their factories from attack by reactionaries. Volunteers in the militia did not live separately from the rest of their class. They did not have their own special barracks or stations like the police but lived their lives immersed in the working-class communities they served. It was common for each individual factory contingent in the mass protests of workers to be headed by the factory committee and deputies to the soviet, followed by the armed factory guard and then the rest of the workers. The role of militias was to be a kind of advance guard of the broader working-class movement. The militias relied on strict standards of admission. "The candidacy of each prospective member," one volunteer recalled in his memoir, *Notes of a Red Guard*, "was discussed at a session of the factory committee, and applicants were often turned down on the grounds that they were regularly drunk, or engaged in hooliganism, or had behaved coarsely with women".[6] The family circumstances of the potential recruits were also taken into account, disallowing sole providers, for instance.

The upheavals in working life, along with expectations for a new way of living, had a big impact on personal relationships. Women would no longer tolerate domestic violence: they had made a revolution, so why would they put up with abuse at home?

Soldiers, too, through elected committees, stood up to their officers. When the government tried to enforce discipline in the army, the newly formed Petrograd Soviet was forced by the sheer rage of the soldiers to pass a new directive promoting a complete restructuring of the army, including the prohibition of disrespectful or demeaning address by the officers, the recognition of the soldiers' committees and the abolition of the death penalty. And when officers purported to represent the soldiers, they got short shrift. John Reed describes a meeting of the Congress of Soviets in Petrograd:

> An army officer attacked the Congress and claimed to be speaking for "delegates at the front". Soldiers in uniform began to stand up all over the hall. "Who are you speaking for? What do you represent?", they shouted. "You represent the officers, not the soldiers. What do the soldiers say about it?" There were jeers and hoots.[7]

The February Revolution purged the entire tsarist apparatus. As one account put it:

> In the Russian provinces, the revolution had destroyed the old administration. Czarist officials, from provincial governor down to the lowliest village policeman, were deposed within a few days or weeks, and some were arrested.[8]

Unfinished revolution

The workers' victory in February did not mean an end to class society. The struggle had only just begun. The situation that resulted from the February Revolution is known as dual power, where workers have challenged the ruling class for power but have not actually destroyed all the vestiges of the institutions used by the old ruling class to maintain their authority.

In Russia, dual power existed between the soviets, set up by workers, and the new Provisional Government. The Petrograd Soviet was the first to assemble even before the tsar had been overthrown, but quickly, soviets were formed in many of the nation's cities, from Finland to the Pacific. In the Spring of 1917, some 400 soviets sprang up; by August, 600, and in October, 900, by which stage they represented about one-third of the population of the Russian Empire.[9] The soviets provided the backbone of the revolution and held reaction at bay. The Petrograd Soviet was an institution of mass working-class democracy, with representation from every big factory and barracks. The masses of workers, soldiers, the poor and the oppressed looked to the soviets for their salvation. Trotsky recalls: "In the eyes of those masses, the Soviet was an organised expression of their distrust of all who had oppressed them".[10]

The Provisional Government in Petrograd was the other contender for power and stood in complete contrast to the soviets. It was a self-appointed body made up of former members of the old tsarist Duma (the fake parliament). On 1 March, the new government elected a ministry staffed almost entirely by wealthy landlords and industrialists and headed up by a prince. The sole exception to this collection of dignitaries was Alexander Kerensky, a member of the peasant party, the Socialist Revolutionaries (SRs), who, as Trotsky says, "was not a revolutionist, [but more of] a provincial lawyer who had defended political cases". The Provisional Government was the government of the bourgeoisie. Its members had done their best to patch up a deal with the tsar to save the monarchy, but they had been overwhelmed by the mass movement. Following the tsar's fall and bending to the spirit of the times, they now spouted revolutionary phrases, but this was only for show. Their entire project was to limit the social gains of the revolution.

The two sides – the popularly elected soviets and the unelected Provisional Government – seemed to be on a collision course. One of the main demands of the February Revolution was for peace and an end to the war. The common people also expected the land to be distributed to the peasants, and workers would control industry. The Provisional Government was opposed to all three. It was terrified of the working class and sought to maintain good relations with Russia's wartime allies, Britain and France. It was determined to fight the imperialist war, maintain the property of the rich and consolidate capitalist rule. For the time being, however, it was in a precarious position – it was a head without a body. Guchkov, the minister of war, admitted in March that:

> The Provisional Government has no real power: the troops, the railroads, the post and telegraph are in the hands of the Soviet. The simple fact is that the Provisional Government exists only so long as the Soviet permits it. The military especially can issue only orders that do not openly contradict those from the Soviet.[11]

This situation could not last indefinitely – either the capitalists and landlords would claw back control, or they would lose their power, and the masses would begin organising a new society. Exploiting classes cannot share power with those they exploit; why would the majority submit to a tiny minority (as the ruling class are) if they had access to power? Both sides were to come to recognise this reality. The history of the months from February to October 1917 is about the struggle to resolve this standoff.

The Provisional Government started with a huge advantage. Even though it exercised no real power in the days after the revolution, the organisation that did, the Petrograd Soviet, endorsed it as the legitimate government of the country despite its refusal to implement the demands that had led the masses to make the February Revolution.

Why did the Petrograd Soviet leadership hand power to the Provisional Government? In short, the Petrograd Soviet, and others that followed in its wake, was dominated by the SRs, a party with its base in the rural and urban petty bourgeoisie, and the Mensheviks, a reformist working-class party. Neither was interested in pushing the revolution beyond parliamentary democracy, a situation in which the soviets would eventually be dissolved. Both were firmly opposed to any transition to socialism. Menshevik leader Irakli Tsereteli, soon to become a minister in the Provisional Government, explained his party's position to Nikolai Sukhanov, a member of the Soviet executive, later to join the radical wing of the Mensheviks:

> Of course, you'll have to talk about the necessity of a compromise with the bourgeoisie. There can be no other road for the revolution. It's true we have all the power, and that the government would go if we lifted a finger, but that would mean disaster for the revolution.[12]

Only in a few naval bases close to Petrograd, the Vyborg district of Petrograd, home to the biggest engineering works, the central industrial belt around Moscow, and Finland, did the Bolsheviks exercise any influence.

The Mensheviks and SRs dominated the soviets in the early months of the revolution for several reasons. First, because the electoral system for the soviets artificially boosted the representation of the soldiers who were more conservative than the factory workers – most of them were, after all, of peasant stock. The Petrograd Soviet, for example, was made up of 2,000 soldier representatives but only 800 worker representatives, despite workers being three times more numerous. Some of the soldier representatives were from the professions – lawyers, journalists and professors – who adopted a socialist label to win support in elections but were no more than liberals. In other cases, they were soldiers themselves but put up by soldiers' organisations, which were still at this stage strongly for the continuation of the war. The system of electing soviet deputies also favoured those from smaller plants with few traditions of militancy and where class relations between bosses and workers were not so sharply polarised as in the big factories. The SRs, in particular, won support from the soldiers and those from the smaller factories. The more general explanation why the Petrograd Soviet voluntarily transferred power to the Provisional Government is the ideological domination of the petty bourgeoisie in the early months of the revolution and the political immaturity of the working class. The petty-bourgeois layers – small proprietors, shopkeepers and minor officials along with the peasants – had been oppressed and exploited for years but awoke with the February Revolution and began to involve themselves in political activity. Their ideology was individualist and pro-capitalist, not collective and socialist. They were for reform, not proletarian revolution. This petty-bourgeois layer, tens of millions strong, shaped mass politics at this stage. The SRs were the natural political representatives of these layers and accordingly drew support in both town and country. Not for the first time, nor the last, reformists were initially the main beneficiaries of a revolutionary upsurge.

The Mensheviks and SRs were helped, too, by the fact that confusion reigned among the Bolshevik leaders in Petrograd. They were for pushing the struggle as far as it would go but believed, in line with party orthodoxy at this point, that Russia must undergo a period of bourgeois democracy before it would be ready for a socialist revolution. In a meeting of the Petrograd Soviet executive committee on 1 March, not one Bolshevik representative opposed handing power to the Provisional Government.

If the Provisional Government depended on the support of these moderate leaders in the soviets, it certainly did not trust them. Its actual power base was the industrialists and big landowners who tried to push back against the working-class offensive. The liberal press, supposedly for democratic rights and progress, also campaigned against the soviets. The Provisional Government declared it would, at a suitable but unnamed date, call a Constituent Assembly that would eliminate the authority of the soviets. The problem the Provisional Government faced was that the insurrectionary mass would not easily be pacified without some redress of the misery and distress that had led to the revolution. But this mass did not yet understand that for this to happen, they had to take matters into their own hands, thereby resolving the contradiction of dual power in favour of the working class rather than the capitalists. It would take time and experience for the masses to understand this. Until then, the Provisional Government had been thrown a lifeline by the Petrograd Soviet executive.

Lenin reorients the Bolsheviks

On the eve of the February Revolution, Trotsky was the only leading Russian Marxist who believed the coming revolution would allow workers to prepare to take power and begin the worldwide struggle for socialism. Lenin had argued that because Russia was so backward, the revolution would be limited to establishing a democratic, capitalist republic.

However, once the February Revolution happened, Lenin abandoned this limited perspective and argued that the working class now had an opportunity to take power. When he arrived back in Russia in early April from exile in Switzerland, he caused a storm within the Bolshevik leadership. The leaders who had been in Russia or returned before April supported the continuation of the war "to defend the revolution" and backed the Provisional Government "insofar as it struggles against reaction and counter-revolution".

Lenin attacked this position, declaring to his comrades who had gathered to greet his arrival in the capital:

> Dear Comrades, soldiers, sailors and workers! I...greet you as the vanguard of the worldwide proletarian army... The worldwide Socialist revolution has already dawned... The Russian revolution accomplished by you has prepared the way and opened a new epoch. Long live the worldwide Socialist revolution...
>
> We don't need any parliamentary republic. We don't need any bourgeois democracy. We don't need any government except the Soviet of workers', soldiers' and farmhands' deputies![13]

Lenin denounced the Petrograd Soviet majority of moderate socialists, accusing them of betraying the workers. He spelled out his position in greater length in the most important document of the revolution, the *April Theses*. In this, he did not argue that the soviets could take power immediately, but, as he explained at the Petrograd Bolshevik conference of 14 April:

> The government must be overthrown, but not everybody understands this correctly. So long as the Provisional Government has the backing of the Soviet

of Workers' Deputies, you cannot "simply" overthrow it. The only way it can and must be overthrown is by winning over the majority of the Soviets.[14]

The Bolsheviks were clearly in a minority; only when the masses overwhelmingly supported the Bolsheviks' call for "All power to the soviets" would it be possible to take power and hold it. Meanwhile, the party had the task of patiently explaining.

Lenin was initially isolated among the leadership of the Bolsheviks, but his efforts to turn the party around to a consistent revolutionary stance were all the easier because the militant worker members now flooding into the party agreed with him. They wanted an end to the war and the introduction of the eight-hour day, and they supported the land being granted to the peasants. They could see that the Provisional Government was not about to make any of these a reality. They protested vigorously against the right-wing positions of Bolshevik leaders such as Stalin and Kamenev, even demanding their expulsion from the party. A mere three weeks after Lenin's arrival, his thesis that the soviets would have to take power was endorsed at a party conference. Ludmilla Stal, an Old Bolshevik, explained: "In accepting the slogans of Lenin, we are now doing what life itself suggests to us".[15]

This episode tells us a lot about the kind of party the Bolsheviks were. It was working-class in composition, whereas its opponent, the Mensheviks, had a more petty-bourgeois membership with fewer working-class supporters.[16] The Bolsheviks had weathered the period of retreat following the defeat of the 1905 revolution better than the Mensheviks because even though both factions suffered from repression, the Bolsheviks' working-class members were more loyal than the intellectuals who had flocked to the Mensheviks in 1905 but who abandoned radical politics once the counter-revolution set in.

As strikes and mass demonstrations revived in 1912, it was the Bolsheviks who came to the fore. This was illustrated by the success of their daily newspaper, *Pravda*, which combined an intransigent revolutionary line with numerous reports from workers chronicling their everyday conditions and struggles. In one year, 11,000 such workers' letters and contributions were published, and the daily circulation of *Pravda* reached 40,000. By 1914, nearly 3,000 workers' groups were contributing funds to *Pravda*, far more than were donating to the Mensheviks' newspaper, confirming the Bolsheviks' leading role among class-conscious workers. By this stage, the Bolsheviks commanded a majority in most unions in St Petersburg and Moscow.

Because the Bolsheviks were an illegal party operating in a country where there were no democratic liberties and no effective trade unions, they did not and could not develop a broad layer of full-time paid functionaries of the sort typical in Western European social democratic parties which dragged them to the right. The Bolshevik leadership and its local cadres were closer to the prison cell or Siberian exile than they were to ministerial posts or to trade union officialdom, and the party had no more than a threadbare administrative apparatus. This made the party relatively (although not absolutely) immune to the kind of bureaucratic routinism evident in the social democratic parties of Western Europe.

The combination of the Bolsheviks' illegal status and its proletarian composition made for an organisational structure radically different from Western European social democracy. In Russia, the absence of parliamentary elections on a geographic basis (Duma elections took place on a factory basis) and the need for secrecy led the Bolsheviks to base their organisation on the factories. This created an intimate relationship between the party and the working class. An old Bolshevik, Osip Piatnitsky, explained:

> In Czarist Russia, the cells...utilised all the grievances in the factories; the gruffness of the foremen, deductions from wages, fines, the failure to provide medical aid in accidents, etc., for oral agitation at the bench, through leaflets, meetings at the factory gates or in the factory yards, and separate meetings of the more class-conscious and revolutionary workers. The Bolsheviks always showed the connection between the maltreatment of factories and the rule of the autocracy... At the same time, the autocracy was connected up in the agitation of the party cells with the capitalist system, so that at the very beginning of the development of the labour movement the Bolsheviks established a connection between the economic struggle and the political.[17]

The Bolshevik Party was not simply the political representative of the working class but an interventionist combat party striving to lead and guide the class in all its battles.

The Bolsheviks were also a party of the youth, particularly among its activist base. This contrasted with the Mensheviks, who relied upon the more respectable, skilled upper strata who looked down on the young Bolsheviks. The relative youth of the membership gave the party a more dynamic and vigorous character and combated any tendencies to conservative routinism. And, as Trotsky argues, "At the decisive moment, the youth carried with them the more mature stratum and even the old folks".[18]

The party was a disciplined body that allowed broad debate and discussion and freedom of criticism but within the bounds of commitment to revolutionary politics. This allowed the Bolsheviks to cohere the most advanced section of the class, the most militant, class-conscious workers, to win over those workers in the middle who were subject to the influence of the Mensheviks and SRs. As Lenin wrote in *What Is To Be Done?*, which set out some principles on which a revolutionary party could be built in early twentieth-century Russia:

> [T]he stronger our Party organisations, consisting of real socialists…the less wavering and instability there is within the party, the broader, more varied, richer and more fruitful will be the party's influence on the elements of the working-class masses surrounding it and guided by it.[19]

Only by insisting on the revolutionary character of the party and the need for all members to be loyal to the revolutionary principle could meaningful debate take place and the party move forward united in action. This discipline did not rule out independent initiative from the rank and file of the party. The same repressive conditions that made unity in action a necessity also compelled the local sections of the party to act for themselves.

The outbreak of World War I threw up major challenges for the Bolsheviks. It exposed the bankruptcy of the reformist Second International, a grouping of social democratic parties across the world that supported the war. Lenin responded to the International's betrayal on a series of fronts. First, he declared the Second International dead and that a new International that would exclude reformists and comprise only revolutionary parties was needed. On a theoretical level, Lenin challenged the fatalist approach of the Second International that saw socialism as simply awaiting the working out of iron laws of history. In contrast to this, Lenin emphasised the role of revolutionaries intervening in the class struggle to push the working class forward. Lenin also sought to come to grips with the new political period ushered in by the first major imperialist war. His book *Imperialism, the Highest Stage of Capitalism*, published in 1916, aimed to show that on a world scale, revolution was now on the order of the day as imperialism marked the beginning of the decline of capitalism and the opening up of the era of "wars and revolutions". It was this belief that underpinned the call for a new International.

Finally, the war inevitably threw up the question of the attitude socialists should take to the state. The Second International believed that a revolution could be made that would leave the existing state apparatus intact. The party's role would be to take over the existing state and undertake a few changes of leading personnel and a certain reorganisation but not to change its structure fundamentally. With such a view of the tasks of the revolution, the centre of gravity of the class struggle must inevitably rest in parliament and parliamentary elections. From this, it followed that the leadership of the party must rest with its parliamentary representatives and that the role of the rank and file is essentially passive. In *The State and Revolution*, Lenin challenged this and argued that instead of taking over the state, the job of the working class and its party was to smash it. That meant a different kind of party, one in which rank-and-file militants are charged not with handing out "how to vote" cards but leading their fellow workers in building their own new state machine. And that meant championing the soviets as the basis for a new workers' state and winning the working class over to this project.

The war did not just force Lenin and his comrades to think through some crucial questions of political strategy but also how to maintain their party in the face of a crackdown on the workers' movement and the flood of militarist and chauvinist propaganda that swept the country. The first 12 months were the toughest, with mass arrests of leading Bolsheviks, including the five Bolshevik Duma representatives who had been the de facto internal leadership of the party (many experienced party leaders, including Lenin, were in exile at this time). Repeated raids on the Petrograd committee, which had assumed the leading role following the Duma arrests, then took out many other party leaders. Many of those arrested were imprisoned or exiled, and many were sent to the front. The party press was banned. Local party organisations were left to fend for themselves with little central direction. Strikes collapsed, and militant Petrograd workers were drafted into the army, replaced by an influx of inexperienced workers from the countryside.

In the latter half of 1915 and into 1916, workers began to recover, and strikes rose quickly. Political strikes became more common. The sailors of the Baltic fleet, most in touch with the Petrograd workers' movement, were radicalising and turning against the war. The Bolshevik Party showed its resilience; local party structures were able to organise despite the lack of contact with Petrograd, throwing themselves into the rising tide of struggle. Membership in Petrograd, the party's strongest centre, grew from 1,200 in July 1915 to 3,000 by the end of 1916; national membership on the eve of the revolution stood at 10,000. They were not yet a mass party, nor were they in a position to direct the coming revolution – in the first days of the Petrograd Soviet, the Bolsheviks had only 40 deputies – but the party had established a footing among the militant sections of the working class even if it still suffered constant harassment by the authorities, a shortage of funds and a lack of intellectuals to write material for the party.

As the February Revolution broke out, the efforts of the Bolsheviks to hold on in the first years of the war paid dividends. They had maintained their organisation and its close connection with thousands of militant workers. Many of these workers had joined the Bolsheviks in the upsurge before the war, and even if many were no longer members in February 1917, they bore the stamp of revolutionary Bolshevism in which they had been trained. So it was that even though the February Revolution appeared to be spontaneous, with no party, not even the Bolsheviks, calling for a rising, Bolshevism played a vital role. Answering his own question, "Who led the February revolution?" Trotsky answered: "We can then answer definitively enough: Conscious and tempered workers educated for the most part by the party of Lenin". It was these workers who helped Lenin prevail against the right wing of the party in April.

Workers' power

The factory committees that mushroomed in the early weeks of the revolution were the wellspring of workers' democracy. Committee members were accountable to their fellow workers. Rules drawn up by city-wide conferences decreed that elections should be held every six months. But an election could be called by the monthly workplace general assembly to which delegates were required to report and in which final authority was vested. Steve Smith comments in his history of the Petrograd committees:

> Members of the committees…viewed their "office" as a means of effecting economic and social change. They…enjoyed no stability of tenure… they were not appointed by some impersonal organisation but elected by and accountable to the workers.[20]

In addition to the factory committees, district and city-wide soviets provided what Sukhanov called "the very crucible of great events, the laboratory of the revolution".[21] Soviets took various forms; a majority comprised representatives of workers or workers and soldiers. Some were exclusively of soldiers, and others of peasants or a mix. Unlike factory committees, which were based on individual enterprises, soviets brought together representatives from multiple workplaces, army barracks, naval bases or villages, and were elected on a pro-rata basis. They varied enormously in size and political sophistication. The Petrograd Soviet of Workers' and Soldiers' Deputies, which was the inspiration for all others, had thousands of deputies, with plenary sessions resembling mass meetings. In Moscow, where separate soviets were established for workers and soldiers, the former had 700 deputies, three-quarters of whom were factory workers, and the rest were office workers and professionals. Other soviets had only a few dozen deputies.

In Petrograd and Moscow, lines of division between the Bolsheviks on one hand and the SRs and Mensheviks on the other were very clear following Lenin's return; in the smaller cities and towns, the distinctions were much less obvious. In Petrograd and Moscow, the Soviets established specialist committees to handle diverse tasks, each with office staff and budgets, but elsewhere, organisation was much more rudimentary. In Petrograd, the executive, elected at plenary sessions of the Soviet, comprised 42 voting members directly elected from the factories and barracks and also non-voting representation from trade unions, the socialist factions of the Duma, district councils and provinces. Some soviets were city-wide, others represented individual districts, some of which, such as the militant Vyborg Soviet in Petrograd, attained national prominence. In June, the first national congress of workers' and soldiers' soviets was convened, bringing together 1,090 delegates from hundreds of workers', soldiers' and peasant soviets.

Like members of the factory committees, soviet deputies were recallable at any time. They remained in the workforce or army, and so shared the consequences of the decisions they voted for in the soviets. Unlike parliamentarians in a capitalist democracy, soviet deputies could not hide behind the actions of courts or civil service bureaucrats – they were working bodies, and deputies had to take responsibility for their decisions. And workers exercised their democratic rights with enthusiasm. If deputies displeased their voters – whether for being too conservative or, on occasion, too radical – they were dumped. The Mensheviks and SRs saw soviets as temporary bodies whose task was to oversee the local organs of government in the interests of revolutionary democracy before passing into history once a Constituent Assembly was elected. In practice, however, soviets quickly became organs of local government, concerned with everything from food and fuel supply to education to law and order, usually competing with rival authorities that had been established for these tasks.

And then there were the trade unions which, in Sukhanov's words, "sprang up like mushrooms" in the months after the February Revolution.[22] More than 2,000 unions were formed over the course of 1917, with membership growing to 2 million by October. Like the factory committees these too held frequent meetings and regular elections. With a few important exceptions, the unions fell under the sway of the Bolsheviks as the year progressed, as workers were drawn to their slogans.

The exact responsibilities of the different layers of representation – factory committees, soviet and trade unions – were the subject of constant debate. Very broadly, the factory committees and, in Petrograd, the central council of factory committees, elected by district factory committees, concentrated on economic and internal factory issues, and the soviets on political problems. In the early days, the soviets took up the fight for workers' industrial rights as well, including the eight-hour day, minimum wages, trade union rights and formation of trade unions, unemployment relief, social security and mediation boards. In March and April, numerous local soviets won the eight-hour day, either by negotiations with the factory owners or, if they refused, as in Moscow, by simply decreeing it.

Later, the soviets extended their functions and, as Sukhanov writes, became "a state within the state".[23] In Sukhanov's account of the Petrograd Soviet: "The populace with all its demands and private, group, social and political interests, turned to it for everything".[24] To tackle the growing food crisis, for example, local soviets adopted stringent measures to alleviate hunger, including imposing bans on the export of bread, introduction of ration cards, searches of the homes of the wealthy for food and supplies. Soviets also took to granting leave to soldiers, disregarding the commanding officer's protests, intervening in labour disputes and even transferring factories to trade unions. In some regions, the soviets administered civil and criminal law, created their own factory militias, paid out of factory funds, organised workers' control over raw materials and fuel for the factories, supervised marketing and determined wage scales. Some soviets expropriated land for communal cultivation. The Kronstadt Soviet in Petrograd, where the Bolsheviks and other radicals won control in April, was the most ambitious of all, electing all commanding officers and, de facto, running the naval fortress.

The factory committees were the closest to their constituents and so were initially the most proactive and the first bodies to register the swing to the left in the working class. By May, Bolshevik motions were winning majorities in the factory committees, and their members were some of the most proactive in them. The soviets did not elect Bolshevik majorities until August. Workers changed their positions through a combination of experience and arguments. Workers' experience of bosses seeking to sabotage production at a time of growing shortages and economic crisis illustrated concretely what the Bolsheviks were arguing: only a workers' government of the soviets could make workers' control of production a reality and end the crisis. Workers' experience with the Provisional Government made them realise that only a soviet government could end the war. That the soviets represented the popular masses across whole districts and cities meant that they had the authority to organise and coordinate the struggles of the entire working class and the oppressed throughout Russia.

The first glimpse of the counter-revolution

The "revolutionary unity" that seized Russia after the February Revolution, in which everyone proclaimed themselves to be for democracy and liberty, did not survive the Spring. It was the Provisional Government's commitment to the imperialist war that began to expose it in the eyes of the masses. On 18 April, Pavel Milyukov, the Cadet foreign minister in the Provisional Government, sent a note to Britain and France, assuring them of his government's total commitment to the war. When Milyukov's note became public, Petrograd was swept with outrage and indignation. On 20 April, a mass demonstration dominated by banners with slogans such as "Down with the Provisional Government", "Down with Milyukov" and "Down with the imperialist policy" marched to where the Provisional Government was sitting. Similar protests erupted in Moscow.

This was the beginning of the struggle that would culminate in October. The deceit of the government was there for all to see. What did it mean? The Bolsheviks warned that the government did not want peace. Could they be right? On the other side, the counter-revolution began its open mobilisation. On 21 April, the centre of Petrograd was filled with supporters of the Cadets declaring their support for the government and the continuation of the war. Army officers and cadets backed them. Clashes broke out with revolutionary workers and soldiers, and shots were fired. General Kornilov, a particularly reactionary member of the high command, moved cannon into the Palace Square, a sign of things to come. The façade of a united nation had been cracked open.

The July Days

Throughout June, pressure was building in Petrograd for an armed uprising to transfer power from the government to the soviets. But Lenin still insisted that to achieve the Petrograd masses' desire for a soviet government, workers in the other industrial cities had to be convinced and more conscious of what was at stake, and the peasantry had to be mobilised into self-activity and a greater awareness of the need to transfer power. They had to understand that the Provisional Government would never meet their demands for peace, bread and land.

In the end, the Bolsheviks could not restrain the Petrograd militants. Some of their own agitators gave the impression they supported an uprising. So Lenin accepted that to minimise the danger, they would have to take part in a mass mobilisation and attempt to prevent it from prematurely overthrowing the government. Beginning on 3 July, hundreds of thousands of workers and soldiers participated in armed demonstrations in Petrograd, some involving clashes with counter-revolutionary gangs. On the 7th, the Bolsheviks called for a retreat, for which they suffered scathing attacks from militants, including some of their own members, for lack of leadership and determination.

Immediately, the government and its supporters saw a chance to destroy the Bolsheviks. They circulated every lie and slander they could dredge up. They wanted to discredit the Bolsheviks to demoralise the masses. The Bolshevik presses were smashed, and the party leaders jailed. Lenin, firmly believing he and other leaders were likely to be shot, went into hiding in nearby Finland.

For a few weeks after the July Days, the Bolsheviks seemed to be hounded on all sides. However, as Lenin had insisted, time was on the Bolsheviks' side. Their enemies could not be content with a witch-hunt against the revolutionaries. They had to smash the power of the workers' and soldiers' soviets. But any move to do this would clarify the reality of dual power in the eyes of the working class.

The counter-revolution comes out of the shadows

After the July Days, the repression became more and more vicious. It was only a matter of time until the counter-revolutionary forces attempted a death blow. The government ordered that regiments and battalions that had taken part in the armed demonstrations be disbanded. General Kornilov ordered that retreating soldiers be fired on with machine guns and restored the death penalty at the front.

Employers were sabotaging production, increasing the suffering and sense of crisis caused by growing hunger and destitution in the war-ravaged economy. They orchestrated a massive campaign of factory lockouts. The chief business organisation stepped up demands for the Provisional Government to dissolve the workers' and soldiers' soviets. In the provinces, land committees were arrested en masse. The capitalists spoke more and more of smashing the revolution. They donated enormous sums of money to Kornilov to fund a military coup. As the Bolsheviks predicted, the reactionaries were teaching the workers what the actual situation was. Increasingly, the question was posed: Who would control the production of wealth in Russia? The working class was becoming increasingly aware that it needed to take control from the bosses.

At first, Kerensky, as head of the Provisional Government, cooperated with General Kornilov's coup plans, hoping that it would leave him free to govern without opposition from his left. However, Kerensky quickly realised that his head, too, would be on the chopping block if Kornilov were successful and turned against him.

But Kerensky could not mobilise the masses to defend the revolution against his recent co-conspirator. That task fell to the Bolsheviks, who urged Russian workers to resist the coup while giving no political support to the Kerensky government. They organised to arm the working class, to mobilise the masses and urged workers to use their power to halt this mortal threat to the revolution.

Kornilov's march on Petrograd galvanised masses of people into action, transforming the situation. Under the leadership of the Bolsheviks, the factory committees of Petrograd organised detachments of Red Guards made up mostly of Bolsheviks and numbering 40,000. A gunpowder works sent a load of grenades to the Red Guards, and the Putilov iron works became a centre of resistance, working 16 hours a day to produce 100 cannon. Unarmed workers formed companies for trench digging, sheet metal fortification and barbed wire fencing. The railway workers switched the tracks, diverting troops from their destinations and sending artillery to the wrong places; they even tore up the tracks in some strategic places. The telegraphers informed the workers of Kornilov's troop movements and held up his communications.

The coup collapsed in four days. "The insurrection had rolled back, crumbled to pieces, been sucked up by the earth," wrote Trotsky in his *History*.[25] An important lesson in revolutionary strategy was established: how to form a united front with forces that, in the long run, have to be discredited and defeated in order to defend the interests of the working class.

The Provisional Government remained a reactionary force, and the SRs and Mensheviks continued to give it support. On 3 September, Kerensky, having replaced Kornilov as supreme commander, issued an order to the army and navy demanding an end to political agitation among the soldiers and sailors. This was an obvious attack on their committees that had arrested reactionary officers. The uproar was immediate, with even Menshevik publications voicing disquiet.

The struggle had taken a giant step forward but had not reached its destiny. That was still to come.

The Bolsheviks win the leadership of the working class

Both right-wing opponents of the revolution and many of those who support it emphasise the role of the Bolsheviks in the victory of October. While the Bolsheviks were important, they were not all-knowing or all-powerful, simply guiding the masses along a straight line to soviet power. Nor did they manipulate the masses into passively accepting their rule.

Every honest account of the months between February and October 1917 reveals in all its complexity how masses of the exploited and oppressed can come to class consciousness, how they can throw off the yoke of oppression and fight for their own rights. The Bolsheviks won the leadership of the workers, soldiers and peasants because their aim of workers' power became the only viable option other than military dictatorship and the destruction of all that the workers had already won. They were the only ones clearly arguing for workers to take power.

The process was uneven. Ruling-class attacks could propel the masses forward. At other times, they pulled them backward. The July Days and their aftermath were a setback. The slander that the Bolsheviks were working for German money sapped the confidence of even the most advanced workers.

Talk of expelling the Bolsheviks from the soviets forced them in some parts of Moscow to leave not only the soviets but also the trade unions. But, paradoxically, in some areas, workers who were only now getting involved, for example, women textile workers, moved directly to join the Bolsheviks and were almost untouched by the reaction.

While the spread of the offensive against the Bolsheviks was wide, it was never deep-seated. The experience of the reaction in some places quickly educated workers to see that the attacks on the Bolsheviks were the preparation for an assault on the workers' revolution itself. Trotsky writes:

> [By the end of July] the position of the Bolsheviks in the Petrograd factories was already restored. The workers were united under the same banners, but they were now different workers, more mature – that is, more cautious but at the same time more resolute.[26]

Mass support for the Bolsheviks and their demand "All power to the soviets" grew after the Kornilov coup. This was reflected in the composition of the soviets. Around the country, workers had realised that the Provisional Government would never implement the central demands of the revolution for peace, land and bread. So, in factory after factory, workers held mass meetings and elected new deputies to the soviets, replacing the previously Menshevik-supporting deputies with Bolsheviks.

The Bolsheviks won a majority in the Petrograd Soviet on 31 August, and Trotsky, who had recently joined their ranks, was elected its president. The Moscow Soviet followed five days later, with a vote of no confidence in the Provisional Government, and then Kyiv, Kazan, Baku, Mykolaiv and several other industrial towns, along with Finnish soviets, where the Bolshevik majorities were even stronger. In some regions, reports came in that the soviet had taken power into its hands. Bolshevik membership soared, from 79,000 at the end of April to over 240,000 by the end of July to 400,000 by mid-October.[27]

The Bolsheviks agitated everywhere for soviet power. Sukhanov describes the situation in the capital:

> The Bolsheviks were working stubbornly and without let-up. They were among the masses, at the factory-benches, every day without a pause. Tens of speakers, big and little, were speaking in Petersburg, at the factories and in the barracks, every blessed day. For the masses, they had become their own people because they were always there, taking the lead in details as well as in the most important affairs of the factory or barracks. They had become the sole hope.[28]

The Bolsheviks called on poor peasants to rise up against landlords and seize land for themselves. Unlike the other political parties, the Bolsheviks encouraged peasants to take direct action rather than wait for the Provisional Government's constantly delayed inquiries into the land question. By August, 482 of Russia's 624 districts had experienced peasant revolts. Bolshevik militants convinced urban workers to champion the needs of the rural poor. They understood that, for workers to take and hold power, they would need to be the recognised champions of all the oppressed. Among the peasantry, the SRs maintained majority support, but by September, over half the SR representatives had split from the party over the question of power. These Left SRs joined the Soviet government after the revolution.

The soldiers, too. In June, 70 percent of the Moscow garrison, many of whom were former peasants, supported the SRs, but by September, 90 percent supported the Bolsheviks. On 30 August, the Petrograd garrison, numbering about 60,000, passed this resolution:

> The Petrograd garrison no longer recognises the Provisional Government. The Petrograd Soviet is our government. We will obey only the orders of the Petrograd Soviet, through the Military Revolutionary Committee.[29]

The path to insurrection

Dual power cannot last. Workers and our rulers cannot simultaneously govern society. One has to take power. The Kornilov coup proved that the ruling class knew this and were determined to destroy the workers' democratic institutions and impose an iron grip on society. For the Russian workers to finally overthrow their rulers, they needed to carry out their own insurrection.

In September, the Bolsheviks represented the most advanced, class-conscious and determined workers in Russia, and they could now, unlike in July, expect to carry the broad mass of workers, soldiers and poor peasants with them. The final blow that defeated bourgeois power was the culmination of class consciousness advancing among the masses and a decisive act in the unfolding class struggle. Before the experience of the Kornilov revolt, the workers and soldiers would not have welcomed or defended a new government. But now they could understand the treacherous role of the compromising socialists and the Provisional Government.

Historians like to point to the lack of mass street mobilisations in October as proof that the revolution was a coup carried out by the Bolsheviks in isolation from the masses.[30] But there was no need for the masses to march in the streets calling for "All power to the soviets"; the soviets were already running most of society, and most of the army had been won to support transferring power to the soviets. Peasant committees were organising the seizure of the landlords' estates. These facts showed that an insurrection could count on the support needed to succeed.

Lenin understood that time was of the essence. The danger was that unless the party moved now that it had won the trust of the masses, the mass of workers and soldiers would retreat into the struggle for individual survival, and their revolutionary consciousness would subside, leaving the way open for a decisive blow from the likes of Kornilov.

But Lenin had to continue arguing inside the Bolsheviks about taking advantage of this rising level of consciousness. In his frantic notes sent to the Bolsheviks from his hiding place in Finland, he attacked the Bolshevik leaders for their hesitation in setting a date for the insurrection. As the clock ticked by, many in the leadership got cold feet, getting tangled up in various manoeuvres by the Provisional Government aimed at buying itself time.

Lenin staked the future of the revolution not only on the decisiveness of the leadership in Russia but on international developments as well. The stakes were high across Europe. Russia had the potential to ignite an international revolution, Lenin believed, and the success of such a revolutionary movement in Europe would be essential to the future development of the fight for socialism in Russia. Without the help of a revolution in a much more industrially advanced country like Germany, the revolution in Russia would fall victim to the country's economic backwardness. This was even more reason that the Bolsheviks had to seize the moment. He was helped in his argument by Trotsky, who had quickly become Lenin's crucial ally on the Central Committee while the latter was in hiding.

On 10 October, the Bolshevik central committee decided that the approaching Congress of Soviets, set down for 25 October, should seize power, and this meant insurrection. However, veteran Bolshevik leaders Lev Kamenev and Grigori Zinoviev publicly disavowed this decision, and there ensued a public debate over whether the Bolsheviks should initiate an insurrectionary uprising. At the same time, there was a growing crescendo of reactionary and moderate socialist papers condemning the Bolsheviks for agitating for an uprising.

In the event, it was a provocation by the Provisional Government that began the final round of mobilisation. Only days after the Central Committee meeting on 10 October, the government suddenly announced plans to move the Petrograd garrison to the Eastern Front. There was uproar, and the garrison proclaimed its lack of confidence in the Provisional Government and demanded the transfer of power to the soviets. On 17 October, a conference of delegates from the front and the city garrison, including representatives from the soviets, openly discussed the need for the transfer of power to the soviets, for peace and for the front-line soldiers to return home. Not that they supported an uprising, but they would support any actions necessary to defend the soviets from the government and other reactionaries.

On Sunday, 22 October, Petrograd Soviet Day, concerts, speech-making and mass meetings took place in factories around the city, and there were massive gatherings in the streets and in public halls from morning till night where old and young, women, men and children, stood patiently for hours soaking up the words of Bolshevik orators, including Trotsky. Trotsky summed up the Bolsheviks' main points: that the government was preparing to surrender Petrograd to the Germans rather than allow the soviets to rule, that the entire world would be engulfed by revolution if they took power, and that only a soviet regime could bring peace, distribute the land and defend true democracy. His words were received with massive applause.

Three days earlier, Trotsky had won an important victory at a mass meeting of the Peter and Paul Fortress, a strategically important Petrograd military centre, which by an overwhelming majority voted that the only military orders that should be obeyed were those from the Military Revolutionary Committee.

The whole situation was leading inexorably to rule by the working class, not only in the major cities but also in the provinces. From 10 October, with an insurrection on the agenda, the Red Guards, the Bolshevik-led workers' militia, enrolled virtually every worker in some Petrograd factories. The commanding staff were all elected. All were volunteers and knew each other, so this was a new form of military organisation emerging from the revolutionary process.

Working women created Red Cross divisions, organised lectures on the care of the wounded and set up bands of nurses in the factories. Automobiles were requisitioned, inventories made of first-aid supplies, and nurses assigned to clinics. All the time, the Red Guards and other organisations were drawing in increasing numbers of non-Bolshevik workers, including those from the Mensheviks and SRs. On 22 October, the Red Guards held a mass conference to finalise their plans for the insurrection.

Moscow was moving to soviet power as well. In response to a wave of strikes, the soviets in that city decreed that henceforth, workers and clerks in factories and shops would be employed or discharged only with the consent of the shop committees. As Trotsky says, "This meant that the soviet had begun to function as a state power".[31]

While the masses were mobilising, the Provisional Government was increasingly isolated and paralysed. Every effort by the government to shore up its position was interpreted by the workers and soldiers as an act of aggression. It tried to cut off the rebellious districts of Petrograd by raising the bridges over the River Neva, precipitating military skirmishes and the defeat of the manoeuvre by armed workers. It also tried to close the Bolshevik printing presses in Petrograd on 24 October, sending reactionary soldiers to smash the equipment and seal the building. This plan, too, was defeated when the Military Revolutionary Committee deployed soldiers to reopen the building, allowing the print workers to resume work.

By its attempts to push the revolutionary movement back, the Provisional Government only opened the road to the insurrection. The preparation, the feverish debates and discussions in the streets, factories and barracks, had prepared vast masses of the oppressed to defend the Soviet, understanding that the defeat of the Bolsheviks would mean the victory of the counter-revolution and the end of their hopes.

That is why the 25 October insurrection looks like not much more than a military exercise when taken out of the context of the previous weeks. There was no more need for mass mobilisations. The only questions remaining were who would prevail and whether the actions of the Bolsheviks to repulse the attacks from the government would galvanise the promised defence. And they did. Trotsky paints a vivid picture of the city of Petrograd on the evening of 25 October:

> In the Vyborg district opposite the headquarters of the Red Guard, an entire camp was created: the street was jammed full of wagons, passenger cars and trucks. The institutions of the district were swarming with armed workers. The Soviet, the Duma, the trade unions, the factory and shop committees – everything in this district – were serving the cause of the insurrection. In the factories and barracks and various institutions, the same thing was happening in a smaller way as throughout the whole capital: they were crowding out some and electing others, breaking the last threads of the old and strengthening the new... At continuous meetings, fresh information was given out, fighting confidence kept up and ties reinforced. The human masses were crystallising along new axes; a revolution was achieving itself.[32]

So much for the right-wing myth that the revolution was only a coup. As Menshevik leader Julius Martov, no friend of the Bolsheviks, put it in a letter to a fellow party member the day after the insurrection: "Understand, please, that before us, after all, is a victorious uprising of the proletariat – almost the entire proletariat supports Lenin and expects its social liberation from the uprising".[33] Even Robert Service, an anti-Bolshevik historian, admits:

> What really counted was that the Bolshevik political programme proved steadily more appealing to the mass of workers, soldiers and peasants as social turmoil and economic ruin reached a climax in late autumn. But for that, there could have been no October revolution.[34]

The Second All-Russian Congress of Soviets

The most striking demonstration of mass support for the Bolsheviks came at the Second All-Russian Congress of Soviets, which began on the night of the insurrection on 25 October. Overwhelming support for the insurrection itself, even among non-Bolsheviks, was clear. Out of the 670 deputies asked their view on power, 505 responded that they were for all power to the soviets. The Mensheviks and SRs, once dominant, had completely squandered their political capital from the February Revolution. At the First Congress of Soviets in June, in which intellectuals and army officers had been prominent, these parties had 600 of 882 deputies. Now, at the Second Congress, dominated by soldiers, workers and peasants from the provinces, the moderate socialists had less than a quarter of the votes, and an overwhelming majority of these were Left SRs who veered towards the Bolsheviks.

There was a simple reason for the fall of the Provisional Government and the collapse in support for those parties that propped it up. British journalist Morgan Philips Price, originally opposed to the Bolsheviks, argued that:

> The government of M Kerensky fell before the Bolshevik insurgents because it had no supporters in the country. The bourgeois parties and the generals of the Staff disliked it because it would not establish a military dictatorship. The revolutionary democracy lost faith in it because after eight months it had

neither given land to the peasants nor established state control of industries nor advanced the cause of the Russian peace programme.[35]

The Soviet Congress opened at 11.45 pm on 25 October. At the same time, Lenin sent a telegram on behalf of the Military Revolutionary Committee to every corner of Russia:

To the citizens of Russia

The Provisional Government has been overthrown. State power has passed into the hands of the organ of the Petrograd Soviet of Workers' and Soldiers' Deputies, the Military Revolutionary Committee, which stands at the head of the Petrograd proletariat and garrison.

The cause for which the people have struggled – the immediate proposal of a democratic peace, the elimination of landlord estates, workers' control over production, the creation of a soviet government – the triumph of this cause has been assured.

Long live the workers', soldiers', and peasants' revolution!

—The Military Revolutionary Committee of the Petrograd Soviet of Workers' and Soldiers' Deputies.[36]

The Congress called on the belligerent countries to start immediate negotiations for a just, democratic peace. Deputies voted to abolish private ownership of land "forever" and decreed that "all land, whether state, crown, monastery, church, factory, entailed, private, public, peasant, etc…will be confiscated without compensation and become the property of the whole people and pass into the use of all those who cultivate it". Lenin, with the humility typical of him and a lack of bravado, simply adopted the land program of the peasant-based SRs and wrote it up as government policy. Do the peasants want the land? Let them organise its redistribution as they demand. The enslaved national minorities of the Russian empire were given the right to independence, up to and including secession. And workers' control over production was decreed as the basis for the reorganisation of the economy for the good of the population.

After October

The overturning of exploitation, placing control in the hands of the exploited, led to an explosion of experimentation in revolutionary Russia. Anything seemed possible, from equal pay to communal childcare, restaurants and housework to free women from drudgery, to control over one's sexuality. The sense of joy enthused poets, artists, architects and engineers to rethink how both the physical world and the imaginary could be transformed not for profits or the comforts and enjoyment of a privileged minority or the glorification of a repressive state but for all. Experimentation in every field burst the limits set by class society, searching for a new truth for a world worth living in.

Some of the legal changes promulgated by the Soviet went far beyond simple economic reorganisation. They opened the possibility of individual freedoms and personal liberation. The Bolsheviks had the oppressed in mind as they legislated these changes. In the first year, the decrees of the Soviet government established universal suffrage, ended the authority of heads of families, abolished the right of inheritance and established divorce and civil laws that made marriage a voluntary relationship free of state and church control. Abortion on demand, introduced in 1920, was the first such reform in the world and in advance of most countries to this day. These gains, backed up by the eight-hour day, equal pay, literacy programs, childcare and communal kitchens, provided the basis for economic and sexual freedom for women – to take control over their own bodies and to take their place in public life.

However, legislating for the possibility of freedom, taking over industry and defeating the old state did not make liberation inevitable. Resources had to be found to make the promise a reality. From the start, feeding the cities was the priority. Hunger had partly driven the radicalisation of 1917, and it could not be wished away. Industry was operating at production levels below those that existed before the war. Capitalists, who had been sabotaging the economy all year, now stepped up their efforts as workers struggled to take control. In the ensuing civil war between the new government and the counter-revolutionary forces, which did not end until early 1921, industrial production dropped to one-fifth of its pre-1914 levels.

And yet the cultural, creative and spiritual energy of the masses was astonishing amid this suffering. Some 125,000 literacy schools were set up, and factories established Education Commissions that put on theatre productions, poetry readings and orchestral concerts that were patronised by huge numbers of working women and men. The schools could not start on time in 1918 because the teachers were debating the latest and best methods of instruction.

It is little wonder that the Russian Revolution inspired workers worldwide. The overthrow of tsarism and the erection for the first time of a society turned upside down, with workers on top and bosses on the bottom, sparked revolutionary upheavals from Europe to the Middle East to Asia. German workers rose up and overthrew the Kaiser, setting up workers' councils like the Russian soviets. Soviets were established in Hungary and Finland. Workers in Italy formed factory councils and, in 1920, came to the brink of revolution before moderate socialists undercut them. For the world's ruling classes, the spectre of the Russian Revolution cast a dark shadow, striking fear into their hearts. "The whole of Europe," fretted British Prime Minister Lloyd George, "is filled with the spirit of revolution". The war and the Russian Revolution also set off or gave heart to anti-colonial revolts in India, Ireland and elsewhere. The Russian working class had lit the torch of revolution, and their achievements in 1917 and the immediate aftermath provide both a vindication of Marxism and an inspiration that serves revolutionaries to this day.

Notes

1.   This chapter incorporates a highly condensed version of Sandra Bloodworth, *How Workers Took Power: The 1917 Russian Revolution*, Socialist Alternative, 2008. Other sources include: Nikolai Sukhanov, *The Russian Revolution: A personal record*, Red Flag Books, 2020 [1955]; Abraham Rabinowitch, *The Bolsheviks Come to Power: The Revolution of 1917 in Petrograd*, Haymarket Books, 2004 [1976]; Oskar Anweiler, *The Soviets: The Russian Workers, Peasants, and Soldiers Councils, 1905–1921*, translated from the German by Hein Ruth, Pantheon Books, 1975; John Molyneux, *Marxism and the Party*, Pluto Press, 1978.

2.   David Mandel, *The Petrograd Workers in the Russian Revolution, February 1917–June 1918*, Haymarket Books, 2018, p.74.

3.   Rex Wade, *The Russian Revolution, 1917*, Cambridge University Press, 2000, p.29.

4.   Sukhanov, *The Russian Revolution*, p.205.

5.   John Reed, *Ten Days that Shook the World*, 1918.

6.   Edward Dune, cited in Jess Lenehan, "The Red Guards in the Russian Revolution", *Red Flag*, 11 December 2021.

7.   Reed, *Ten Days*.

8.   Anweiler, *The Soviets*, p.134.

9.   Anweiler, *The Soviets*, p.113.

10.   Leon Trotsky, *History of the Russian Revolution*, Pluto Press, 1977 [1933], p.213.

11.   Trotsky, *History*, p.217.

12.   Cited in Sukhanov, *The Russian Revolution*, p.243.

13.   Cited in Sukhanov, *The Russian Revolution*, pp.256 and 263.

14.   V.I. Lenin, "Report on the present situation and the attitude towards the Provisional Government", April 1917, *Collected Works*, Vol. 24, p.146.

15.   Trotsky, *History*, p.342. "Old Bolshevik" refers to those who had been party members since the 1890s or 1900s.

16.   The following account of the Bolshevik party draws heavily from Molyneux, *Marxism and the Party*.

17.   Cited in Molyneux, *Marxism and the Party*, p.67.

18.   Cited in Molyneux, *Marxism and the Party*, p.68.

19.   V.I. Lenin, *What Is To Be Done?*, 1902.

20.   Smith, "Petrograd in 1917".

21.   Sukhanov, *The Russian Revolution*, p.79.

22.   Sukhanov, *The Russian Revolution*, p.205.

23.   Sukhanov, *The Russian Revolution*, p.286.

24.   Sukhanov, *The Russian Revolution*, p.286.

25.   Trotsky, *History*, p.736.

26.   Trotsky, *History*, p.768.

27.   Dave Sherry, *Russia 1917: Workers' revolution and the festival of the oppressed*, Bookmarks, 2017, p.147. Estimates of Bolshevik membership vary widely, but no account disputes the rapid rise through the year.

28.   Sukhanov, *The Russian Revolution*, p.465.

29.   Trotsky, *History*, p.1147. The Military Revolutionary Committee was the body set up by the Petrograd Soviet to defend the revolution from reactionary attacks.

30.   See, for example, Orlando Figes, *A People's Tragedy: The Russian Revolution: 1891–1924*, Jonathan Cape, 1996.

31.   Trotsky, *History*, p.1124.

32.   Trotsky, *History*, pp.1078–9.

33.   Quoted in Tony Cliff, *Lenin: The Revolution Besieged*, Pluto Press, 1987, p.2.

34.   Robert Service, *The Bolshevik Party in Revolution, 1917–23*, Barnes and Noble, 1979, p.62.

35.   Morgan Philips Price, *Dispatches from the Revolution in Russia 1916–1918*, Pluto Press, 1997, p.88.

36.   Rabinowitch, *The Bolsheviks*, pp.274–5.

Chapter ten

The defeat of the Russian Revolution[1]

We do not live in a state but in a system of states, and the existence of the Soviet Republic side by side with imperialist states for any length of time is inconceivable. In the end, one or the other must triumph.

—Lenin, 1919, cited in Leon Trotsky,
The Third International after Lenin, 1928

I N THE LAST CHAPTER, WE LOOKED AT THE RUSSIAN REVOLUTION, in which millions of workers and peasants rose up to throw out the rotten autocracy that had ruled Russia for 300 years. The revolution showed the capacity of the working class to organise society in a completely new way, without bosses. But today, when people think of the Russian Revolution, often the first thing that comes to mind is the figure of Joseph Stalin and the dictatorship that ruled the country for most of the twentieth century. Not workers' liberation but workers' oppression. Not freedom but totalitarianism. Not soviets but gulags. The enemies of the Russian Revolution, comprising not only outright reactionaries but liberal and social democrats too, have put forward a series of reasons for this outcome – that workers are too stupid to run society, that Lenin and the Bolsheviks were megalomaniacs who cruelly duped the working class into supporting them, that October was a coup made behind the backs of the working class, that the use of violence corrupted the revolution and led directly to Stalinist terror, or even that the Russian people had known nothing but "strong rulers" and could not cope with democracy. Whatever the reason, they all come to the same (useful but completely fallacious) conclusion – that a revolution that liberates the working class is an illusion. Whether they argue that society today is the best we can hope for or that only by gradual parliamentary change can workers improve their lot, the upshot is the same – revolution is a sin.

Such arguments are regurgitated with monotonous regularity. It does not matter that they lack any credible historical evidence; they depend for their widespread acceptance not on their resemblance to the truth but on the power of those who put them forward. Those with money or a prestigious position in the academy, or MPs or trade union leaders who make careers out of selling out the working class, despise the idea of workers running the world and will continue to do their best to discredit it. Understanding the actual reasons for the defeat of the Russian Revolution is critical if we are to see through the right-wing argument that socialism is doomed to fail or fall victim to dictatorship.

Marxists start with an explanation rooted in the world economy and the world imperialist system that permits no escape from its ruthless logic short of an international revolution. The leaders of the Bolsheviks were always insistent that the Russian Revolution was part of a Europe-wide struggle. The outcome of that struggle would seal its fate. Trotsky, addressing the deputies of the Second All-Russian Congress of Soviets on 25 October, explained: "Either the Russian revolution will raise the whirlwind of struggle in the West, or the capitalists of all countries will crush our revolution".[2] Lenin repeated the point in March 1918: "[T]he absolute truth is that without a revolution in Germany we are doomed".[3]

Why is it so important that working-class revolutions spread, and why is what Stalin called "socialism in one country" a contradiction in terms? Socialism is not a utopia that can be conjured up by sheer willpower. Like all other societies, it requires the material basis that makes its existence possible. Socialism is a classless society based not on the subsistence existence of pre-class societies but on the technologies and level of productive power that class-based societies have developed. Socialism was impossible in the Middle Ages or in the time of the slave societies of ancient Greece and Rome. Only with the abundance associated with the rise of capitalism could the productive surplus be used to raise the living standards of all, not just a minority. Only with the creation of a large working class, such as had come into existence by the late nineteenth century, could capitalism be brought down and replaced by an egalitarian system. In the absence of abundance, the only things that would be equalised would be poverty and want.

So, by the beginning of the twentieth century, the material basis for socialism existed worldwide. But that did not mean individual countries could build socialism while the rest of the globe was dominated by capitalist competition. Because it is an international system, capitalism has created an international division of labour. No one country is self-sufficient. As early as 1847, Engels had written:

> Will it be possible for this revolution to take place in one country alone? No. By creating the world market, big industry has already brought all the peoples of the Earth…into such close relation with one another that none is independent of what happens to the others.[4]

The interlocking of economies means that a workers' state, unless joined by others reorganising production collectively to provide for human needs, cannot advance to socialism. Any attempt to forge a socialist society within the borders of a single country will end up being strangled by its backwardness. And, as we shall see with Stalin, "socialism in one country" was only ever a cover for the seizure of power by a rising bureaucracy with no interest in seeing the working class ever run things.

The situation facing the Bolsheviks

The prospect of the Russian Revolution spreading into the European heartland was entirely realistic. The combination of mass revulsion at the horrors that capitalism had unleashed during World War I and the inspiration provided by the Russian working class sparked a six-year wave of revolt that spread across the European continent from Ireland to Poland, from Finland to Italy. It was not only the Romanov tsars who lost their thrones; the same fate befell the Hapsburg royal family in the Austro-Hungarian empire, the Turkish sultan and the German Kaiser. The revolt was not limited to Europe; the revolution gave heart to workers in every country, including distant Australia.

The Communist Party (the renamed Bolsheviks) did all it could to foster the revolution in other countries and to maintain as many of the advances of the workers' state as possible. The Russian Communists established a new Communist Third International (the Comintern) in 1919 to replace the discredited Second International that had betrayed workers by supporting the imperialist war. Comintern Congresses brought revolutionaries together from across the world, and the Bolsheviks intervened in them to educate the new generation of international revolutionaries in the politics, strategies and tactics that could bring victory to their movements.[5]

At home, things were grim, and the new Communist government faced problems on every front. By the end of 1917, the Russian Revolution faced harsh economic conditions because of the combination of war and capitalist sabotage. By early 1918, industry had collapsed, famine was rife and disease widespread. Within a few months of the insurrection, the new workers' state was subjected to reactionary counter-revolution led by the former generals, landlords and capitalists, known as Whites, in opposition to the Reds in government. The personnel of the old state sabotaged basic administrative functions. The civil war and threats from within could have quickly been suppressed but for their backing by foreign armies from across Europe, the US, Canada, Japan and even Australia, which swept through the beleaguered nation, putting the revolution in mortal peril. Hoping this would cause the total collapse of the Communist government, the imperialists also imposed a blockade on trade and weapons. Further, as part of its peace deal to end the war with Germany in March 1918, the new Soviet government had to surrender Ukraine, the country's breadbasket.

The results of the civil war and blockade were catastrophic. Fuel became scarce, and railroad transportation – the country's lifeblood – was reduced to a shadow of its pre-war capacity. What meagre resources there were went toward fighting the counter-revolutionary armies. By the end of 1920, factory production had declined to 13 percent of its 1913 level and iron ore to less than 2 percent. The situation called for desperate measures. Straining every sinew, raising and training a new Red Army, extracting every ounce of grain from the peasants to feed the cities and army, and diverting industrial production almost entirely to military ends, the Communist government fought with their backs against the wall.

The civil war and economic collapse had not just economic but political consequences for the security of the revolution. If socialism is workers' control of production, by 1921 in Russia, there were neither workers nor production. The most militant Bolshevik workers had left the factories to fight against the White armies or to work for the new government. On top of those who went to fight, hundreds of thousands of workers fled the towns for the country in search of food. In three years, Petrograd lost 60 percent of its population, and Moscow lost nearly one-half.

The dramatic shrinkage of the working class and the destruction of the economic life of the country had devastating effects for the revolution. With people forced to scavenge for a living, they were in no position any longer to take part in the political life of the new workers' state. As Lenin told the Party Congress in 1921: "Owing to the war and to the desperate poverty and ruin, the working class has become declassed, i.e. dislodged from its class groove, and has ceased to exist as a proletariat".[6] For a revolution that had depended on the mass participation of the working class in the working of a new society, this was a dire threat to its survival.

Without material help from a revolution in a wealthy country, the problems could not be overcome. To hold on while they fomented revolutions in Europe, the Communists used the mechanisms of the state, even bringing in specialists from the old regime to organise departments and industry. It was not their goal, but it was necessary and defensible as a temporary state of affairs and while their international policies were aimed at international revolution.

An additional problem was that the Communist Party, by its very success in forming a government, had now attracted thousands of careerists who saw the party as a ticket to personal advancement. The core that had withstood tsarist repression and had been tested by the fires of 1917 was now only a small minority. This had serious consequences for the health of the Communist Party. Lenin wrote in 1922:

> If we do not close our eyes to reality, we must admit that at the present time the proletarian policy of the Party is not determined by the character of its membership, but by the enormous undivided prestige enjoyed by the small group which might be called the Old Guard of the Party.[7]

The hardships imposed on the population by economic collapse, civil war and the measures adopted by the government to resist, including the forced grain requisition from the peasants to feed the cities, created discontent. However, so long as the victory of the Whites was a threat, such discontent was muted. A White victory would have meant not the introduction of a democratic parliamentary system but a bloody terror. The Communists, and anyone suspected of Communist sympathies, would have been massacred in their tens, if not hundreds, of thousands. The landlords would have returned to seize their land from the peasants, and every democratic gain of the revolution would have been reversed. Trotsky said that had the counter-revolution won in Russia in this period, "fascism" would have been a Russian word.

By the end of 1920, the counter-revolution had been smashed, and the Whites had turned tail and fled. Now, the suffering experienced by the Russian masses was increasingly laid at the door of the Communist Party. This was the basis of a revolt in March 1921 by sailors at the Kronstadt military base, the gateway to Petrograd. The Kronstadt sailors of 1917, who had been a centre of revolutionary zeal and a firm base for the Bolsheviks, had gone to fight the Whites and were no longer at the garrison. Their replacements were new sailors, recently torn from the countryside and who had not been shaped by the experience of taking part in the revolution. Their demands, most evidently the demand for an end to the grain seizures and the introduction of free trade in grain, reflected their peasant origins. Their demand for "Soviets without Communists" was seized upon by every White general who understood the significance of a government defeat at this strategically located base. Facing the loss of the fortress, the Communist government sent the Red Army to storm it. The result was the deaths of many of the Kronstadt rebels.

Kronstadt showed the problems the workers' state faced and expressed the increasing hostility of the peasants to the revolution now that the threat of the return of the landlords had vanished. Urgent measures were needed to minimise this opposition if the workers' state were to survive. Lenin spelt out what was necessary if they were to build socialism at the Tenth Party Congress in March 1921, shortly after the crushing of the revolt:

Here industrial workers are in a minority, and the petty farmers are the vast majority. In such a country, the socialist revolution can triumph only on two conditions. First, if it is given timely support by a socialist revolution in one or several advanced countries... The second condition is agreement between the proletariat, which is exercising its dictatorship, that is holds the state power, and the majority of the peasant population.[8]

With these two problems in mind, the Party Congress introduced the New Economic Policy (NEP) that ended grain requisitioning from the peasants. Instead, the peasants would be taxed and able to use whatever profits they could make as they decided. In other words, it allowed the re-introduction of the market. That created something of a breathing space but could not halt the rise of Stalin to dominance. This required the first of Lenin's conditions: an international revolution to halt the degeneration at home.

It was the absence of a successful workers' revolution elsewhere in Europe in the years after 1917 that ensured the defeat of the Russian Revolution. Trotsky and other Russian revolutionaries had expected defeat, if it came, through the physical destruction of the workers' state by counter-revolutionary foreign armies. But the Bolsheviks triumphed in the civil war that followed the revolution. Rather than being overthrown from outside, the revolution was destroyed from within – by the processes set in train by its isolation.

By the mid-1920s, the revolution faced pressure from the world capitalist system on every side. The result was what Trotsky called "a long period of weariness, decline and sheer disappointment in the results of the revolution". As the spirit of self-sacrifice that had made victory possible gave way, "pusillanimity and careerism" took its place.[9]

This was the context in which the new bureaucracy under Stalin took power, along with its increasingly authoritarian practices. After a stroke, Lenin was bedridden through 1923 and finally passed away in January 1924. On his death, Stalin, a relatively minor Bolshevik leader in 1917 but who by 1922 had emerged as party General Secretary, took over the leadership. Nothing was inevitable about this transition, and it had certainly not been Lenin's preference. Lenin did not have confidence in Stalin; he moved to have him removed from his role in the party's leadership before he (Lenin) died. But Stalin had the support of the state and party bureaucracy behind him, and

Trotsky, who had a much greater claim to the leadership, failed to challenge Stalin's seizure of power.

Barely was Lenin dead when Stalin announced that the party's aim was now "socialism in one country", a complete reversal of what had long been party policy. From then on, Stalin and his henchmen conducted a vitriolic campaign against the idea that the revolution's fate depended on the success or failure of revolutions in the West. They condemned it as alien to the true traditions of Lenin and the Bolsheviks.

The theory of "socialism in one country" was not a call to hold on until the international revolution came to Russia's rescue but a reactionary, anti-Marxist utopia, the foundation stone for the ideology of a new rising bureaucracy ruling over the ashes of the revolution. That is why Trotsky included a lengthy appendix to his *History of the Russian Revolution* in which he showed that the entire Bolshevik tradition had been one of internationalism and complete opposition to the national chauvinism that went hand in hand with the promotion of "socialism in one country". This was true among not only leading Bolsheviks but also the rank-and-file members and even those workers, soldiers and sailors influenced by them.[10]

Stalin's strategy was not simply the self-serving policy of a new leader keen to cement the loyalty of a bureaucracy wary of the renewal of international revolution for fear of what it might do to their own positions. In the absence of a strategy of international revolution, the Stalinist bureaucracy had no alternative but to force up the rate of exploitation at home, the distinguishing feature of "socialism in one country", if it was to defeat the threat posed by the big imperialist powers such as Britain and Germany. Everything was now to be subordinated to military competition with the West.

The turning point of Stalin's counter-revolution came in 1928 with the announcement of the first Five-Year Plan, which set excessive goals for industrial growth and marked the triumph of the new state bureaucracy conscious of its own needs and interests. The plan was accompanied by the beginning of the forced collectivisation of the peasantry, aimed at squeezing the maximum surplus from agricultural production. Russia's workers and peasants were drafted into the service of breakneck industrialisation, super-exploited for the sake of Russia's industrial development. Before this period, economic growth had been accompanied by improvements in living standards. Now, wages and social spending were entirely subordinated to the siphoning of the maximum amount of surplus wealth into expanding heavy industry. Forced labour was employed on a mass scale, entire populations were uprooted, and millions died in the state terror used to carry it through.

It was as if the period of primitive accumulation – the expropriation of the peasantry, chattel slavery, and so on – before the Industrial Revolution in Britain was condensed in Russia into a period of several years instead of a few centuries. "We are fifty or a hundred years behind the advanced countries," Stalin declared to an audience of factory managers in 1931. "We must make good this distance in ten years. Either we do so, or they crush us."[11]

"Socialism in one country" was the ideology used by the new ruling bureaucracy to justify a program of accumulation on the backs of the Russian workers and peasants. Apologists for the Stalinist regime say, what else could they do? The workers' state had to survive in a hostile world. But this is precisely the point. To survive in that hostile world is to capitulate to its rules and economic dynamic.

By the early 1930s, nothing of the revolution remained: the working class was politically destroyed, atomised at the workplace by the introduction of incentive schemes such as piecework and bonuses and driven to exhaustion by speed-ups in the factories and mines. The counter-revolution had definitively triumphed.

Trotsky's struggle against Stalin

Many accounts of the degeneration and ultimate defeat of the Russian Revolution put it down to a version of Original Sin. Stalinism was not a break from Bolshevism, this theory goes, but its logical continuation, and Stalin was the logical successor to Lenin.

That this theory is rot is easily proven by the fact that for Stalin to triumph, he had to wipe out almost the whole of the old Bolshevik cadre of any stature from the revolutionary years. One by one, virtually every one of those who stayed in Russia was executed in the Great Terror of the 1930s or committed suicide in despair. Trotsky, who had been exiled in 1929, was eventually assassinated at his home in Mexico by one of Stalin's agents in 1940. If, as the revolution's enemies claim, Stalinism arose as the consequence of dictatorial features of the Bolshevik Party, why did the party's entire leadership have to be removed in this way?

The fact was that Stalin had to deny, debauch and overturn every Marxist tradition of the party to consolidate his bureaucratic rule. He could do this, not because he was right, not because he was more politically astute than others, or because he was the inheritor of Lenin's authority, but because the revolution was isolated and the working class broken: this was the determining factor in Russian politics.

Trotsky, Stalin's most consistent and determined rival, needed to appeal to a class-conscious working class that could mobilise to defend the soviets' democracy, that could defend their conditions and limit the bureaucracy's growing power. The working class, as we saw, was severely depleted and exhausted from the deprivations of the civil war, and many of the most class-conscious were the ones to fight and die on the front lines.

Nevertheless, grassroots opposition to Stalin persisted. In 1927, a turning point in the development of the new state, Stalin's regime was under considerable pressure. Illegal and semi-legal meetings were happening around the country, and opposition literature was widespread. A crowd of 100,000 at a rally to commemorate the tenth anniversary of the October Revolution cheered Opposition members aligned with Trotsky. Opposition activity was apparent from Leningrad to Ukraine, Transcaucasia, Siberia, the Urals and Moscow despite ever-increasing repression and intimidation.

However, for Trotsky and his supporters to defeat Stalin, it would have taken a revolutionary upsurge by the working class, and these shows of defiance were far from that. This returns us to the key question: that of the international revolution. The most drastic consequence of the developing bureaucracy was the counter-revolutionary influence of the increasingly reactionary and bureaucratic Russian party on the Comintern. From the Fifth Congress of the Comintern in 1923, the increasingly bureaucratised party, which still retained its influence over revolutionaries from other countries, used this influence to promote not revolutions overseas but the interests of the bureaucratic apparatus in Moscow. The last thing Stalin wanted was a new revolutionary wave in Europe or Asia, as that might have led to a revival of the confidence of the Russian working class and a revival of the revolution at home.

In Germany, a bitter five-year struggle, which began with a sailors' mutiny in Kiel in November 1918, had created several opportunities for a revolutionary breakthrough. But, lacking a revolutionary party, the German working class could not settle accounts with the capitalists. The German struggle of 1918–23 completely confirmed the need for a revolutionary party to be built long before the outbreak of the revolutionary struggle if the working class was to emerge triumphant. It was only in 1918 that leading German revolutionaries decisively broke from the rotten Social Democratic Party to form their own party. Events rushed upon them long before they could develop their party into something capable of leading a revolution. Inexperienced and lacking authority in the working class, they repeatedly misjudged the situation confronting them and failed to strike decisively in 1923 when revolutionary opportunities opened up. In China, too, workers could have broken through in the mid-1920s, but the implementation of Comintern policy resulted in a reactionary nationalist government taking power, which destroyed the mass working-class base of the Chinese Communist Party in the major cities.

By the end of the 1920s, the revolutionary wave had given way to the consolidation of the Stalinist bureaucracy not only in Moscow but also, under its direction, in Communist parties worldwide. Increasingly nationalist in outlook, led by time-servers and sycophants and guided by politics that now had no relationship to the Bolshevik traditions of workers' power, the Communist parties had ceased to be an instrument of revolution. Anyone who raised doubts or supported Trotsky was hounded from the Communist parties or expelled.

Was there an alternative to the rise of Stalin and the counter-revolution? Once Stalin's clique got control and it was clear they were abandoning the revolutionary goals of the party, Trotsky and his supporters followed the only alternative open to genuine revolutionaries who still supported the Marxist idea of socialism as the self-emancipation of the working class. They began to organise opposition to these developments. They fought on every front: the question of democracy, the question of policies adopted by the Comintern, domestic policies that were shifting the balance from consumption to accumulation, and on questions of theory.

In countries where they opposed the local Communist parties, Trotsky's supporters were hounded, branded "Trotsky-fascists" and even physically attacked to isolate them in the workers' movement. Their contribution to revolutionary Marxism remains one of the most inspiring achievements of the movement. Their sacrifice, their determination to stand by the fundamental ideas of Marxism and to defend the interests of the working class, kept alive the central tenet of Marxism: that international workers' self-emancipation is the only basis for socialism. They kept alive what not just the Stalinists but also every capitalist and their hangers-on wanted to see snuffed out. The historical tragedy was that without a successful revolution somewhere else, the rise of a repressive bureaucracy was inevitable.

The 1917 Russian Revolution remains the high point of working-class power and stands as proof that the working class can overturn capitalism and start on the path toward the reconstruction of society for the good of humanity. The defeat of the revolution, however, reminds us that people make history, but not in conditions of their own choosing. No matter how heroic their actions are, even the strongest-willed revolutionaries cannot alter circumstances that are overwhelmingly stacked against them. Russia gave us only a brief but brilliant glimpse of workers' power. Sadly, the Stalinist bureaucracy that rose on its ruin for decades gave real socialism a bad name – one it does not deserve. Polish-German revolutionary Rosa Luxemburg's defence of the Bolsheviks in 1917 reads as the best epitaph on the revolution's enduring significance:

> By their determined revolutionary stand, their exemplary strength in action, and their unbreakable loyalty to international socialism, they have contributed whatever could possibly be contributed under such devilishly hard conditions...

> Lenin and Trotsky and their friends were the *first*, those who went ahead as an example to the proletariat of the world; they are still the *only ones* up to now who can cry with Hutten: "I have dared!"

This is the essential and *enduring* in Bolshevik policy. In this sense, theirs is the immortal historical service of having marched at the head of the international proletariat with the conquest of political power and the practical placing of the problem of the realisation of socialism and of having advanced mightily the settlement of the score between capital and labour in the entire world. In Russia, the problem could only be posed. It could not be solved in Russia. And in this sense, the future everywhere belongs to "Bolshevism".[12]

Stalinism after Stalin

The theory of socialism in one country did not disappear with the death of Stalin in 1953. The theory has also been central to the ruling ideology of the one-party dictatorships that have called themselves "communist" and which modelled themselves on the USSR, from Eastern Europe to North Korea. None of them was created by workers' revolutions, making it even clearer, if proof were needed, that this kind of state had nothing to do with the traditions of Marxism and the self-emancipation of the working class. It was closely associated with the mistaken notion that socialism can be measured by the degree of state control of the economy.

Such a notion is utterly false. Countries where most of the means of production are concentrated in the hands of a state bureaucracy but where workers have no control over that production have nothing to do with socialism. Workers' revolts in Eastern Europe – including the forming of workers' councils in Hungary in 1956, similar to the 1917 soviets – were the practical proof that these societies, which had been erected after the Soviet invasion and based on the Stalinist model, were socialist in name only.

The same holds true for planning. A socialist society seeks to end the anarchy of the market by introducing conscious planning. But planning alone doesn't equal socialism. There are already elements of planning under capitalism. There is planning within firms, within the Pentagon, in Australia Post and so on. But none of these forms of planning eliminates the anarchy of the market. Instead, they are driven by it. There is state planning in North Korea, but the plan is shaped by the country's negotiation of its precarious position within the world economy, of which it is a small, isolated patch. The planning isn't democratic or fully under the planners' control. In these examples, the planning is designed to maximise output and profit at the expense of the worker, not to meet human need. Imagine the tremendous organisation and planning involved in executing a major US-led war, and you get some idea of what might be possible if all that energy were used to feed, house, clothe and educate everyone on the planet.

Whether socialism exists, therefore, does not depend on this or that form of property (private ownership or nationalisation) or on the existence of planning, but on whether the society is in the hands of the associated producers – the working class. Rather, the aim of workers' power is to implement a series of economic and social transformations that do away with all class distinctions and create a society whereby the state – an instrument of class domination – gradually fades away.

As Engels wrote: "The proletariat seizes the public power, and by means of this transforms the socialised means of production, slipping from the hands of the bourgeoisie, into public property". The economy, now under workers' control, socialises the means of production so that production and distribution can be carried out according to a rational plan that meets human need. "In proportion as anarchy in social production vanishes," Engels continued, "the political authority of the state dies out."[13]

To be successful, this process requires that socialism be international. "Socialism in one country" remains a contradiction in terms.

Open admiration for Stalin is now rare on the international left. Nonetheless, Stalinism has left a residue on contemporary left-wing politics. In chapter six, we discussed contemporary "campism", the idea that the world is divided into two camps, that of the US and its allies and that of the US's opponents, with the latter given a stamp of approval as somehow constituting an "anti-imperialist camp", regardless of the often odious nature of governments in this camp. Campism has its origins in the Stalinist Comintern's division of the world in the 1930s into progressive and peace-loving nations and reactionary and warmongering nations. There was nothing principled about this division. Stalin labelled as peace-loving those such as Britain and France that ran the world's two bloodiest empires. They were called "progressive" only insofar as

Stalin believed he could inveigle them into a diplomatic and military alliance against Germany. In 1939, all this was turned upside down when Stalin signed a pact with Hitler. Moscow now condemned British and French imperialism and partnered with Hitler to carve up Poland and the Baltic states. Campism today is equally cynical, substituting bourgeois great power politics for the genuine internationalist traditions of socialism.

Perhaps the biggest Stalinist hangover, however, is the popular front, the idea that the working class should form an alliance with a section of the capitalists to advance the nation's interests, a renunciation of the socialist principle of working-class independence. The popular front, like the campism with which it often overlaps, also originated in the 1930s Comintern. To cobble together an alliance with the capitalist governments of Britain and France, Stalin had to demonstrate to them his bona fides as a trustworthy partner. This entailed proving to them that the USSR had abandoned the Comintern's project in the 1920s of encouraging revolutionary challenges in their spheres of influence. Stalin now told Communists in Britain and France and their extensive empires to collaborate with their own ruling classes. If blocs of nations could be forged based on their supposedly peace-loving nature, that also entailed blocs of classes within those nations. Class struggle was out; class collaboration was in. Communists in Britain and France were told to fly their national flags, support militarisation (to safeguard peace, of course) and champion unity of all classes, except possibly a few die-hard reactionaries who opposed an alliance with the Soviet Union. In the United States, the Communist Party threw its lot in with the Roosevelt administration and sabotaged moves within the labour movement to form an independent workers' party, which would have transformed American politics. Stalin instructed communists in Spain to smash the revolutionary working-class upsurge that had greeted an attempted fascist coup against a newly elected government to reassure the British and French governments that their investments in Spain were safe. During World War II, after Germany invaded Russia, Stalin told Communists in Allied countries to go all out for the war effort, including by breaking strikes. In India, Communists were told to put off the national independence struggle because it undermined the British war effort, completely discrediting the party.

The popular front survived as official Communist strategy even after the

US-British-Soviet alliance fell apart soon after World War II. It was adopted by almost all the anti-colonial movements, many of which were guided and often funded and armed by Soviet (or, sometimes, Chinese) communism. It remains an influential force in "progressive" politics today, a term itself imbued with the popular front. Much of the US left is still captured by the Democratic Party, which remains a thoroughly capitalist party run in the interests of the ruling class. In anti-war campaigns, classless appeals for "peace" or for the United Nations to intervene to stop wars that do not target the class system responsible for war are rooted in the Communist popular front strategy of the 1950s and 1960s. The popular front approach also underpins much environmental campaigning that seeks alliances with friendly, supposedly green capitalists or involvement in UN summits where environmentalists try to persuade big corporations that an environmentally sustainable future is in their interests. Attempts to create an all-class alliance against fascism or far-right governments and presidential candidates in Europe and Latin America also reflect popular front politics – as if capitalist parties have any principled objection to fascism or can be reliable allies in the fight against it. The Yes campaign in the 2023 Voice to Parliament referendum, with backing from the trade unions, the ALP and big capitalists, was a popular front in action. This led to an anodyne campaign that shrank from any serious fight against racism and which the capitalists nonetheless abandoned in the closing months, as its likely defeat became apparent.

The defeat of the Russian Revolution was the greatest tragedy of the twentieth century. It was responsible not only for barbarism in the Soviet Union itself but also for the degeneration of the international socialist movement. The Communist parties, founded in many cases by those inspired by the 1917 revolution, were transformed into big monolithic propaganda machines that argued that socialism meant a single-party authoritarian dictatorship and had no interest in workers' struggle. They wrecked every workers' movement they intervened in, opened up the path to fascism in Germany, and discredited the name of socialism. Stalinists were elitist, hostile to working-class democracy, and totally distorted the legacy of Marxism. If anyone promotes Stalinism today, they obstruct the vital project of building a genuine movement for working-class self-emancipation.

Notes

1. This chapter includes extensive extracts from Sandra Bloodworth, *How Workers Took Power: The 1917 Russian Revolution*, Socialist Alternative, 2008, and Paul D'Amato, *The Meaning of Marxism*, Haymarket Books, 2014.

2. Leon Trotsky, *History of the Russian Revolution*, Pluto Press, 1977 [1933], pp.1184–5.

3. V.I. Lenin, "Political Report of the Central Committee, March 7", speech given to the Extraordinary Seventh Congress of the RCP(B), March 6–8, 1918, *Collected Works*, Vol. 27, p.98.

4. Friedrich Engels, *The Principles of Communism*, 1847.

5. The rise and fall of the Comintern is covered in: Tom Bramble and Mick Armstrong, *The Fight for Workers' Power: Revolution and Counter-Revolution in the 20th Century*, Interventions, 2021.

6. V.I. Lenin, "The New Economic Policy and the Tasks of the Political Education Departments. Report to the Second All-Russia Congress Of Political Education Departments October 17, 1921", 1921.

7. V.I. Lenin, "Conditions for Admitting New Members to the Party: Letters to V.M. Molotov", 1922.

8. V.I. Lenin, "Report on the Substitution of a Tax In Kind for the Surplus Grain Appropriation System", speech given to the Tenth Party Congress, 15 March 1921.

9. Leon Trotsky, *The Revolution Betrayed*, Pathfinder Press, 2002 [1936], p.86.

10. Trotsky, *History*, Appendix II, "Socialism in a Separate Country?", pp.1219–57.

11. J. Stalin, "Speech to industrial managers, February 1931", academic.shu.edu/russianhistory/index.php/Stalin_on_Rapid_Industrialization.

12. Rosa Luxemburg, "The Russian Revolution," in *Rosa Luxemburg Speaks*, Pathfinder Press, 1970, pp.394–5.

13. Friedrich Engels, *Socialism: Utopian and Scientific*, 1880.

Chapter eleven

The revolutionary party
and our project today

> The Communists, therefore, are on the one hand, practically, the most advanced
> and resolute section of the working-class parties of every country, that section
> which pushes forward all others; on the other hand, theoretically, they have
> over the great mass of the proletariat the advantage of clearly understanding
> the line of march, the conditions, and the ultimate general results of the
> proletarian movement.
>
> —Marx and Engels, *The Communist Manifesto*

WE FACE A SYSTEM based on oppression, exploitation, war and environmental catastrophe. All other political parties accept this status quo, even if some are for tinkering with it. We need mass revolutionary parties worldwide that can challenge this entire system and lead a revolution to its socialist conclusion. Such a party is not built simply to win parliamentary elections but to lead workers' struggle and mass movements and to drive them forward.

A series of revolutionary movements in the twentieth and twenty-first centuries have repeatedly shown the harsh reality that without a mass revolutionary party at the helm, such movements go down to defeat. The contrast between the experience of Russia in 1917, with the Bolsheviks providing essential leadership to the Russian working class, and Germany in 1918–23, when an experienced revolutionary party with deep roots in the working class was missing, makes this case most clearly. But why is this a general rule, and what are the factors at work that are responsible for it?

Even as a mass workers' struggle is on the ascendancy, many factors can sabotage it. Opposition from the ruling class to a rising tide of workers' struggle may take the form of co-option – whereby partial concessions are offered and sweeteners held out to particular groups of workers or certain leaders; or repression – whereby the ruling class turns to arrests and if these are not enough, bullets. Often, both are practised. In the first phases of an upswing, before workers begin to see through the tricks of the ruling class and before they understand their strength, they are susceptible to both.

The effectiveness of ruling class tactics is significantly enhanced when workers lack a revolutionary party to fight them. This is because workers have to deal not only with the outright capitalists and their parties but with counter-revolutionary forces within their ranks. No matter how spontaneously struggles break out, often with no forethought as to where they might lead, reformist and liberal forces, both long-established and newly formed, will seek to divert the struggle into a dead end. In Australia, the chief such force is the ALP, whose leaders dread the radicalisation of the working class because it threatens their role as parliamentary representatives aiming to take charge of the capitalist state. Alongside them stand the trade union leaders who can see their role as mediators between labour and capital jeopardised by workers who no longer want to submit to the bosses.

During the Kerr coup in 1975, the left-wing trade union leaders did the most to snuff out the gathering outrage and channelled workers' resistance into the parliamentary elections – only they had the credibility to win the argument for passivity with the militant workers. In Egypt in 2011, the revolutionaries faced opposition from both the die-hard supporters of the dictator President Mubarak and those who posed as their friends. In Egypt, these "friends of the revolution" included not only those who were part of the state machine, such as the army's high command, but also those whom the old regime, including the Islamist organisations and the middle-class liberals, had persecuted. Even though divided among themselves, they collectively defused the popular revolt and ushered in a period of reaction.

Liberals and reformists do not want to see the working class assume state power. "Trust us," they cry, "and we will see that your just demands receive satisfaction. But first, you must all go back to work and resume production. The students must stop occupying their campuses and return to their classes".

Of course, the ruling class backs the reformist forces with all the tools at its disposal when the outright conservative parties cannot squash the revolutionary movement. The media will give unstinting sympathetic coverage to attempts by reformist and liberal groups to douse the revolutionary ardour of the masses, portraying them as "responsible" and counterposing them to the "wreckers", "anarchists" and "outsiders" who want the struggle to go forward. They will promise all sorts of consultation and inquiries into the workers' grievances to get the workers to go back to work.

There opens up quickly in any mass workers' struggle a battle for the hearts and minds of the working class. The reformist forces – the ALP and union leaders in the case of Australia – will have a ready-made audience for their arguments because workers' consciousness starts out broadly sympathetic to reformist ideas. Further, these forces have a long-established place in society; they have the entire weight of tradition behind them.

If reformist consciousness predominates in the Australian working class taken as a whole, this does not tell us the entire story. It is better to see working-class consciousness as mixed, with both supportive and antagonistic ideas to the capitalist system. There is always a minority of workers who crawl to the boss; most likely, such workers will also be the most racist and nationalist and hold a range of other reactionary ideas they have absorbed uncritically from the right-wing media and other capitalist propaganda. The broad mass of workers experience a shifting mix of ideas, perhaps with basic trade union consciousness but holding to some right-wing ideas as well. This broad middle layer is the natural constituency of the reformist organisations that play on this contradictory mix of working-class and capitalist ideas. Another minority, by definition small at all times short of a revolutionary upsurge, will see the need to smash the system and understand the need to combat racist and other right-wing ideologies if the working class is to unite successfully in struggle. The point of a revolutionary party is to bring together this last group, what Marxists call the *vanguard* of the working class, to wage a fight for leadership of the working class in opposition to the reformists and, of course, the capitalist system itself, which the reformists defend.

What are some characteristics of a revolutionary party?

First, and most obviously, it must be built based on revolutionary socialist politics. The system of world capitalism that we confront today cannot be overturned by any means short of mass insurrection, a thoroughgoing revolution on an international scale that systematically dismantles the vast apparatus of capitalist class rule and replaces it with new institutions of workers' power and popular control. A socialist movement that refuses to confront this reality is building on sand. We need a party of militants who understand the magnitude of our tasks.

Parties that claim to be revolutionary but fudge their politics by abandoning political positions that are momentarily unpopular or that try to blur the line with reformist politics to appeal to more workers can only play a destructive role because they confuse workers about the tasks ahead of them and the nature of the enemy to be overcome. They can only lead workers to a dead end, possibly with disastrous consequences.

The political foundation of a revolutionary party dictates its character and methods of operation. The struggle for socialism has to be led by the working class – not by peasant armies, radical nationalists, students, intellectuals, oppressed minorities, bands of armed guerrillas, or "the people" in general. Because of this, any genuine, mass socialist party must have a mass working-class membership concentrated among the core of industrial workers. Without this, it is impossible to lead a workers' revolution. Not that the revolutionary party must be only made up of workers. Other social layers – such as students, intellectuals and the unemployed – should find a place in such a party. Indeed, in a country like Australia, a party that did not have a mass base among students, for example, would face serious difficulties. But this does not mean that the party is in any sense an alliance between the interests of students and workers, as a campaigning movement might be. Students and other non-working class elements in the party are welcome as members on the basis that they commit themselves to a working-class program.

The ALP, being a reformist party, sees parliament as the focus of its efforts. Its goal, to win a parliamentary majority, determines its internal structure – the parliamentarians and trade union leaders run the show – and its primary task: electioneering. The role of the ALP membership is to hand out how-to-vote cards in elections and, for the more active, become involved in the apolitical factional battles to determine who will win preselection ballots.

A revolutionary party has a totally different view. For it, the critical battleground of politics starts not in parliament but with the fundamentals of the class struggle – the battle between capital and labour in the workplaces and on the streets. The party aims to win over the working class to socialism in that struggle and forge a movement that can take on and defeat the capitalist state. So it must be organised accordingly. The basic organisational unit of the party is the workplace or campus branch, not the geographical electorate.

A revolutionary party is made up of activists, not bureaucrats. Unlike the ALP, the revolutionary party is not ruled over by its representatives in parliament or trade union leaders, should it have some in its ranks. Instead, it subordinates them to democratic control by the party members and the elected party leadership. The mass membership of the party is not simply there to hand out how-to-vote cards for the politicians. Instead, the rank and file of the party form a collective wing of the workers' movement, fighting for leadership of the class on every political question and in every battle. To do this, every member needs to be a leader. This means intervening politically – selling the party's publications, arguing with people to break them from pro-capitalist ideas and win them to socialism, and to the right orientation on the immediate question of the day. There is no room in the revolutionary party for a passive, paper membership or people looking for a cosy bureaucratic position – party members must be active and self-sacrificing.

The revolutionary party needs to be centralised. This is because the enemy – the big capitalists, the media, the police, the politicians, the courts and the prisons, the government bureaucracy and the military – form a coordinated, centralised body of military, social and ideological force organised to defend the interests and the rule of capital. The party cannot imagine this reality away; its forces need to be similarly centralised if they are to be effective.

Centralisation, to be clear, does not mean bureaucratisation or rule by a small, unelected clique. It means, rather, that the party can act decisively and swiftly when the need arises. Centralisation refers to the process of bringing together the experience of militant workers and students from all over the country to develop a clear sense of the national situation. Once familiar with the national situation, with all its unevenness, a national leadership, elected by and responsive to members, can then make decisions to guide the party's practice, taking into account local variation.

Decentralisation, often advocated as a way to empower the membership of parties or movements, only paralyses the party when decisiveness is needed, if authority is dispersed across the country with no unifying body. Not only can an organisation run on such lines not advance in one step, but the decisions that each local committee takes are developed with no recognition of the broader circumstances, significantly increasing the chances of mistakes and needless duplication of efforts. Delay and disorganisation significantly reduce the organisation's chances of successfully fighting a highly organised capitalist offensive.

The revolutionary party is centralist so it can respond quickly and throw its forces into the struggle. Sometimes, this means defending the barricades or going out on strike in a united fashion or launching an insurrection. But much more commonly, the party will need to carry an argument into the struggle to win the working class to a particular view or away from a course that will lead to defeat. This need to act is also part of the argument for a mass party. To carry through an argument – to organise a mass strike once you have won support for your position – requires serious forces on the ground, not merely good ideas.

But as well as being centralist, the party must be *democratic*. It is not enough simply for the leaders to decide and for others to have the discipline to follow the party line. Why is this? First, a party cannot get its members to win other people to a position unless most of them actually understand the issues and are confident they are arguing the right thing. If you only put a position because of blind obedience to the party, you will not be convincing. Maximum involvement in party debates and decision-making is a requirement if members are to be committed to those decisions and to be confident to go out and argue for them.

Discussion and debate are also important for rank-and-file party members to feed in experiences that are crucial for forging a picture of the state of the struggle across the whole country, across various industries and campuses, to help work out what the key arguments are, what is the readiness of each group of workers to act, what obstacles the party will face. The process of communication within the party is, therefore, a two-way street – bottom-up and top-down.

Centralisation and democracy are not counterposed. That is why the Bolsheviks could navigate the ebbs and flows of the struggle in 1917 – the leadership was in tune with the mood of the advanced workers and, when it was not, as in the period before Lenin's return in April and again in the weeks leading up to the insurrection, Lenin could use his knowledge of the sentiment among such workers to win the argument within the leadership.

Finally, vigorous democratic debate is also the best means to build a leadership that can establish its political authority to give orders and have them carried out, not because of bureaucratic submission, but because the leadership has the confidence of the mass of members.

For democracy to work in a mass party, the membership also needs to be educated in the history, theory and practice of Marxism. This is another point of differentiation between the methods of a reformist and revolutionary party. Of course, the ALP has a mythology with which it attempts to imbue its supporters, but it *is* a mythology, not the reality about the history or the current objectives of the party. After all, how could the ALP cohere its working-class supporters around the truth – that the party's purpose is to run Australian capitalism in the interests of the rich and at the expense of the people who voted it into office?

The revolutionary party has no interest in concealing its true aims and objectives from its mass membership or the working class. In fact, it is a prerequisite for the party's success that workers come to understand the truth about their position as a class and the correct relationship of the different political parties to themselves and other classes in society. The revolutionary party must make itself the memory of the working class. It must be the chronicler and interpreter of its victories and defeats, the vehicle whereby the lessons of the past are transmitted into the struggles of today.

So, while it is crucial that the party develop a large layer of experienced and leading members (cadres) who are dedicated to the party and who can assimilate the program and the orientation of the party and give it stability and depth, educational work goes well beyond that, and even beyond the party's rank-and-file membership. One strength of capitalism in the West is that its assumptions and its worldview permeate almost every aspect of life. Workers view things through a framework given to them by bourgeois society. The revolutionary party needs to win what Gramsci called the battle for *hegemony*. The party must systematically attempt to make Marxism the lens through which the vast bulk of workers and oppressed view the ups and downs not only of monumental struggles but also of every aspect of their lives. Achieving this means systematically educating the mass of workers in socialist politics – popularising Marxist theory in ways accessible and convincing to people well beyond the ranks of the party itself.

In periods of difficulty and retreat, a deep-rooted understanding of what you are doing and why you stand where you do is crucial. Many years after the events, a Polish former Stalinist, Leopold Trepper, made this point when writing about the Trotskyists who resisted Stalin in the 1930s, when so many had not:

> They fought Stalinism to the death, and they were the only ones who did. By the time of the great purges, they could only shout their rebellion at the freezing wastelands where they had been dragged in order to be exterminated... Today the Trotskyites have a right to accuse those who once howled along with the wolves. Let them not forget, however, that they had the enormous advantage over us of having a coherent political system capable of replacing Stalinism. They had something to cling to in the midst of their profound distress.[1]

To carry out its mission, the revolutionary party must maintain its independence from all other political parties and organisations (including class organisations like trade unions). On the other hand, the party must always strive to unite the working class and then unite the working-class movement with other progressive social struggles. How does this work? First, unity. The revolutionary party must fight all the divisions in the working class that serve the ruling class and which it fosters. Therefore, the party must be determined in its attempts to overcome divisions based on race, gender, sexuality and nationality, as well as those between different trades and occupations, between skilled and unskilled workers, between old and young, and so on. Second, the party should strive to unite with other forces in struggle regardless of its principled disagreements with them. So the revolutionary party should work in trade unions – even reactionary ones – to fight alongside broad layers of workers, even the most backward. It should seek to form united fronts with reformist organisations around specific goals and specific struggles. While most workers still look to reformist leadership, the party must support those reformists against openly bourgeois forces. As long as the mass of workers looks to parliament, the revolutionary party, one with thousands of members and a real hearing in the working class, must take part by running in elections and attempting honestly to get its own candidates elected.

Beyond the working class itself, the revolutionary party should seek alliances with other forces that can aid the struggle against capital. It should not shirk alliances with different sections of the petty bourgeoisie or with the leaders of anti-imperialist national struggles or struggles of oppressed minorities. But in all of this, the revolutionary party must maintain its own independent standpoint, both organisationally and politically. Seeking alliances with other forces does not mean capitulating to them politically. It does not mean dropping or moderating the party's criticisms, let alone dissolving the party organisationally. For this reason, freedom of criticism is paramount in any agreement or alliance the revolutionary party enters into. With the reformists, the united front is designed not simply as an effective measure of joint struggle against capital – although it is that – but also a means by which the misleadership of the reformists can be exposed, and workers won from their banner to the revolutionary one. The slogan summarising this approach is "march separately, strike together".

The revolutionary party needs to have an international perspective. It will be built in each country primarily as a national party. This is the only way mass parties can be built. Because capitalism is organised based on different nation-states, that is the terrain of the class struggle which is given to us. But while capitalism is organised based on nations, it is also an integrated world system. As Marxists have always maintained, and the experience of the Russian Revolution proved, socialism cannot be built in a single country. In the final analysis, the battle between labour and capital is a global battle, and the working class will not be victorious until we have defeated the capitalist class on a global scale. And because the forces of global capital will unite to resist workers' revolution, a party needs to be integrated with revolutionaries in other countries to develop an overview of the international situation and to advise on the strategy and tactics of the revolutionary movement in every country.

As the experience of Russia and Germany showed, the revolutionary socialist party needs to be there *before* the struggle starts, because an organisation with the confidence and authority to lead is not born spontaneously. The party is built through the continual interplay of socialist ideas and experience of the class struggle. For merely to understand society is not enough: only by applying these ideas in the day-to-day class struggle, in strikes, demonstrations, campaigns, will workers realise their power to change things, and gain the confidence to do it. At certain points, the intervention of a socialist party can be decisive and can tip the balance towards change, towards a revolutionary transfer of power to the workers, towards a socialist society. But simply waiting until the revolution before taking the first steps to build a revolutionary party is leaving it too late, something that generations of revolutionaries have found out to their cost. History does not wait for revolutionaries to catch up to meet the needs of the hour.

Finally, although the aim of a revolutionary party is to lead a working-class revolution, this does not mean that it ignores the demand for economic and social reforms to improve the lot of the workers within the capitalist system. Such demands are the starting point from which all workers' struggle develops. It is not just that socialists welcome the material benefits that might arise from such reforms as a victory for the workers and a defeat for the capitalists. It is also because during the struggle, which involves the mobilisation of the working class in strikes and mass demonstrations rather than simply the tabling of a motion in parliament, the eyes of the working class can be opened up to the prospect of winning more. Their confidence in their own strength is enhanced. Things that yesterday seemed remote now seem possible. This process does not lead in a straight line to revolution, but without this process getting underway, no progress towards any revolutionary transformation of society is possible.

For socialists to stand aloof from the fight for reforms would rightly condemn them to irrelevancy; they must instead prove themselves to be the most ardent fighters in this struggle to win over workers to the project of revolutionary change. As Rosa Luxemburg put it:

> The practical daily struggle for reforms, for the amelioration of the condition of the workers within the framework of the existing social order, and for democratic institutions, offers to the Social Democracy [i.e. a Marxist party] the only means of engaging in the proletarian class struggle and working in the direction of the final goal – the conquest of political power and the suppression of wage labour. For Social Democracy, there is an indissoluble tie between social reforms and revolution. The struggle for reforms is its means; the social revolution, its goal.[2]

An important distinction must be made between the fight for reforms and *reformism* as an ideology and practice that takes shape as reformist parties. A revolutionary party must remain highly critical of the reformist project, which both seeks to restrict the demands for reform to what the capitalist class will tolerate and prioritises the parliamentary process in place of the class struggle as the mechanism for social change. Focusing *only* on parliamentary reform means that not only will the outcomes be inferior to what workers might achieve by wielding their economic and social power, but the workers' movement will not be strengthened in this process. Apart from any other consideration, in the absence of such a strengthening of the working class, the ruling class is better positioned to roll back reforms later.

In summary, to overthrow the capitalist system, we need a *mass revolutionary party*. Such a party will consist, for the most part, of working-class members. It will comprise the most advanced and most self-sacrificing workers – the vanguard – to fight for leadership of the class. A mass party must be centralised and able to intervene in a united and disciplined fashion. It will also need to be democratic, to convince members of the strategy and tactics decided by the party and to commit them to it, to inform the process of decision-making and to establish a leadership with authority. The membership will need to be educated in the theory and practice of Marxism, both through reading and discussion and through experience in struggle. Cadres, members with the capacity to lead, will be essential.

The revolutionary party will need to be independent of other political parties while fighting for the unity of the working class from a class struggle perspective. The party should seek to form alliances with other non-working-class organisations, for example, in the fight for national liberation or against racism, but should never subordinate itself to such organisations. The party should have an international perspective because internationalism is necessary to combat racism and national chauvinism and because the working class is inherently international, while not forgetting that the struggle mostly occurs on the terrain of national politics. Finally, the revolutionary party must be energetic in pursuing reforms by using revolutionary means – mass struggle – to win workers away from their loyalty to reformist parties.

Socialist Alternative's project[3]

Socialist Alternative is not a revolutionary party. We are far too small, and our roots in society and in the labour movement in particular, are currently far too weak to offer a mass alternative to the ALP or Greens. Nevertheless, what we do today can be important in laying the groundwork for that vitally needed party. While our numbers are small, Socialist Alternative is the largest revolutionary group in Australia since the 1920s. We are the only socialist group with a national presence and an expanding membership. Founded by a few dozen comrades based overwhelmingly in Melbourne in the mid-1990s, the organisation has grown to over 500 activists nationwide. While this is nowhere near what we ultimately need, it is an important achievement in a context where the broader left has disintegrated.

Socialist Alternative is building an organisation of active members. There is hardly a campaign in Australia that does not involve our comrades. We are known for leading campaign groups against racism and fascism, for refugee rights, for Palestine, for climate justice, for LGBTI rights and against education cuts.

While it is not easy to achieve victories in the neoliberal era, we have had a few big ones. We led the street movement for marriage equality, beginning with rallies of only a few dozen but culminating after many years in rallies thousands-strong, before the ultimate victory in the 2017 referendum. We led a militant student movement in 2014 that defeated the Abbott government's attempt to impose $100,000 university degrees. In 2019, Socialist Alternative led demonstrations of tens of thousands in response to the bushfire crisis when Prime Minister Scott Morrison holidayed in Hawaii. Even where our efforts have not resulted in victories, we have nonetheless mobilised thousands to protest injustice. In 2020, we initiated a 15,000-strong rally in support of abortion rights in Melbourne after the US Supreme Court struck down *Roe v. Wade*.

While many campaigns have had popular support, we are also not afraid to take controversial positions when it is right to do so. Socialist Alternative has always stood four-square behind the Palestinian cause in the face of intimidation by state and federal political leaders, police commanders, university administrations, and media such as the *Age* and *Sydney Morning Herald*, all of whom try to disparage Palestinian solidarity as antisemitism or support for terrorism. In 2011, 14 of our members were arrested as they took part in a Boycott, Divestment and Sanctions protest campaign against the Max Brenner chain of stores and then dragged through the courts. In 2023, in the biggest wave of pro-Palestine protests in Australian history, Socialist Alternative branches and individuals were central to organising, chairing and speaking at mass rallies nationwide. While Socialist Alternative championed public health measures taken during the COVID-19 pandemic, we were not prepared to accept governments opportunistically using these measures to stamp out outdoor political activity that involved no threat to public health; in 2020, our members were taken before the NSW Supreme Court by police for calling a Black Lives Matter demonstration in defiance of such unwarranted restrictions on public assembly.

While rebuilding trade unions is a longer-term project that doesn't always have the same public profile, it is a vital task that cannot be shirked. The organising efforts of Socialist Alternative members in workplaces across the country have made an impact and won them respect and recognition, as outlined in chapter five.

Perhaps the most significant effort of recent times has been our campaign to get a socialist elected to parliament through the Victorian Socialists (VS). This giant effort has involved reaching out to well over a hundred thousand voters across Melbourne through door-knocks, public meetings, protest actions and more. At the Victorian elections in 2022, VS did not win a seat but recorded over 50,000 votes, the highest vote for a socialist party for many decades. It is possible that in the coming years, VS may win one or more seats in the state parliament.

All of this has been possible only because of the steady growth in size and experience of our organisation. Without committed socialists working tirelessly to fight for both immediate goals and long-term transformation, Australia would be a more passive, more right-wing and less hopeful place.

Every person reading this book has a role to play in constructing a socialist movement that can make a difference to the world right now. If we had a few hundred or a few thousand more members, the possibilities for action would multiply.

The purpose of a socialist organisation, however, is not only to fight the latest government attack or build a union presence at work. The point of a socialist group is to overthrow the system. We have seen from history that failing to do so can have disastrous consequences. The obstacles range from repressive laws and armed police all the way to progressive-seeming organisations that work to undermine our movements from within. These might be NGOs, reformist politicians and treacherous union leaders who are always eager to contain and diffuse popular anger.

Challenging these types of politics and organisations is crucial to building effective campaigns around various issues. Moderates often oppose the most minimal social and industrial activism for fear of alienating their friends in high places. The climate and refugee NGOs are the most typical examples of this trend, hibernating whenever Labor is in government. The same can be said of the public sector trade unions that fear damaging Labor's electoral fortunes far more than they fear the wage cuts being imposed on their members.

The same battle of political ideas between radicals and moderates unfolds in revolutionary moments. For now, though, we are far from that point.

There are two big traps that socialists can fall into in moments when revolution is not on the immediate agenda. One is to lose sight of this long-term goal and reduce ourselves to the level of pragmatic reformists. The other is to daydream about a revolutionary future while doing nothing to bring it any closer. It is easy to make the first error when engaged in a struggle around something immediate: this is the pressure "not to make the perfect the enemy of the good" that we hear so much about. There is also a temptation to make the other mistake, as demonstrated by the internet left, where seemingly ultra-radical anarchists and Stalinists exist in isolation from any real-world resistance.

A socialist organisation, even a relatively small one like Socialist Alternative, can help avoid these traps. We are a group of people committed to organising resistance while also preparing politically and theoretically for the bigger challenges. The more people are involved in such a group, the more likely it is that the skills, knowledge and political principles accumulated through generations of class and social struggle can be passed on and built upon in a way that can shape future radical struggles. Ultimately, it will determine whether our side wins or loses.

Therefore, the most important task of any socialist organisation is to grow. Only by building a mass socialist movement can we have a real impact on working-class politics. Small groups of radicals can occasionally punch above their weight by going viral or by calling well-timed demonstrations that draw out tens of thousands. But to organise a serious challenge to capitalism, we need socialist activists and organisers embedded in every workplace, university campus and social struggle.

For this reason, every serious revolutionary must be an aggressive recruiter, both to the ideas of socialism and to an organisation that can make those politics a force in working-class life. Participation in regular weekly meetings to discuss the politics of the day and democratically decide on our approach to political questions and activity on the streets, in workplaces and on campuses is an essential part of members' work.

It is easy to be pessimistic about our chances of ultimate success. We face the genuine prospects of economic crisis, climate disasters, fascist governments and a new world war. But the only thing more enraging than capitalism is nihilism. Nobody can guarantee the victory of the working class, but there is no excuse not to be part of the only movement that has a decent shot at fixing the root causes of society's problems once and for all.

Conclusion

Let us draw some threads together from this book by way of a summary and conclusion. Capitalism has to go. It condemns itself as a system, in the prophetic words of Marx, because amid the riches labour creates, the capitalist class cannot even assure the survival of humanity, let alone the survival of the poor. Further, even as many hundreds of millions around the world lack basic subsistence, the rich are getting ever richer and have no concern for those they exploit.

The working class has an interest in overthrowing the capitalist system because it produces the wealth of the world and yet has no control over it and does not reap the rewards for its efforts. But the working class is not only a suffering class. As history has proven repeatedly, the working class can rise and fight back. Its role in production is both the source of its exploitation and the foundation of its power – without our labour, nothing moves, and no profits come forth.

When the working class rises up, it faces not only the boss of this or that workplace but the whole concentrated power of the capitalist state. At its core, the capitalist state is the means used by the capitalist class to repress the working class and to protect the ill-gotten gains of one group of capitalists from others. The state is not a neutral body, therefore, but a coercive body that must be overthrown if humanity is to progress. Tinkering with the system through parliament will not be enough; the ruling class will never give up its power through an act of parliament.

The working class needs a revolution if it is to take power. This must mean more than a shuffling of the figures at the top; it means the wholesale transformation of the existing social order. Such revolutions occur not because of a conspiracy but because of crises in the system that force the working class to act and paralyse the ruling class. A revolution is needed, not only to smash the power of the capitalist class, but because in the struggle for radical social and economic change, the working class creates the new institutions that become the basis for a workers' state, and in this process becomes aware of its own power.

Revolution may seem an unlikely prospect in Australia, but any review of the history of this country confirms the recurrence of political and economic crises and upsurges of working-class struggle. These have never led to a revolutionary challenge, but Australian workers have shown no lack of courage and determination in their fight for change. Further, Australia is part of the world system, and, more than ever, political developments overseas will have a big impact here.

Socialism will involve the working class taking over the running of society democratically. The abundant productive potential inherited from capitalism will finally be fully realised as production is organised based on human need, not private profit. As society is reorganised on this basis, the foundations of class society will be eliminated, and with it, communism will become a reality. "Human nature" is not an obstacle: we are not hard-wired to compete selfishly. Not only is there ample evidence of people behaving cooperatively even in today's competitive, class-ridden society, but for most of human existence, egalitarianism was the rule.

Australia is an imperialist power. The ruling class uses its economic and military might to advance its agenda throughout the Asia-Pacific region and beyond. In coming years, we are likely to see the Australian military working hand in hand with the US to push back against China's growing presence in the region. This contest between rival imperialists threatens devastating consequences for the people, possibly even a nuclear war. Our task in Australia is to halt the US-led war drive without in any way conceding to China's own imperialist ambitions. Any so-called humanitarian interventions by the Australian military are simply a cover for the interests of Australian capitalists and the state. When people in countries that are oppressed by imperialism rise up to demand national self-determination, their struggle has a progressive character, both in weakening imperialism and in raising the potential for workers in imperialist countries to break from support for their own rulers.

Oppression is the systemic subjugation of particular groups, not simply abuse or patronising language or depictions in the media, although those are features of it. Oppression relates not only to women, migrants, Indigenous and LGBTI people but the working class as a whole. The basis for oppression is the needs of the ruling class: to divide the working class, limit its horizons and lower its wages, justify invasions, colonialism and war, and reinforce the nuclear family structure that reproduces the working class at low cost. Oppression is, therefore, an ineradicable feature of capitalism. Socialists support all struggles against oppression because such struggles help to break down divisions within the working class. However, for oppression to be smashed, capitalism has to be overthrown, and the working class has to lead.

The Russian Revolution was the greatest event in modern history. It tells us that even in the most difficult circumstances of war and hardship, the working class can overthrow a powerful state machine and impose its own rule on society. However, such a struggle will not be possible unless led by a mass revolutionary party attuned both to the end goal and the shifting sentiments of the working class.

That the workers' state in Russia was overturned and replaced by a monstrous dictatorship is no indictment of socialism but a warning that unless revolutions spread internationally, they will be choked from either within or without. Those governments that later came into existence and which claimed to rule on the Russian model have nothing to do with socialism. Socialism is not state ownership but workers' power.

Finally, the working class needs its own revolutionary party if it is to win the battle against capitalism. Such a party has to bring together the most advanced sections of the working class, not to isolate themselves, but to win the argument for revolution among much broader sections of the working class.

Socialist Alternative may be small today. Our goal – to play our part in creating a revolutionary working-class party hundreds of thousands strong in the future – may seem ambitious. But there is no other way than to start where we are right now, with the tools we have at our disposal. We cannot put this task off to the distant future. We cannot simply wait for the "right moment" before we start. Nor can we simply wait for someone else to do the job; neither the ALP nor the Greens has any interest in smashing capitalism – they only want to run it and keep the bosses happy. No, we need to build a proudly revolutionary party that can settle accounts with capitalism once and for all. There is so much to fight for, and so much activism to throw ourselves into in the here and now. We cannot let capitalism continue to degrade and oppress. We urgently need all those who oppose it to involve themselves in the project of revolutionary socialism. The time to start building such a party is now, and we want you, if you have been convinced by what you have read in this book, to join us in this task. Together, we have a world to win!

Notes

1. Quoted in Alex Mitchell, *Come the Revolution: A Memoir*, University of New South Wales Press, 2011, p.320.

2. Rosa Luxemburg, *Reform or Revolution*, 1908.

3. This section was written by Omar Hassan and first published as "Why you should join Socialist Alternative", *Red Flag*, 16 November 2022.

Socialist Alternative's Statement of Principles

1. Socialist Alternative is a revolutionary Marxist organisation. We stand for the overthrow of capitalism and the construction of a world socialist system.

2. By socialism, we mean a system in which society is democratically controlled by the working class and the productive resources of society are channelled to abolishing class divisions. Only socialism can rid the world of poverty and inequality, stop imperialist wars, end oppression and exploitation, save the environment from destruction and provide the conditions for the full realisation of human creative potential. A system under the democratic control of the working class is the only basis for establishing a classless, prosperous, sustainable society based on the principle "from each according to their ability, to each according to their need".

3. Stalinism is not socialism. We agree with Trotsky's characterisation of Stalin as the "gravedigger" of the Russian Revolution. The political character of the regime established by the Stalinist bureaucracy in Russia most closely resembled that placed in power in capitalist countries by victorious fascist movements – an atomised population ruled over by a ruthless bureaucratic dictatorship masquerading behind social demagogy. We stand in the tradition of the revolutionaries who resisted Stalinism, and we fight today to reclaim the democratic, revolutionary politics of Marx, Engels, Luxemburg, Lenin, Trotsky and others from Stalinist distortion.

4. Socialism cannot be won by reform of the current system or by taking over the existing state. Only the revolutionary overthrow of the existing order and the smashing of the capitalist state apparatus can defeat the capitalist class and permanently end its rule. A successful revolution will

involve workers taking control of their workplaces, dismantling existing state institutions (parliaments, courts, the armed forces and police) and replacing them with an entirely new state based on genuinely democratic control by the working class.

5. The emancipation of the working class must be the act of the working class itself. Socialism cannot come about by the actions of a minority. The struggle for socialism is the struggle of the great mass of workers to control their lives and their society, what Marx called "a movement of the immense majority in the interests of the immense majority".

6. For workers to be won to the need for revolution and for the working class to be cohered organisationally and politically into a force capable of defeating the centralised might of the capitalist state, a revolutionary party is necessary. Such an organisation has to cohere in its ranks the decisive elements among the most class-conscious and militant workers. Laying the basis for such a party is the key strategic task for socialists in Australia today.

7. It is not enough for a revolutionary party to organise the vanguard of the class. For capitalism to be overthrown, the majority of the working class must be won to revolutionary action and the socialist cause. It is not enough to simply denounce the non-revolutionary organisations and political currents in the workers' movement. Revolutionaries have to engage reformist organisations via the method of the united front in order to test the possibility for united action in practice and demonstrate to all workers in a non-sectarian way the superiority of revolutionary ideas and practice. We support all demands and movements that tend to improve the position and self-confidence of workers and of other oppressed sections of the population.

8. Socialists support trade unions as the basic defensive organisations of the working class. We stand for democratic, militant, class struggle unionism and reject class collaborationism. We also stand for political trade unionism – the union movement should champion every struggle against injustice.

9. Capitalist exploitation of the working class and the natural world has created a situation where the profit system threatens the habitability of the planet. We oppose attempts to halt climate change and environmental destruction through measures that place the burden on working-class people and the poor. We demand instead fundamental social and political change that directly challenges the interests of the ruling class. The environmental crisis can only be solved under socialism, where the interests of people and the planet are not counterposed.

10. Socialists are internationalists. We reject Australian patriotism and nationalism and fight for international working-class solidarity. The struggle against capitalism is an international struggle: socialism cannot be built in a single country.

11. The imperialist phase of capitalism has ushered in an era of military conflict that has no precedent in human history. The core element of imperialism is the conflict between imperial powers, or blocks of capital, which attempt by military, diplomatic and commercial means to divide and redivide the world in their own interests. In the conflicts between imperial powers (open or by proxy), revolutionaries do not take sides, least of all with our own ruling classes. Nor do we call for the resolution of inter-imperialist conflict by the "peaceful" methods of international diplomacy. Instead, we fight for international working-class solidarity and unity and embrace Lenin's revolutionary call to "turn the imperialist war between nations into a civil war between classes". In the case of wars waged or diplomatic pressure exerted by military threat by the imperial powers against colonies and non-imperialist nations, we oppose the imperial power and defend the right of national self-determination.

12. Australia is an imperialist power in its own right. Through its own economic and military strength and in alliance with US imperialism, Australian capitalism seeks to politically and militarily dominate its region and project power more broadly. This gives revolutionaries in Australia a special obligation to stand in solidarity with struggles of workers and

the oppressed in our region against Australian imperialist intervention and control.

13. We recognise Aboriginal and Torres Strait Islander people as the first people of Australia. We acknowledge that sovereignty was never ceded and condemn the crimes of genocide and dispossession committed by European colonists and the Australian state. We support the struggle for land rights, sovereignty and economic and social justice for Indigenous people.

14. We oppose all immigration controls and support open borders. We fight to free all refugees from detention and for the right of asylum seekers to reach Australia. We oppose racism towards migrants. In particular, we reject racism towards Muslims, whose right to religious and political freedom is routinely attacked on the spurious grounds of "fighting terrorism".

15. We oppose all oppression on the basis of sex, gender or sexuality. We oppose all forms of discrimination against women and all forms of social inequality between men and women. The struggle for freedom from exploitation and freedom from all forms of oppression includes the liberation of lesbians, gay men, bisexual, transgender and intersex people. We fight for an end to all legal and social discrimination against LGBTI people and all forms of sexist discrimination. We support full reproductive freedom for all women.

16. All these forms of oppression, and others like the oppression of the young, the disabled and the elderly, are used to divide the working class and to spare capital the expense of providing for the needs of all members of society. Combating them is an essential part of building a united working-class struggle that can win a socialist society. Only a socialist revolution can bring about the genuine liberation of the oppressed and the ability of every human being to realise their full potential.

Further reading

General texts

The Revolutionary Ideas of Karl Marx, by Alex Callinicos.

The Meaning of Marxism, by Paul D'Amato.

Capitalism

The Communist Manifesto, by Karl Marx and Friedrich Engels.

Wage Labour and Capital, by Karl Marx.

A Crime Beyond Denunciation: A Marxist Analysis of Capitalist Crisis, by Sandra Bloodworth.

"To have and to hold on to: wealth, power and the capitalist class", by Sam Pietsch, in Rick Kuhn (ed.), *Class and Struggle in Australia*.

"From exploitation to resistance and revolt: the working class", by Diane Fieldes, in Rick Kuhn (ed.), *Class and Struggle in Australia*.

Karl Marx's Theory of Revolution, Vol. 2 (The Politics of Social Classes), by Hal Draper.

The state

The State and Revolution, by V.I. Lenin.

Karl Marx's Theory of Revolution, Vol. 1 (State and Bureaucracy), by Hal Draper.

The Labor Party: A Marxist Analysis by Tom Bramble and Mick Armstrong.

"Illusions of equality: the capitalist state", by Rick Kuhn, in Rick Kuhn (ed.), *Class and Struggle in Australia*.

"Police state: the politics of law and order", by Tom Bramble, *Marxist Left Review*, 17.

Workers' struggle and revolution

Reform or Revolution, by Rosa Luxemburg.

Revolutionary Rehearsals, edited by Colin Barker.

The Fight for Workers' Power: Revolution and Counter-Revolution in the 20th Century, by Tom Bramble and Mick Armstrong.

"Lenin and a theory of revolution for the West", by Sandra Bloodworth, *Marxist Left Review*, 8.

Socialism

Socialism: Utopian and Scientific, by Friedrich Engels.

The Two Souls of Socialism, by Hal Draper.

The Civil War in France, by Karl Marx (about the Paris Commune of 1871).

What is the Real Marxist Tradition?, by John Molyneux.

Trade unions

Trade Unionism in Australia: A History from Flood to Ebb Tide, by Tom Bramble.

"Can the working class still change society?", by Tom Bramble, *Marxist Left Review*, 2.

"Our unions in crisis: how did it come to this?", by Tom Bramble, *Marxist Left Review*, 15.

Imperialism

Imperialism: The Highest Stage of Capitalism, by V.I. Lenin.

The Right of Nations to Self-Determination, by V.I. Lenin.

The Neighbour from Hell: Two Centuries of Australian Imperialism, by Tom O'Lincoln.

"Biden's plan for the US empire", by Tom Bramble, *Marxist Left Review*, 22.

"AUKUS and the US alliance: Australian imperialism in the Indo-Pacific", by Tom Bramble, *Marxist Left Review*, 23.

"Vietnam: How we won last time", by Anne Picot, *Socialist Review*, 4.

Class and racial oppression

Socialism and Indigenous Liberation, by Jordan Humphreys.

"Racism in Australia: who's to blame?", by Tess Lee Ack, *Marxist Left Review*, 4.

"Racism: whitewashing the class divide", by Phil Griffiths, in Rick Kuhn (ed.), *Class and Struggle in Australia*.

Black Liberation and Socialism, by Ahmed Shawki.

The failure of identity politics: A Marxist analysis", by Sarah Garnham, *Marxist Left Review*, 22.

"The political economy of immigration to Australia", by Jordan Humphreys, *Marxist Left Review*, 17.

Women's and LGBTI oppression

The Origins of the Family, Private Property and the State, by Friedrich Engels.

"The origins of women's oppression – a defence of Engels and a new departure", by Sandra Bloodworth, *Marxist Left Review*, 16.

"Marxism and women's liberation", by Louise O'Shea, *Marxist Left Review*, 7.

"The roots of sexual violence", by Sandra Bloodworth, *Marxist Left Review*, 10.

Rebel Women in Australian Working Class History, edited by Sandra Bloodworth and Tom O'Lincoln.

"The roots of gay oppression", by Norah Carlin, *International Socialism Journal*, 42.

Revolution is for Us: The left and gay liberation in Australia, by Liz Ross.

The Russian Revolution

The History of the Russian Revolution, by Leon Trotsky.

Ten Days that Shook the World, by John Reed.

The Russian Revolution 1917: A Personal Record, by Nikolai Sukhanov.

How Workers Took Power: The 1917 Russian Revolution, by Sandra Bloodworth.

Lenin: All Power to the Soviets, by Tony Cliff.

Lenin's Interventionist Marxism, by Tom Freeman.

"Lenin vs 'Leninism'", by Sandra Bloodworth, *Marxist Left Review*, 5.

The defeat of the Russian Revolution

Russia: From Workers' State to State Capitalism, by Chris Harman, Peter Binns and Tony Cliff.

The Comintern, by Duncan Hallas.

Lessons of October, by Leon Trotsky.

The revolutionary party and our project today

What is to be Done?, by V.I. Lenin.

The Socialist Movement: Our History, by Corey Oakley.

From Little Things, Big Things Grow: Strategies for Building Revolutionary Socialist Organisations, by Mick Armstrong.

"What kind of organisation do socialists need?", by Corey Oakley, *Marxist Left Review*, 5.

"The origins of Socialist Alternative: summing up the debate", by Mick Armstrong, *Marxist Left Review*, 1.

www.ingramcontent.com/pod-product-compliance
Lightning Source LLC
Chambersburg PA
CBHW032050020426
42335CB00011B/273